Roll Models
People Who Live Successfully Following Spinal Cord Injury
And
How They Do It

Richard Holicky

Edited by Barry Corbet

Supported by Grant #496 from the PVA Education Foundation.

Order this book online at www.trafford.com
or email orders@trafford.com

Most Trafford titles are also available at major online book retailers.

Supported by the Paralyzed Veterans of America
Education Foundation: Grant #496

Print information available on the last page.

ISBN: 978-1-4120-4022-8 (sc)

Trafford rev. 10/09/2018

 www.trafford.com

North America & international
toll-free: 1 888 232 4444 (USA & Canada)
fax: 812 355 4082

CONTENTS

Acknowledgements

This project was funded by the Education and Training Foundation of the Paralyzed Veterans of America. Thanks to Barry Corbet who not only guided me through the writing and bears credit for making this coherent and readable, but more importantly has for years provided me with a model of a life on wheels lived with humor and grace. Thanks to Michelle Bergman for constant help in file and photo conversions and transfers. Susie Charlifue, Denny O'Malley, Bonny Sims, Pam Bechtel, Linda Singer, Susan Solnick, Kenny Hosack and many others at Craig Hospital provided referrals and help. Kathy Hulse and Lester Butt gave me valuable and much needed information, support and advice. Thanks also to Scott Richards at Spain Rehabilitation, Minna Hong at Shepherd Center, Jeff Cressy at Rancho Los Amigos, Mario Prietto at Homeboy Industries, Michael Countee with Project Peace, Richard Patterson and Janie Whiteford at Santa Clara Valley Health Center, Chris Vertiz at Schwab Rehab Hospital and Care Network, Mercedes Rauen of NSCIA of Illinois and Diane Grzymko at Kessler Rehabilitation Institute. Many others helped along the way. Finally and most importantly, I thank those profiled here for sharing their time, their knowledge, their lives.

About the Author:
Richard Holicky has been writing about spinal cord injury and disability issues for well over a decade. As a researcher, writer and peer counselor at Craig Rehabilitation Hospital he studied and wrote extensively on spinal cord injury and aging, and authored a book and numerous articles for family caregivers. He's also worked as a teacher, counselor and mediator in the Denver area since breaking his neck in a 1989 skiing accident. Prior to injury he was, alternately, a teacher, farmer, woodsman, hard rock miner, writer, youth worker, teacher and community organizer.

About the Editor:
Barry Corbet has spent more than 30 years in service to spinal cord injury survivors and professionals, first as a film maker, later as an author, and for over a decade as editor of *New Mobility* magazine. His book, *Options*, penned in 1980, is still considered required reading and the best available primer for newly injured individuals; his films inspired a generation. Barry's back was broken in a 1968 helicopter accident. He lives in the foothills of the Colorado Rockies.

About the Artist:
Charmaine G. Brown has exhibited extensively in New Mexico and throughout the Southwest. She has twice been awarded a New Forms Regional Initiative Grant funded by the National Endowment for the Arts, as well as grants from The Rockefeller Foundation, The Andy Warhol Foundation for the Visual Arts, and most recently a Quality of Life Grant by the Christopher Reeve Paralysis Foundation. Charmaine lives and works in Albuquerque, NM and became paraplegic in a 1984 automobile accident.

About the artwork:
Much of the art seen throughout the book comes from the *Royal Flush* exhibit, a series of full size satin quilts and three dimensional installations. Other work comes from *Circus Display* and DIS-CARDS, a nationally distributed postcard disability awareness campaign. ∎

PREFACE

Spinal cord injury happens to people of all kinds. It doesn't just happen to people with proven abilities who know they have what it takes to keep their heads above water. It happens to kids from slums, high-school dropouts, people with no visible family support. It happens to anybody. Some do well. Some don't.

What, if anything, do people who do well with spinal cord injury have in common? There are many who thrive without big liability settlements, vibrant health or long-term disability insurance, without an advanced degree, a good job to return to or an outstanding IQ.

And what does doing well mean? Evidently, it doesn't always mean working, bringing home a paycheck and having the usual toys. It doesn't always mean the American dream of wife, kids and a house in the suburbs. Sometimes it means the simple pleasures of being content with life, having a measure of self-esteem and looking forward to each new day. There are countless people with spinal cord injury who live happy, ordinary lives but don't fit rehabilitation's traditional definition of success—full-time employment, few major medical complications and fewer hospitalizations.

There are also countless survivors who have thrown in the towel, who spend their days watching television and waiting to get a pressure sore. What's the difference between these two groups of people? Is it a knack for reinvention? Is it attitude? A set of beliefs? Good habits or relentless ambition? Are those who do well just too young and naïve to know they're not supposed to be able to live in the world and like it?

What enables people to be happy? What do they have in common? These pages offer some answers.

I met Tom when I was in rehab. He was a C6 quad and had used a chair for more than a dozen years. Though he needed help each day, he drove, ran a business, owned his own home and ran around with more than his share of women. He laughed a lot, raised some hell and I never heard him complain. As I got to know him, I began to suspect that regaining a life might be possible. If he could do it, I thought, maybe I could. Tom was kind enough to come around and visit from time to time and even took me out to lunch and dinner, my first real ventures into public places. He showed me that people wouldn't shy away and that I might still have things to offer.

Tom was my mentor, and that was my good fortune. He told me how to deal with government programs and insurance companies and get the benefits they owed me. He told me where to find the best deals on medical equipment and was quick with tips for finding attendant care and accessible housing. He knew the law and how to use it. He was my guide in this strange new land. Most important, he showed me that my life could be about more than just my wheelchair. He gave me hope that life could still give me satisfaction and purpose. By showing me his life and how he lived it, he gave me a vision of what my life might be.

This book contains a group of Toms—young and old, male and female, quad and para, employed and not—and they can help you just as my Tom did me. These Toms were injured in many different ways, are of different races, live in different parts of the country. Most are quite happy with their lives, proud of how they've lived them and moving forward into the future rather than looking back at the past. I spoke to each at length, first by phone, then in person, and asked them the questions I remember having myself when I was injured plus some more that have come up since. I wanted to know the specific things they did, believed or learned that had helped them do well. I wanted to see if there was anything vaguely resembling a Seven Successful Habits of Highly Successful Wheelers. Some of the questions I asked varied only slightly—biggest fear versus biggest obstacle, most difficult things to deal with versus biggest losses of SCI. Small changes in questions often brought out a large change in responses.

None of these Toms are in perfect harmony with their disabilities. Some are still figuring things out, still getting used to their wheels and finding their way. Others have made their mark and are now concerned with what aging has in store for them. I intentionally avoided "superstars" and people who had unusual advantages. Instead I looked for ordinary people living ordinary lives, people who had successfully wrestled their demons and won their victories on their own merits. I wanted to hear how they had traversed the immense distance between where they started after injury and where they are now. I didn't want to hear it from healthcare professionals. I wanted to get it from the horse's mouth.

This isn't a random sample of people with spinal cord injuries. I chose people doing well. Unlike the majority of spinal cord injury survivors, many here work and many have been to college. Still, few are people of privilege and many come from humble roots. What separates most of them from many survivors is their commitment to growth and happiness. They looked at their lives after injury and made a choice to live them well.

In telling their stories, I've tried to show what their lives are like *today*. Almost everyone spoke of despair and hopelessness early on; few anticipated what life with a spinal cord injury could offer. Yet they persevered and prospered. Through them, I've tried to present a picture of the possible.

No one book can offer all the answers and the best we can hope for is some direction, a few hot tips and a shining example or two. None of the suggestions contained within is guaranteed to work for you. However, every tip listed worked well for some one and often for quite a few.

Methodology

This project was funded by the Paralyzed Veterans of America's Education and Training Foundation. What I've done is not hard research, but rather anecdotal information gathered in a somewhat methodical and organized manner. My goal was to provide people in rehab or later with a group of role models with whom they might identify.

Two groups of SCI survivors helped me define the concept of success and how to identify people to interview. I found people through rehabilitation hospitals, chapters of both the Paralyzed Veterans of America and the National Spinal Cord Injury Association, through friends and associates in the disability community and through word of mouth. In all, I spoke to about 400 people and choose 53 from the 200 who expressed an interest in participating.

I chose people based on a combination of personal factors and demographics, such as age, level and origin of injury, gender, race and geographical location. I consciously avoided people who received big settlements, and looked for people who were happy with themselves and with their lives and felt, by their own standards, that they were coping well.

I talked to each person at length on the phone, then met each in person. In telling their stories, I've tried to present glimpses of where they've been, how they got here and a picture of what their lives are like today, with an intentional emphasis on the present in order to show both possibilities and just how far they've come.

It is with regret that I must note the passing of two of the individuals profiled on these pages. Glenford Hibbert and Audrey Begay both died shortly before publication, though neither of their passings were related to their injuries or subsequent disabilities. Medical and rehabilitation advances over the past 50 years have insured that life expectancy following SCI now approaches that of the non-disabled population. I celebrate both Glenford's and Audrey's lives and can only trust the reader will draw valuable lessons from them. ∎

A Glossary of Terms

AB, ABs: Ablebodied people, a.k.a. nondisabled people. We were all there once.

ADA: The Americans with Disabilities Act, landmark civil rights legislation passed in 1990 guaranteeing people with disabilities full and equal access to society and protection from discrimination on the basis of disability.

Cath, Cathing: Catheterize, catheterizing

CIL or ILC: Center for Independent Living or Independent Living Center. These are organizations that promote and enable living independently in the community. They dispense information and assist clients in accessing services and assistance programs within their communities. They're usually government-funded but mostly run by people with disabilities. They provide their services free of charge.

Chair: In this book, synonymous with wheelchair.

Crip or Gimp: In-group terms used with affection by some people with disabilities, but unwelcome when used by nondisabled people.

ICU: Intensive care unit.

Medicaid: Federal/state medical insurance program for impoverished and disabled people. This is the insurer of last resort, and covers in-home personal care in some states, durable medical equipment in most, and prescription drugs in all. Eligibility is subject to strict earnings limits.

Medicare: Federal healthcare program for the elderly and disabled. Most people with SCI who qualify receive Social Security Disability Insurance. Medicare's coverage is less generous than Medicaid's and, starting in 2005, offers only bare-bones drug coverage.

NSCIA: National Spinal Cord Injury Association, a nationwide SCI information and support center with chapters in many states. A good early information source. See resources for other groups that can help.

PASS Plan: Plan for Achieving Self Sufficiency, a little-used Social Security program that allows recipients of SSI to work and have earnings over the limits. It sets aside excess earnings for work-related expenses, such as future educational expenses or work-related expenses like computers and vehicle modifications.

PAS: Personal Assistance Services, aka. Attendant services.

PVA: Paralyzed Veterans of America

SCI: Spinal cord injury.

SSI: Supplemental Security Income, the Social Security Administration's welfare program for people with low incomes. Recipients must meet strict income and asset restrictions in order to qualify, and monthly payments are very low. For many, the primary benefit of SSI is Medicaid eligibility.

SSDI: Social Security Disability Insurance, Social Security's long-term disability insurance for people who worked for some time before becoming disabled. Benefits are determined by pre-injury wage levels. Unlike SSI, this program has no asset limits. One key feature of SSDI is eligibility for Medicare.

Section 8 Housing: Relatively inexpensive government-subsidized housing for low-income people. Only a small portion is accessible. Eligibility is determined by income. For those who qualify, monthly rent is set at one-third of monthly income. Qualified applicants far exceed available units.

SO: Significant Other

Tetraplegia: Synonymous with quadriplegia.

UTI: Urinary tract infection, a common complication of SCI.

VASCI: Violently acquired spinal cord injury

VR or Voc Rehab: Vocational Rehabilitation Services. The Vocational Rehabilitation Act requires each state to provide assistance to residents with disabilities to help them find and qualify for employment. Voc Rehab has a long history of assisting people with college tuition and other education-related expenses like books and transportation. ∎

DEMOGRAPHICS

The number of people living with spinal cord injury nationwide is estimated at approximately 250,000, with about 11,000 people sustaining new spinal cord injuries each year.

Abbreviations used below: AA=African American; MVA=Motor Vehicle Accident; GSW= Gunshot Wound; SO= Significant Other

SCI by Gender:			By Race:			By Origin of Injury:		
	Nationally	This Book		Nationally	This Book		Nationally	This Book
Male	79%	76%	White	63%	63%	MVA	44%	45%
Female	21%	24%	AA	26%	21%	GSW	22%	24.5%
			Hispanic	5.6%	11%	Sports	8%	19%
			Asian	2%	4%	Falls	22%	6%
			Native Am	.2%	2%	Other	2%	6%

The proportion of injuries due to motor vehicle crashes and sporting activities have declined while the proportion of injuries from falls has increased steadily since 1973. Acts of violence peaked in the mid 1990s but have subsequently declined.

By Level of Injury:				
	Nationally	This Book	This Book:	
Tetraplegia	50%	51%	Average age at injury	21.5
Paraplegia	48%	49%	Average yrs. post-injury	17.2
n/a	2%		Total years of experience	931

Single	25		21 of 53 participants are in committed relationships	
Married	14		that began after injury	
Single w/SO	9			
Divorced	7	5 post-injury	Parents	20	11 became parents post-injury
		(2 remarried)	Single Parents	11	3 women gave birth

Because people are typically young at time of injury, a disproportionate number are single.

Employed full time	32	Attended college	41
Employed part time	9	Presently attend college	7
Significant volunteer work	39	Students full time	5
Unemployed	4	Hold 2 or 4 year degree	31
Retired	3		

Forty-eight of 53 participants have worked at least part time

Unemployment rates are extremely high for people with SCI. This group, selected because its members have done well, bucks that trend. Most have worked, volunteered extensively and pursued higher education.

CHAPTER ONE
Early Thoughts

"I was afraid that when people saw me in a wheelchair they'd feel sorry for me and not see me as that person I felt I still was."

Cathy Green

"At first I thought everything would be different. I was surprised that my money still had the same value."

Vincent Dureau

"Before I was injured, no one could keep up with me and I wanted something that mattered. I asked for a big challenge and disability gave me that."

Keith Davis

"It's OK to not be OK with this. You don't have to like or accept this; you just have to reconcile yourself to the parameters."

Karen Hwang

"I didn't need this to become a better person."

Susan Douglas

Getting started after spinal cord injury can be terrifying. At least it was for me. Like most people new to SCI, I was the first wheeler I'd ever met and I couldn't imagine what life would be like. All the time I was in rehab I struggled to sleep, to focus, to just calm down. I wanted answers, like how I was going to get out of bed and get dressed each day, how I was going to find someone to help me or find accessible housing in a mountain town of 2,000 souls, and how I was going to keep my job if I couldn't drive. I wanted to know if I really had a future with a girlfriend who was having second thoughts about being with me and filled with guilt because she was having them, or if I'd be alone for the rest of my life if she left. I wondered and worried about work,

sex, living on my own and whether any of my friends—the ones I marathoned and skied and rafted and biked with—would want to spend time with me. I was afraid I'd become a pariah, someone (or worse yet, some*thing*) to be avoided or feared because of the chair. Could I make new friends? How? Would my life have any meaning? If so, then what? I got more panicky each day as my date of discharge neared.

When I talked with my fellow inmates I discovered most of them had the same fears and concerns. A few might have had an answer or two, but most of us left rehab clueless and, at best, with unformed plans, inaccurate expectations and erroneous beliefs. I left the hospital thinking:

- I'm not strong enough emotionally
- This might be a fate worse than death
- I'll never have any quality of life
- I'll never work again
- I'll never have fun again
- I'll never be loved again
- Life will lose its meaning.

About a year after discharge I was at Craig Hospital doing some outpatient physical therapy when a guy about to be discharged cornered me and pointedly asked, "Hey, I'm going home next week. What should I expect? What's it really like?"

For some reason he thought I was doing OK and would have some answers. In truth, I was still struggling to get through my days, filling them with volunteer work and laying the necessary groundwork to go back to school. I'd get up each morning, feed my girlfriend's two boys and drive them to school, then pick one of them up from kindergarten three hours later. I ran errands, did grocery shopping, laundry and occasionally cooked a meal. My relationship with my girlfriend was shaky; I was prone to temper tantrums and angry more often than happy. My main accomplishments that first year were learning all my self-care well enough that I no longer needed to pay a daily attendant, and going from no plan to a half-assed one. And I was supposed to know what it's really like?

The best I could offer was, "It's not going to be anything like you expect, so maybe you shouldn't have any expectations at all."

Fourteen years later, I think I could have been more eloquent but the message wasn't too far off-base. Most of my early beliefs and expectations have been proven dead wrong. Spinal cord injury isn't what I thought it was or what I thought it might be.

What I know now is that all the emotions most people feel in the first few months after injury are totally real and reasonable. I know SCI is about as big a curve ball as life can give us, yet I also know we don't need to be saints or heroes to get past it. I know there are many people who have gone before who are willing to talk and share and help. I know there's no need to field this curve ball all alone.

The people on these pages have lived with SCI and shared their stories. They don't see themselves as inspirations or even doing anything unusual. Instead, they say they're ordinary people, living ordinary lives—lives they've reinvented and made into something slightly or greatly different than their pre-injury lives—that enabled them to move back into life, work, love, sex and adventure. Most of them confirm all the platitudes we heard in rehab—life goes on, you can still have fun, everything is still possible. They say the lives they have now didn't come easy, that they worked hard to get where they are. Few offer a timetable for getting there, but they all offer the same observation: "If I can do this, anybody can do this."

As I met with people, I asked each of them the same questions, beginning with the fears and emotions they'd felt soon after injury and worked through the years to the present day. I've included the questions and listed the answers given most frequently.

This is a chance to compare notes and see what other people thought about early on, what they worried about, what they thought would happen and what they did about it all.

Q: What were your thoughts immediately following injury?

- "I was kind of optimistic. I thought that things would be OK and that I'd figure this out."
- "I was totally depressed and afraid. I thought everything was over."
- "All I could think of was 'How will I survive?' I didn't have a clue as to how I was going to take care of myself or my family."
- "I wanted to know if I was going to be alone forever. Could I have sex or kids or find a partner?"
- "I was in total denial. If I didn't think about it, I didn't have to worry."
- "I was just getting by day to day. I never thought about the future."
- "I wanted to die."

Sound familiar? Most in this group remember the fear and anxiety they felt right after injury, but most also remember a hint of optimism.

"I just sort of went day to day and thought of it as a new beginning," says Jason Graber. "I wasn't all that fazed by not walking."

A good deal of that kind of optimism came from not fully understanding what had happened or how spinal cord injury could and would affect their lives. Felipe Antonio was just happy to be out of bed and learning how to do things. Keith Davis saw it as a welcome challenge. Others, like Charlotte Heppner, couldn't believe all the physical implications of SCI—bowel and bladder and UTIs and pressure sores and all the rest: "I just kept thinking, what else can happen?" Most of us are stunned and numb those first few weeks. We just don't know what to think. On these pages, the words "bad dream" come up a lot.

Sometimes, as reality sinks in, our hopes and expectations sink as well. Rather than seeing this as a bad dream, we see it as just plain bad. Sobering stuff, this spinal cord injury. It's no wonder our optimism heads south in a hurry. For most of us, at least initially, the more we learn the worse the picture becomes.

But for this group, even though their optimism faded as the reality of their situations sunk in, few fell into total despair. Optimism and an inclination to ask questions about what might be possible served them much better than deep depression. There's a lesson here.

Q: What were your initial thoughts, reactions, and impressions about SCI and what the future would be like?

- "I was depressed and thinking this was a fate worse than death."
- "Total denial. I was very angry. All I could think was 'Why me?'"
- "I was uncertain about most everything. Would I be able to work, be independent?"
- "Mostly I was overwhelmed."
- "I was optimistic. I figured I'd be OK."
- "I was so afraid about the future, about taking care of myself, about everything."
- "I had no frame of reference; I didn't have anything to compare this to."
- "I was still worried and wondering about relationships, marriage and sex."
- "I was still living day to day."
- "I saw this as an opportunity; it was my second chance."

"I thought life was pretty much over," says Paul Herman.

"I wasn't sure I wanted to live like this," Kevin Wolitzky says of his early days after breaking his neck.

These depressed reactions are understandable, especially since we're bombarded by media messages about physical perfection, extreme makeovers and pity for anyone less than above average. We don't get much help from nondisabled people, and some may even expect us to be suicidal. It could be denial or hope

springing eternal, but the majority in this group managed to at least suspend judgment about their new lives until they had more answers. They said doing so helped.

Like most of us, Eric Gibson knew nothing about SCI. He wondered what life on wheels would be like and how he would deal with it. Vincent Dureau, Jason Graber, Jamie Peterson and others took life day by day, focused on learning all they could and tried not to think past tomorrow. Susan Douglas, Amit Jha and Cathy Green looked forward to getting back to school soon.

If there's good news here it's that even with some time to digest the full extent of what had happened to them, less than a third of these people said they felt totally depressed or hopeless. The key for many was that even though they were scared, uncertain and clueless about what to expect, they asked questions. As they did, and as they got answers, they slowly gained confidence, grew more comfortable, began to understand their situations and tackle their self-care problems.

Most of us get past our early fears and negative images of disability by asking questions and getting answers.

As the Roman historian Livy wrote, "We fear things in proportion to our ignorance of them." Most early uncertainties revolve around what we *don't* know. And the universal factor that eases anxiety and makes things begin to look possible, this group says, is talking to each other, to rehab professionals and—most of all—to experienced wheelers.

Most relied on the pros for answers while they were still in the hospital. When someone told Joel Irizarry he couldn't have kids, he got scared: "But I got that cleared up real fast by talking to a real doc." He got the information he needed quickly. Once Phillip Mann got to a quality rehab center and saw what was possible, he made good use of a knowledgeable staff to learn as much as he could. Matthew Seals remembers the PT who taught him many of his fundamentals: "She drove me like a drill sergeant. I needed that." The best advice

Keith Davis got was from a rehab nurse who told him that because he was young and would heal fast, he should go out and do things: "What I heard was that the chair wasn't a big deal, that I shouldn't worry about all the bad things that could happen."

Attitudes and outlooks often change even more when people meet experienced wheelers—or even relatively short-term wheelers—who are willing to listen, answer questions and provide some assurances. That's how Pat McGowan learned: "Henry [a seasoned quad] took me under his wing and taught me how to secure benefits and deal with government bureaucracies. He really helped me." There's comfort in knowing you don't have to figure it all out on your own.

Angel Watson had no real image of what it meant to be in a chair: "All I thought of was the little old lady in the window." The first time she saw a successful wheeler who laughed and had a job and a life, she began to see more possibilities.

Stark reality motivates some. Michael Slaughter kept expecting to wake up from his bad dream, but when that didn't happen he eased his anxiety by learning as much as he could. Like others, he found that his fears became less overwhelming with familiarity, discussion and example.

Not everyone gets through despair and hopelessness quickly. Don Dawkins spent years avoiding other wheelers until he finally joined a support group, where old-timers helped him come to grips with his anger and denial. "Old-timers don't coddle you," he says. "And most of the time they give you what you need."

Something else is clear from this group: We move at our own speed and in our own ways, and some of us take awhile before we can begin to question how SCI is affecting our lives and what we should be doing about it. ∎

Charmaine Brown, *Circus Display, 1998*

First Things First

The road to successful living with SCI has an on-ramp and it's paved with attention to detail. A common thread in this group is that they learned the basics of self-care, benefits, housing and transportation before they tackled issues like employment, dating or home ownership. Makes sense, really, like putting on clothes before wheeling out the door, cooking food before eating it or tackling grade school before college. Many compare life after SCI to a second birth and childhood. They say you have to lay the foundation before throwing parties in the castle of joy.

Psychologist Abraham Maslow proposed a ladder of needs most human beings must climb on the way to fulfillment and happiness. It works pretty well for the ablebodied set. Maslow says we must meet certain basic and fundamental needs before moving on and meeting needs with more potential for reward. The higher up the ladder we climb, the more gratifying the rewards become.

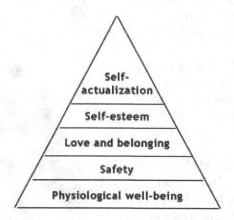

People with SCI start with basics like eating, shelter, security and a sense of predictability (e.g. accessible living quarters, a bathroom routine that works, skin integrity, reliable attendant care). Only after we've met those basic needs can we move on to higher rewards, and eventually maybe even that promised land Maslow calls self-actualization.

If we don't meet basic needs first, they'll dominate us and continue to bite us in the butt. Spontaneity and self-esteem are hard to come by when you're panhandling on a street corner or lying in your urine waiting for an attendant who's late again. Career fulfillment doesn't often come to those who can't get dressed for work. Love seldom comes to those who hate themselves. First things first.

That's how the people on these pages did it. They learned all they could about spinal cord injury and self-care so they could stay healthy. With basics taken care of, they moved on to transportation, relationships, careers and recreation.

What they tell you in rehab is true: If you want a life, learn the basics. First things first.

Maslow's Hierarchy of Needs
and
Challenges Following Spinal Cord Injury

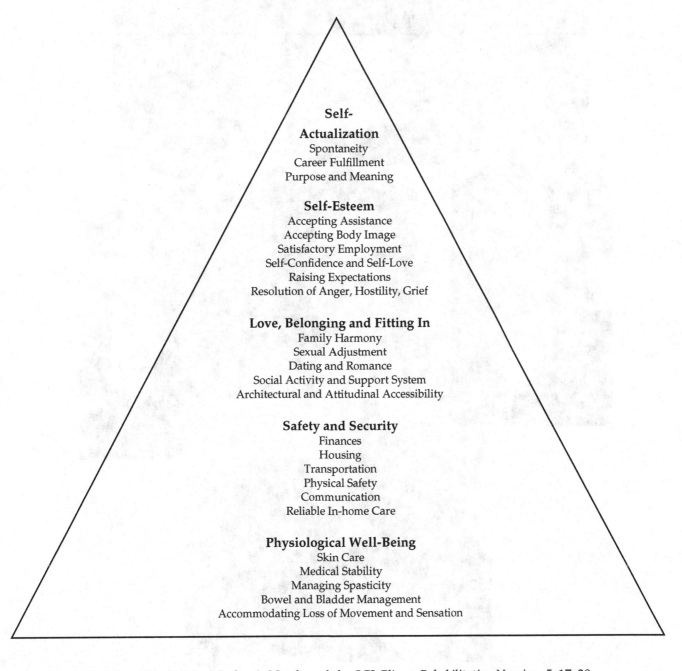

Self-Actualization
Spontaneity
Career Fulfillment
Purpose and Meaning

Self-Esteem
Accepting Assistance
Accepting Body Image
Satisfactory Employment
Self-Confidence and Self-Love
Raising Expectations
Resolution of Anger, Hostility, Grief

Love, Belonging and Fitting In
Family Harmony
Sexual Adjustment
Dating and Romance
Social Activity and Support System
Architectural and Attitudinal Accessibility

Safety and Security
Finances
Housing
Transportation
Physical Safety
Communication
Reliable In-home Care

Physiological Well-Being
Skin Care
Medical Stability
Managing Spasticity
Bowel and Bladder Management
Accommodating Loss of Movement and Sensation

Adapted from Stark, P.L., Maslow's Needs and the SCI Client, *Rehabilitation Nursing*, 5, 17–20 with permission of the Association of Rehabilitation Nurses, 4700 W. Lake Avenue, Glenview, IL 60025-1485. Copyright © 1980. ∎

11

Clockwise from top: Benj Anderson, Steve Ferguson, Audrey Begay & family, Robert Statam, Wardell Kyles, Anne Marie Hochhalter, Ryan Odens, Patty Rivas (middle).II

Ryan Odens

"All I've ever wanted to do was farming," Ryan Odens says. "I figure I'll always be doing it." Ryan is a modern-day farmer. Rather than rising with the roosters like his ancestors, he sleeps in until 7:30 or 8 and knocks off about 5 p.m.

That's what he told me but as we talked it became apparent that this 9 to 5 schedule of his only applies from November to March. That's when chores are limited to moving snow, feeding livestock, maintenance, ordering and selling seed, and his personal favorite, taxes. From late March through May, he and his brother Nick are usually at it until 10 p.m. or midnight working the ground and planting their 1,300 acres of corn and soybeans.

From September until the snow flies they're busy harvesting, often until well past midnight. The summer growing season is easier and they knock off about 5:30 or so, after spraying and cultivating, caring for about 30 head of stock, maintaining equipment, or mowing and putting up hay. He and his brother work as hard as any farmers; their hours are just slightly different.

If that seems like a lot of responsibility for this 25-year-old from Little Rock, Iowa, it's because it is. He's an old 25, less carefree and a bit more focused on the future than most men his age. He's seen some major changes since his injury in the fall of 2000.

He'd been drinking the night he rolled his truck and was thrown from it. Luckily, the accident started a small brush fire and attracted some attention. Help came and he was in acute care within an hour. He'd broken several ribs and both wrists, torn up his shoulder, fractured his C1-5 vertebrae and damaged his cord at T3-4. All this left him, as he puts it, "one bungled-up mess."

Following surgery a few days later to install rods from C7 to T7, Ryan was shipped off to Sioux Falls for four weeks. It's just as well that he has little memory of that stay. Doctors had him wearing both a hard collar and a shell brace. The pain was pretty intense and many of his medications caused allergic reactions. He was in and out of the intensive care unit four times with problems ranging from urinary tract infections to fluid build-up in his lungs. One bungled-up mess, indeed.

He still wasn't certain what all had happened, and stayed that way for some time. His doctor told his mother that there was no need to tell him about the paralysis, that eventually he would figure it out on his own. He did, but he never gave up hope of walking.

With a Little Bit of Help ....

Return of function came to Ryan in a big way during his four and one-half months at Craig Hospital. He took his first steps in a pool about eight weeks after injury and slowly progressed from the chair to a walker. Within eight months he got back to farming, which was also about the time he began using forearm crutches. Now he's down to a cane. Because the rods limit his mobility, his gait is very deliberate and anything but fluid, and his impaired balance means a stiff wind can knock him over.

13

When we go outside, I have to wheel quite slowly so he can keep up.

All through rehab Ryan was sure he'd continue farming once he was home. He stuck with therapy that first winter—he still does some PT—and was ready for planting by spring. "There are definitely worse things than spinal cord injury," he says. "I figured I did this to myself and I'd get through it myself." Well, maybe not entirely by himself.

Family and friends have given him enormous support, most likely a repayment to him for his sharp sense of humor and ability to put others at ease. And when they saw how serious he was about getting back to farming, they stopped worrying and began treating him as the same guy he'd always been.

"If my friends had abandoned me," he says, "all this would have been a lot harder. They came and got me and took me places after I got home even if I didn't want to go. They treated me the same and that's what's helped the most. That and getting back to a normal routine as quickly as possible. Feeling like I was contributing to what needed to be done helped a lot, too."

Luckily his family already owned a clutchless tractor, and that got him back in the fields in time for the spring planting.

He had other help. While he was still at Craig, his counselors connected him with Easter Seals of Iowa, hoping they'd help get him back in the fields. Easter Seals did some assessment, and then contacted Voc Rehab to tell them what Ryan needed. VR ponied up for an ATV to get him around the farm and lifts to get him onto the tractor and the combine. They put a concrete floor in the machine shed so he would have a solid, level surface for doing maintenance, and tossed in electric gate openers as well. Easter Seals gave him a lift so he could get in and out of his home, and paid for some modifications inside. With the physical barriers eliminated, he was good to go and the rest was up to him. He tells me this kind of help from agencies is common in Iowa and not tied to any level of physical function.

"Both Easter Seals and Voc Rehab tried to get me to go back to school," Ryan says, "but farming was all I was interested in." More proof that he hasn't changed.

The Fields of Home

Ryan's return to farming was a learning experience, an exercise in frustration with a dose of depression on the side. He struggled with getting around through the mud and learning how to do things differently, and he was still concerned with how others perceived and judged him.

Because farming is such hard work and keeps him on his feet throughout the day, his injury is far more limiting than if he worked in an office in front of a computer. Though he's fairly strong in the morning, he tires quickly and can't do nearly as much of the heavy lifting as he once did. He was still working on his balance and strength using a stationary bike and a Stairmaster. That first year or so was hardly a cakewalk.

But mentally, Ryan was up to the hard work of farming, doing it so well that within two years he was named the Easter Seals Farmer of the Year, and was the subject of numerous newspaper and magazine articles.

These days, during the summer when he has some slack time, he spends his evenings helping out friends with their dirt-track racing stock car, doing maintenance, tire or body work. He goes to the races on weekends, coordinating what needs to be done in the pits. When he's not farming or doing the racing thing, he's spending time hanging with his many friends at clubs, bars or restaurants, doing what twenty-somethings do. He likes to snowmobile during the winter and plans his trips to Denver for reevaluations around the Broncos cheerleaders' visits to Craig.

Ryan continues to work on his walking and says he's exercising all the time. "I think I'm still getting stronger," he says. "Seems like I can do more around the farm."

And other places too. Always looking for something to do, he's now selling insurance on the side. A cousin of his is in the business and has been hounding him to give it a try.

"Life, farm, commercial. You name it, I sell it. It's OK."

Ryan's a mix of playful energy, youthful enthusiasm and the accelerated maturity that often comes with the hard times of something like SCI. The mix gives him the willfulness of a youngster with the wisdom of someone successfully dealing with adversity.

"The deal is that people are depending on me," he says. "I don't have a choice, I've got to work, and the working helps a lot. When my dad died, no one thought my brother and I could run the farm, but we did. When I got hurt most everyone assumed I wouldn't walk or go back to work. What gets me out of bed every morning is my will to succeed and my desire to prove those people wrong. When people tell me I can't do something, that's when I really try. Knowing I'm not supposed to be able to do something really gives me a reason to do it."

Has SCI changed Ryan at all?

"Oh, yeah," he says. "I look at life and people differently. Work is less important to me and it's hard to take life for granted. I'm quicker to help people now."

What about the future?

"Things can always be worse and they can always be better. I live day to day. But I'm still a little kid; you know, 'first you crawl, then you walk.' I'm still getting better, getting stronger."

Do you see a reason behind all this?

"A lot of people say everything is part of God's plan," Ryan says, "but if that's true, how can He expect anyone to deal with this? Most of the time I believe that God doesn't give people more than they can handle, but sometimes I think that's a bunch of crap too. I've seen people fall 75 feet down a silo and walk away. Some of this stuff is pretty random. Return of function is kind of like making money—you can work real hard and still be poor. I kinda think my walking's a miracle." ■

Charmaine G. Brown, *A Royal Flush*, 2004

15

Robert Statam

Robert Statam believes that disability has given him a second chance at life. It came at the age of 39, and he's running hard with it.

"I spent years abusing alcohol and drugs and never once thought I could be brave enough to get off that roller-coaster ride," he says. "I never dreamed this was how it would happen. Disability gave me an opportunity to start out fresh and find what I wanted out of life. Most people don't get that chance. I got so many things going right for me now, I'm real optimistic about the future. I'm feeling about 80 percent whole and getting better. The wheelchair may have saved my life."

He tells me this with the wide-eyed, smiling enthusiasm of a kid who's just learned to read or swim or drive. Through all his travails he remains a happy, grateful, enthusiastic guy. He's dealt with most of his demons and is focused on living each day with a belief in himself and his ability to deal with what life throws him.

"People always see me happy and with a smile on my face," he says. "I don't worry much about things. We all have bad stuff happen to us in life and this is one of them for me. I know there will be others; that's part of the journey."

Robert's medical odyssey began in 1999 with an arthroscopic surgery for back pain at Hines VA Hospital in Chicago. The procedure went well and he was good to go … for a couple of weeks. What followed was a bad made-for-TV movie: weeks of intense back pain, physical therapy, a series of steroid shots. When he began losing function he was diagnosed with a bulging disc. Five months later, in the hospital waiting for surgery, he stood up, heard something pop, and fell back onto the bed. Nothing worked from the waist down. Though nurses gave him morphine for pain, he wasn't checked by a doctor until the next day. No one could tell him exactly what had happened.

Following surgery and two months of therapy, he regained some bowel and bladder function and was able to walk with a walker. After discharge from Hines and a two-month stay in a nursing home, he went to live with his brother.

"As soon as I got there, the phone rang," Robert recalls. "It was a treatment facility for drugs and alcohol. They had a bed for me, so I went there for six weeks of treatment."

Finally, after more than six months, he was out of medical facilities but not yet out of the woods. He still had chronic pain, diabetes and heart disease to deal with, and he was still discouraged and worried about what would happen next. It took him two years to find subsidized housing on the South Side of Chicago.

Perseverance

These experiences would enrage most people, but somehow Robert kept his smile, tried to stay positive, sucked it up and toughed it out. I wondered how he managed to do it.

"Seeing how much my family cared and how much they were doing for me helped me let go of the anger," he says. "I couldn't continue to be mad and at the same time accept what they were trying to do for me. Then I started looking around and seeing what other patients were able to do, what was possible for them. I also watched for what not to do. Things slowly improved. For a while I thought I should be able to deal with all this on my own, and all the time there were people around with answers to most of my questions."

Drawing motivation from others, Robert began to push himself into potentially uncomfortable situations—on public transportation and in places where he was exposed to public attention. Over time, his confidence and social skills grew.

He became assertive enough to question medical professionals and government officials. He learned the ins and outs of obtaining SSDI and VA benefits. He secured housing, appealing denials along the way. His learning curve for this life with disability may have been plodding and tedious, but it got him where he was going.

Robert eventually learned enough that he wanted to share his knowledge. Then it was back to Hines VA to work as a peer counselor.

"I tell people not to give up hope and to work to stay positive," he says. "I tell them my story and how I found out that I could still be happy, that I'm happier now than before. I tell them how quickly things happened for me once I began trying new things like sports, computers and spending time with other people in chairs."

In addition to his counseling, Robert takes four days a week of computer and typing classes. That structures his time and teaches him skills he can use in the future. While he's retraining, he relies on SSDI and some VA disability compensation to cover his expenses.

"It's just me," he says. "I don't need much and I keep things simple. It's okay for now."

Turning Point

Robert feels that entering the resident drug and alcohol recovery program is what turned his life around.

"That's what really did it and changed things for me," he says. "I did group and individual therapy, and began to make sense of my drinking and drugging. The longer I was there the more I was able to see and understand my part in it and own up to my past mistakes and behavior. The group stuff helped me let go of a lot of my anger and shame about dependency. I started having fun again. Now my mind is about 100 miles ahead of drinking and I'm not bothered by it any more."

Nearly four years later, he's still clean and sober.

"I gave up thinking my way of life was the only way of life; I found out I could still have fun without drinking or using. When I saw that I was still enjoying myself even though I've got this disability, I thought, 'Well hell, nothing's impossible now.'

"Now it's time for me to help other people," he says. "I'm looking to make it all work and give back."

He does give back—as a peer counselor at Hines, as a board member and the coordinator of the VA Veterans Services of the local PVA chapter. He serves on the advisory council of the Chicago Transit Authority and works on his building's tenant council committee addressing accessibility issues and organizing events.

Drug and alcohol abuse cost him a long-term relationship, but when he got sober, other doors opened—counseling, Bible study, disability advocacy and computer classes. What works for Robert now is staying busy, out in the world and meeting new people, filling his hours with activities that make him feel good about himself.

He got an additional lift from wheelchair sports, and has competed in the annual PVA Wheelchair Games twice.

"Seeing so many vets out there *doing* gave me a very warm feeling," he says. "These guys have given me a lot of support, the confidence that I could do things and that I didn't need to be ashamed or embarrassed about being disabled. They've helped me deal with sexual dysfunction and bowel and bladder stuff. I've learned how to take care of myself, and take responsibility."

What's been hardest for him?

"Well, the physical losses and the pain. For a while I thought I was going to be able to get by without the chair, but that doesn't look like it's going to happen. The pain attacks are very severe; the bowel and bladder is always a hassle. Maybe the hardest part was the lack of companionship. At first that was very hard, but now I like the solitude and I like myself. I'll spend evenings doing homework and playing on my laptop. Sometimes I'll go to movies or the mall. I'll take what I've got."

Robert says he's always looking forward to something. Computer school is going very well for him; it's fun and he's learning. He feels he needs another year or two of getting used to both the chair and sobriety before he begins shopping for a partner. Down the road he's hoping to own some property.

"I'm discovering things I never thought I'd like," he says. "I like myself more. It might sound like baby steps, but it's working for me. There's *always* hope. I've found that if I keep on keepin' on, eventually it pays off. I feel like I'm becoming the man I always should have been.

"It's been about four and a half years and my life has been filled with new experiences. I've grown tremendously. Traveling and attending conferences have allowed me to get involved in advocacy for the rights of the disabled and learn how the government operates. There's no end to the impact one person might make.

"I have learned how to deal with my medical issues at my own pace and don't seem to let anything keep me down. The more I keep busy the less time I have to think about my problems. I look at it like this: we all only have one life to live so let's love the life we live today, and if you should have a second chance at life, don't worry about yesterday." ∎

Charmaine G. Brown, *A Royal Flush*

Audrey Begay

When Audrey Begay and her brother Arthur saw a young woman crossing the street in a wheelchair about seven years ago, they were filled with pity and sympathy.

"We talked about how hard that must be," she remembers. "That was before we knew even half of all that's involved with being in a chair. I made Arthur promise me then that if I ever ended up like that he would kill me, no matter what. I promised to do the same for him."

Two weeks later she was in a Durango, Colo. hospital, on a ventilator and in a coma, with a C4-5 spinal cord injury. If that's not spooky enough, her accident happened on Halloween while she was dressed as Frankenstein's bride. Her brother never pulled the plug and Audrey's not complaining.

Returning home from that Halloween party, Audrey slipped on a patch of ice outside her home, where she then lay for several snowy hours before her roommate found her and called 911. By the time she got to the hospital she was paralyzed from the neck down, her lungs were collapsed and she was barely breathing. Her coma lasted for nearly a month.

Following fusion surgery and six weeks of acute care, Audrey moved on to Denver for rehab at Craig Hospital. Her brothers and her mom took turns staying there with her. She was able to lose the vent and learn some skills, but the bottom fell out of her world on Valentine's Day. Her fiancé broke off their engagement, telling her coldly that with mountains to ski and trails to bike, he needed to move on.

"This chair," he said, kicking the tires, "is just so unattractive."

"I'm happy right now and at peace with myself," Audrey says. "I never thought having a husband, a daughter, an apartment, any of that stuff, was possible. Now I have them all. Before I was injured I was a wild Indian running around the country. I was depressed and suicidal. I'd broken all the mirrors and light bulbs in my apartment and hung blankets on the windows. I had no friends, no car, no job; I was gone."

Audrey's telling me all this as we sit in the suburban Denver apartment she shares with Adrian, her partner of nearly five years, and their three year-old-daughter. Unlike that pre-injury apartment, which overflowed with her depression, this one is filled with comfortable furniture and the necessary toys—television, VCR, computer. Her days are filled with mothering Hannah on her own while Adrian is off working his medical internship.

On weekends, or when Adrian is off and has free time, they check out local museums or go out to listen to music. Other times, she relaxes by either reading or writing. And now that one of Adrian's daughters from a previous marriage has moved in with them, Audrey is doing a crash course in step-parenting.

With the help of her aide, who comes each morning to get her dressed, out of bed and in her chair, Audrey's up and going by 8 a.m. to have breakfast and keep track of the little one. Often she and Hannah go out for walks or to the playground to be with other kids. She is a housewife in every sense; she does the laundry and cleans the house. Due to her limited function—both arms are impaired and she uses a power chair—housework consumes much of her day. It's worth it, she says, because it keeps her busy and feeling productive.

Her incomplete injury left her with some use of her legs, enough that she can use her standing frame for an hour each afternoon. Home by 4:30, Adrian takes over parenting duties while Audrey spends time with her aide doing self-care until 6 or so. After dinner and some family time, she spends a couple of hours reading or working on her book until crashing at about 10 p.m.

Finding a Life

Audrey has already said that when she had her accident in 1998 she was broke, dependent and suicidal. These days she seems happy, optimistic, hopeful. How did that happen? The hard way.

After her discharge from Craig, the entire family—Audrey, her mom and two brothers—moved into a Denver apartment. With little money and no furniture, they all slept on pillows on the floor and one of her brothers turned her several times a night. Being broke, eight hours from home and trying to deal with catastrophic injury put everyone on edge. The more her family fought, the more Audrey withdrew and felt like a burden. Eventually she locked her door and hid in her room.

"That's when my brother Arthur said, 'Time to get your head out of your ass, Audrey.' He dragged me out to coffee shops and restaurants or up to the mountains and out on trails. He pushed me hard. It was scary—I was very self-conscious, but I went and it was fun. Things started getting better then."

They also got better when she began dating and saving money to move out on her own. Then Adrian, whom she had met when he was a personal care assistant at Craig, called and asked her out.

"I was always nervous about leg spasms and things," she says, "but he knew all

about them and never cared. I wasn't as nervous with him." They became friends quickly and over time began dating. He helped her fill out subsidized housing applications and took her to see apartments where she might live on her own. Eventually she found one that worked.

"It was great," she says. "I loved living on my own and being away from my family. I really needed that and found out I was stronger than I thought."

The life she wanted demanded new strengths. She had to cope with all the changes without help. Things took longer and required more patience. She needed to wear different clothes. She needed to get out and do for herself.

"I had to accept myself,' she says. "That's hard, but I did it."

After a year of dating, when Audrey became pregnant, she and Adrian found another place and have been living together since. Hannah arrived by cesarean section after a normal pregnancy. Motherhood has been a bigger, scarier and harder challenge than she'd expected, one that totally turned Audrey's life around.

With Adrian working each day, she's been a full-service mom from the start, changing diapers as much with her mouth as with her hands. Terrified of dropping her baby, and just as scared of letting others see how afraid she was, Audrey faked it. She acted much more confident than she felt, but in time she learned it all.

"Being a mom in a chair is hard work but you learn to improvise," she says. "The physical stuff was OK, but it was so emotionally draining."

Said like most new moms, disabled or nondisabled.

True Independence

Though she's in a power chair, has little hand function and needs aides every morning and afternoon for transfers, dressing and bathroom functions, Audrey speaks of feeling much more independent now than before she was injured. *More* independent?

"I have mental independence," she insists. "I rely on myself and keep going. I

20

have goals. I expect days to be good. Life's hard, but I'm happier now than I was before I got hurt.

"I'm responsible for my health, my self-care and for being happy. SCI is still like a roller coaster and I still have to hang on and roll with stuff like UTIs and skin sores but I'm doing it. That's new for me. Hannah's my motivation, what gets me out of bed each morning and keeps my mind off me. She makes me responsible."

That motivation and responsibility has driven her to learn to use a computer and finish high school online. Now she dreams of going to college once her daughter's in school.

About a year after her injury, she began writing about her pre- and post-injury experiences and now spends a couple of hours a day at it. Her writing serves as a physical and emotional meditation, a way to sort out and understand what's happened and what the sum of her experiences mean. This is a common exercise for many who go through traumatic events, a way to make sense of things for themselves. While it might resemble therapy, it's way cheaper.

Audrey's life may not be gum drops and lollipops but she finds it far fuller and richer than she ever imagined it could be and her writing has helped her get there.

"I don't think anyone ever gets fully adjusted to SCI, but I know I can make it what I want it to be. It's not about having money or being physically independent. I had a friend who had both, but she couldn't adjust and she killed herself. You can sit around feeling miserable or you can find ways to make life easier."

Note: Audrey passed away unexpectedly in June of 2004. She'd been in good health. ∎

Charmaine Brown   *A Royal Flush*

Steve Ferguson

Steve Ferguson was getting his life together in 1996, working a maintenance job and about to start a new job with Federal Express. He had his child support straightened out and was committed to being a better dad. He'd been straight for several months and was trying to put drugs behind him when someone he knew talked him into making a buy. The deal went bad and he was shot. He spent six weeks in a Washington, D.C. hospital, then six months in the National Rehabilitation Hospital (NRH), also in D.C. Complete C5 injury; complete life change at 32.

Now, seven years later, he's working part time, seeing his daughter regularly and instructing the drum and bugle corps of a church marching band. Getting shot didn't stop him from getting his act together. It may have helped.

"I'd grown up with the shooter ," he says. "I'd hooked him up with the buyer, but when he took off without paying and the dealer couldn't find him, he shot me and tried to run me over. We used to be friends and then he tries to kill me. I was angry with him for changing my life."

Quickly understanding that he would now need daily assistance, Steve began working hard at NRH to learn all that was necessary about his care, as well as everything it would take to supervise those who would provide it. He learned how to keep himself healthy.

"I realized that no one would know my needs or wants unless I knew what they were and could tell people. I learned about my care so I could teach it to others. Now that I have to be my own best advocate, I'm much better at communicating."

With few options for independent living, Steve went straight from rehab to a nursing home in Maryland within commuting distance of D.C. He sees the facility as a crib and plans on living there until he figures out how to live on his own. He's never heard of the Olmstead Act, which requires services—such as the ones he needs—to be given in the least restrictive setting, and he doesn't see his limited choice of living arrangements as a political matter.

Why a nursing home?

"I have to have at least 12 hours of care a day," he says. "I need help with dressing and transferring; I need to be turned two or three times a night. Right now, the hassles of living here aren't as bad as what I'd have to deal with if I lived in downtown D.C. The way things are, I think living on my own would be too hard."

Regaining control of his life in the nursing home environment is a challenge, but apparently not more than he can handle. He packs a lot into the small room: a music system, a microwave, a small refrigerator and a computer. Therabands and a skateboard for strengthening his arms sit next to the television and VCR. The sip-and-puff device you see below his chin in the photo allows him to use his speakerphone. A sign reading "If you move it, put it back;

if you open it, close it; if you break it, fix it" reminds his aides who's in charge. And because he's off-grounds and in the city most days of the week, he's not around enough to go stir crazy.

Marching Therapy

Steve played bongos, the cymbals and a scratchboard by the time he was nine, joined the drum corps and began playing with the McCollough Royal Knights Marching Band when he was 12, and became the drum instructor in 1989, 12 years later. Though his chair gets in the way sometimes, music has remained a big part of his life after injury and he went back to directing the Royal Knights as quickly as he could. The band, he says, has been his salvation. He shows me a trophy for outstanding service, easily 30 inches tall, which speaks to the band's appreciation of his directing talent.

"They helped me get back into things and gave me a reason to go back downtown," he says. "I was their big brother, their cuz, their uncle. We were tight. We gave each other unconditional love and they came and played for me while I was in the hospital. Going back to instructing them after my injury helped me feel like I could still do things. That's helped me a lot."

He's still directing and has even traveled to Charlotte, N.C. for the annual church marching band competition. On the trip, the kids provided his care. If the videos he showed me are any indication, his band matches up well with high school bands competing on a national level. He hums along as we watch the tape of him, in uniform and in his chair, leading them through their steps. He's proud of the work he's done with them and his passion for both music and kids is clear

"I feel good seeing all the positives from that band. Music is the only thing that keeps some of those kids off the street. I've taught them a lot, from drumming to being polite. I'll take these kids over a woman anytime."

Continuing to direct hasn't been easy. About three years after injury he was asked to step down and assume a consultant role,

a move that he feels was directly connected to his use of a wheelchair.

"That messed me up bad," he says. Eventually he followed some of his drummers who had moved to a rival band. He now instructs two nights a week and still spends a lot of time with the kids.

Not content just to teach, Steve continues to learn as well. Looking for more formal music training, he got Voc Rehab to pay for some courses at the University of D.C. Getting out, interacting with others and pushing his endurance all helped him get used to the chair. He enjoyed the learning, challenge and structure and liked how the classes tested his abilities. He sees more school in his future.

Mentoring Himself and Others

More than the band and music occupy Steve's time. He's a peer counselor at NRH with the Disabling Bullet Project, a program designed specifically for people living with violently acquired spinal cord injuries (VASCI).

"I was used to mentoring because of the band," he says. "I got involved with this program because I wanted to help and needed something to do. I started when I was still in rehab and turned it into a part-time job. As I was trying to make others stronger, the mentoring made me stronger because I had to come to terms with this stuff."

Steve presently works with five young people with VASCI, meeting with each once a week to answer their questions and talk about their concerns. Sometimes he takes them out to movies or video parlors; other times they'll take in an NBA Wizards game. In a perfect world, he'd expand the present inpatient-only program to outpatients as well.

He counsels on violence prevention with the D.C. chapter of the Chicago-based ThinkFirst program and Project Peace, both of which are geared to junior and senior high school students. He tells them about himself and how he deals with the physical and social aspects of living with a disability.

"I enjoy teaching kids that their actions

and decisions have consequences," Steve says. "I use myself as an example and show them the consequences of my foolish choice. Getting shot was a real reality check for me. I had to think about what I was doing and how I was living my life."

He's also worked as a research intern at NRH, gathering data about how the violently acquired injuries of others have affected their families, friends and lovers. The information he compiled is distributed by the hospital to people with new and old injuries.

Steve's face lights up when he speaks of his daughter Montez. Now 13, she was six when he was shot. "She's adjusted like a soldier," he says proudly. When his daughter's mother was uncooperative about visits, he sought subpoenas, went to court and eventually secured parenting time so he could see Montez twice a month and have her in his life.

"All that court stuff was a hassle," he says, "but it was worth it. Now we spend every other weekend together. I either call MetroAccess to pick me up or ride my chair the half mile to the subway to go get her. Sometimes we go out to a movie, other times we'll go back to my place to hang out and play video games. She's not afraid to help me with things like meals. She accepts the chair and it just doesn't seem to make much difference to her."

Getting to this point of resolution and peace hasn't been easy. His biggest challenge has been to forgive the guy who shot him. "I was angry that I let this happen to me but I can't change it," he says. "It took me about four years to forgive him and be able to say so out loud, but I had to do that if I wanted to get out of the depression. Things got better when I did. Church helped me too. Now my mind isn't so cluttered with anger and the 'Why me?' stuff any more. If I didn't let go of the past, I'd still be bitter; if I worry too much about the future, I'll never get strong."

Lessons learned?

"Every action has consequences," he says. "Being in a chair has taught me to be more assertive and to know everything about my care so I could teach it to others. I'm moving on. I've taken some classes and I'm working. If I can do it, so can other paras or quads. Nobody's going to come and give you opportunities. You gotta go for them."

One year update: Steve just finished up driving lessons and is in the market for a set of wheels. Next on his agenda is finding an apartment. "Things are looking up and keep getting better." ∎

Anne Marie Hochhalter

Pessimists will often tell you that the light at the end of the tunnel is only the headlight of an oncoming train. Anne Marie Hochhalter spent her first two years on wheels feeling like a deer trapped in that headlight, wondering what else might go wrong. Life and all its difficulties just kept piling on.

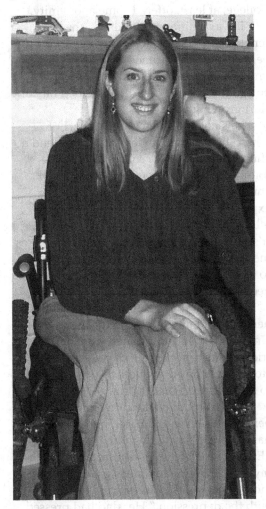

In April of 1999, when Anne Marie was 17 and a junior at Columbine High School in Littleton, Colo., she was one of dozens of students injured in a school shooting that shocked the country. Shot twice, she almost died from internal damage that required multiple surgeries. Her back was broken at T12. After six weeks in ICU and another six in acute care, she made her way to Craig Hospital for two months of very public rehabilitation under the intense eye of the local, national and international media.

By October, she returned to Columbine for a couple of classes each day to complement the tutoring she was getting at home. When her mom died later that month, the media barrage was renewed and even more intrusive than before. Most of us grieve in private; the Hochhalters had to do so with the entire country watching.

Over the course of the next three years, on top of the shootings, her injury and losing her mom, she had to face two moves, intense chronic pain attacks and medication that made her depression worse rather than better. When her dad remarried, she found herself living with three new stepsiblings.

"When you put all those things in a list," Anne Marie says, "it's like, wow, how did I do that?"

Now we're in Westminister, just north of Denver, in the townhouse Anne Marie shares with a roommate. Though it's still a couple of days before Thanksgiving, the Christmas tree is up, stockings are hung and the place is loaded with good cheer. After I meet Molly the dog, we sit in the living room, near her piano, where she tells me about tunnels and light.

The Tunnel

She speaks of her injuries and surgeries in a calm, detached manner, perhaps because she's told her story so many times. Most of her pre-rehab time remains lost in a morphine and Versed fog, so she picks up when she got to Craig.

"I was still in shock when I got to rehab," she says. "It helped that Richard and Sean [fellow students also injured in the shootings] were there and we were going through this together. I learned how to do everything, like cook and take care of myself, but never really thought I'd ever use any of it. I was very nervous about going home. I was really shy and self-conscious before the shootings happened, so the media being around all the time was very hard."

Local newspapers and television stations carried stories of the shootings every day for months, and though the hospital did a good job of protecting the kids from the media, the press was ever-present. In October, just as the attention began to fade, Anne Marie's mother died of a suicide.

"She was bi-polar and watching her go downhill was so hard. The media was so unfair after she died and just wouldn't leave us alone. It was hard, and still is. I can live a normal life in a chair but I can't without my mom."

Her mom's death plunged Anne Marie, her younger brother Nathan and her dad into dark places. Operating on autopilot, she spent the next year healing, learning to live with nerve pain attacks, struggling with being in her chair all day, and looking for a memory-free environment. The family moved to a different home in the community and later to a mountain town nearly an hour's drive away.

Throughout that first winter without her mom, she tried to learn to walk with braces. She felt a lot of pressure from her family and friends to not give up, even after a PT told her walking wasn't practical. "We all had some hope because I can move my legs a little, even though I can't use them," she says. "My dad wanted so badly for me to get better, to walk. There was still so much pressure. Until I accepted that I wasn't going to walk—which was way before everyone else did—I felt like my life was on hold. That's no way to live.

"When we moved to a small town in the mountains, I didn't know anyone and felt very uprooted," she says. "I wasn't doing anything, mostly because there's not much to do there. I had a lot of pain in my rotator cuff from using the hand controls, so I couldn't drive. I lost contact with my friends in Denver and was sleeping 10 to 15 hours a day from my medications."

Cumulatively, the shootings, paralysis, her public rehabilitation, and the death of her mom, combined with the pressure to walk, improper medication, chronic pain and physical isolation, were a good formula for depression. To Anne Marie, it all felt like backsliding.

"When my dad remarried, we moved again and now I had two stepbrothers and a stepsister. Instead of all these changes, I just wanted to hold on to everything I'd lost. I felt like I was in this deep dark hole. I didn't think about getting a ladder; I just wanted someone to come get me out. Living in the mountains was not a happy time in my life."

The Light

Anne Marie had begun community college a year and a half after the shootings and being away from Columbine helped, even though several of her nondisabled classmates attended the same school. College, at least, offered some anonymity.

"It was a different mindset," she remembers. "People were paying money to be there and appearance wasn't very important. It was a very accepting environment and being there helped me to start growing up."

She's never been very religious, but when she accepted an invitation to attend a church service with a college friend, she found support and comfort there. "This church was very different from what I expected. There was music and joy and fellowship. It was great and very helpful. It's a big part of my life now because it gives me something to believe in. It doesn't have to be God or religion, but I think everyone needs to believe in *something*."

But just as she began to feel better about herself the family moved to the mountains. Unable to drive and isolated from her friends, she dropped out of college and stopped attending services. It was a struggle to keep her eyes on the prize.

"As I learned to take care of myself more, being in the chair got easier, and as that happened, I'd try to do more," she says. "Eventually I got more comfortable with myself. Changing my meds gave me lots more energy and let me start to function with the depression." Her dad had pressed her hard—almost coerced her, she says—to find a way to drive, and she's not sure she ever would have without that pressure. And once she learned how to cope with the pain attacks, she began to feel safer about driving.

Before the shooting she wore glasses, had braces and was sure everyone was critical of her appearance. When the braces came off and she got contacts, she went from being shy and thinking everyone was looking at her to using a chair, being outgoing and *knowing* everyone was looking at her. How can that be?

"The media thing sort of pushed me into the spotlight," she says, "even though I never did an on-camera interview. People seemed to treat me better after the shootings and never made fun of me. I know the chair isn't my fault so I'm not self-conscious about it and I don't feel judged as much. It actually might have helped some. Everything I've done has been one more baby step that helped me feel more in control. I wish I could have done things quicker, but I'm not sure that was possible. Now I'm surprised by all I can do."

Packing up, finding a townhouse and moving back to Denver to live on her own were all major steps to freedom. By changing her circumstances, she changed her attitude and her life.

"Once I moved back to Denver and was on my own, I began to see the blessings and appreciate all I had, like the love and support from my family and my friends and knowing I could rely on God. My life wasn't on hold anymore and I went back to school."

She also knows she has a way to go. She's still using a sliding board and has one of those "I've fallen and can't get up" alarms, most likely a remnant of all the time spent in the tunnel.

Blessings

Throughout our conversations, Anne Marie keeps coming back to faith, family and friends as important keys for her. She speaks repeatedly of feeling blessed.

She's had some material advantages. A small insurance settlement and donations from people all over the country pay for big-ticket items such as her truck and school,

and provide a reserve for her future. Until she's working full time, she'll rely on SSDI, Medicare and a part-time job to pay the bills.

"I keep reminding myself of how much I have so I don't just keep asking for more," she says. "For a long time I thought my life was horrible, but I know that things can always be worse and that everything I have could be taken away in an instant as it was with the shootings. I have so much. My trust gives me some security and allows me to be independent. I could live in Africa or some other place where I'd be ridiculed, beat up or treated horribly for being disabled. I'm not a millionaire or set for life, but I've got so much more than most people in my situation. I can't complain about my life.

"I can say all these things now," she quickly adds. "Until a year or so ago I was in a downward spiral of 'Oh poor me, I'm so worse off than everyone else.' I didn't believe people when they told me things would get better.

"I don't know if this happened for a reason, but I know my injury helped get me to Christianity and to be a better person. I don't ask why or try to understand, but if this hadn't happened I'd still be living at home and struggling to pay for college.

"I think we can choose how we react to this. It's made me stronger and I've learned that I can take a lot. It's awesome when people tell me that how I'm dealing with this now gives them hope. That's given me a way to give back.

"I focused on all the negatives for way too long. All that did was bring me down and I didn't like feeling that way. Focusing on the positives is what works for me now. Being in a chair is natural now, like I've always been this way, and that's really cool. I can't imagine how hard it would be to hate being in the chair every day." ■

Wardell Kyles

The first thing most people notice about Wardell Kyles is his smile, probably way before they see his chair. This is one of the happiest guys I've ever met, and after talking to him for only 20 minutes I had to stop and facetiously ask him if he was on drugs.

"I'm just happy to be alive," he says. "I'm seeing the world through different eyes now. Life is good and I'm having a ball."

Wardell's life has changed dramatically since he was shot in a messy drug deal and served a year in a state correctional facility. Now, at 40, he's not what I expected an ex-con to be. But then, my expectations were probably about as accurate as the ones most ablebodied people have for us wheelers.

Five years ago he woke up in the hospital with a T4 injury, his wrist and ankle shackled to his hospital bed. For some unexplained reason, he was unable to move either his arms or his legs. His weight plunged from 200 pounds down to 118. He says that when professionals explained that his leg spasms had nothing to do with return of function and that he would not walk again, he wanted to die.

After two weeks at Cook County Hospital in Chicago, Wardell was transferred to rehab at Oak Forest where, over the course of the next few months, he regained arm function. He was arraigned while still there and made his first court appearance while he was still in his hospital bed. He knew he was going to do time. His physical therapist had worked with convicts before and she gave him a crash course in what incarcerated life on wheels would be like, teaching him his self-care, grilling him on what to do and showing him what would happen if he failed to take care of himself.

He went to prison with many skills still unmastered and much of what he now knows has been self-taught. Because the standard prison chair had fixed armrests, he had to relearn transfers, falling down daily in the process. Having to get by on two catheters a month for his intermittent catheterization program, he fought UTIs the entire year.

Wardell remembers who helped him the most. "My PT Debbie. She told me I would have to stay strong and she wouldn't let me say no. I listened because I knew it would be sink or swim. She got me ready."

While in prison he watched other crips doing second and third stretches, and they all had problems—pressure sores, UTIs, all the usual complications. Watching them taught him what not to do. He learned to be assertive with a smile and to claim his rights. He filed grievances to make both the gym and the yard accessible.

"I'm different now," he says. "I've got a different perspective. The penitentiary actually helped me. I saw guys in chairs who were there for the second or third time, some for life. I decided that wasn't going to be me because I wanted more. I can't explain why, but since I got out I'm much happier and much more interested in helping people."

Improvise, Adapt, Overcome

Not every newbie can turn his life around. How did Wardell manage it?

"First guy I met," he says, "was this wheeler who'd been to college, and he told me about opportunities and possibilities, stuff I never knew even existed. Then I bumped into someone I used to run with who had become a minister. I figured if these guys could turn their lives around, I could too. And there's Debbie, my PT. She taught me so much about independence and health maintenance. I think what helps the most is always being around positive people."

Wardell developed a mantra while in prison—improvise, adapt, overcome—and it served him as well after his discharge as it did when he was locked up. Since subsidized housing is scarce in Chicago, he moved back in with his parents. He wins the sweepstakes for most inaccessible housing, a second floor apartment with no elevator. He scoots up the flight of stairs while dragging his chair behind him, then goes back down to close the door. He reverses the process to go out, which is almost every day.

Typically, he gets up around 5 a.m., reads a little from the Bible, then does a short workout with free weights. After visiting with his mom he's off to a fitness center. If his upper body is any indication, he pushes himself hard.

How does he find living with his parents?

"They usually want to do too much for you and that can make you lazy and more dependent," he says. "I'm still trying to find subsidized housing and have been on the list for two years. That should happen pretty soon and then I'll be able to say good-bye to those stairs."

As soon as Wardell was released, he began volunteering his time. He hooked up with the Disabling Bullet Project at Oak Forest Hospital, a mentoring program at the Rehabilitation Institute of Chicago and a kids summer program. He's particularly proud of the mentoring. Once it was funded, he was the first person to be hired.

Every other Saturday he's at juvenile halls (he calls them Bad Boy schools) speaking to kids already in the system. He works with the Chicago Public Schools as part of a youth violence-awareness program, and does contract work for the district. Now he goes into middle schools, high schools, youth facilities and specialty schools for kids with disciplinary problems.

"Those last ones are my favorites," he says. "You know, even though they're young, they know the truth and you can't BS them. It's rough in the inner city, it really is. You gotta make an impression early."

His peer mentoring with the Oak Forest prevention program grew into a part-time job and now he's up to 16 clients. He volunteers for the local chapter of NSCIA, speaking about disability issues. After one of those gigs, someone gave him an old, converted van. Later, when someone else gave him another van, he passed the first along to an acquaintance with a new injury. He's also been given a standing chair.

All this volunteering, speaking and mentoring has interfered with Wardell's plans to go to school and become a certified personal trainer. He had visions of working with people with disabilities and ultimately running his own gym, and had already convinced Voc Rehab and the Department of Human Services to cover most of the expenses. Plans for school aren't out the window, but now he's considering some changes in the course work.

"I like working with kids so much that I'm thinking about taking a couple counseling courses instead," he says.

From ex-con to college graduate?

"I don't think so. I went to college for a couple years after high school because I loved to run and had an athletic scholarship, but it wasn't for me. It's not for everybody."

The Main Attraction

Something that *was* for him was Moving Mountains, a weekend outdoor adventure empowerment program for people with disabilities. Wardell found it a very positive experience.

"That was a reality check for me," he says. "I went in not only wanting to do everything, but to be first in everything. That program was humbling and began to teach me the limitations of my body."

He travels with the Paralyzed Veterans of America (PVA) for football and weightlifting competitions, flying or taking the train to Minneapolis, Atlanta, Columbus and San Antonio. He likes the travel and seems to always find the perks, such as free meals when Amtrak dining cars are inaccessible. The traveling, he says, is an adventure.

"I'm always looking to learn from other people. I'm a lot bolder since I was shot. Hey, what else can happen to me?"

A case in point is dating women.

At first, Wardell had his doubts about what kind of woman would want to be with a guy in a chair wearing a diaper. Now he laughs at those concerns. His biggest surprise has been women coming on to him.

"Makes no sense," he says, "but for some reason, women are drawn to the chair. They're always around me and meeting new ones isn't a problem. As far as sex goes, it was trial and error for me. I tried Viagra; I tried the pump; I talked to a lot of other guys."

When he shows me a bunch of his photographs, they're all the same. They're all Wardell and two or three or four women, all smiling up a storm. And as we sit outside waiting for his ride, he flashes a huge smile and a greeting—"Hi, how are you doing?"—to every woman who passes by. Invariably they respond with a smile and warm words. Wardell's the attraction, not the chair.

"I just can't help myself," he says. "I'm thinking I need to be married, so that's my next project. I just have to get an apartment first."

For the present, he's happy with who he is. "This has given me a chance to evaluate my life," he says. "Most of the guys I see in chairs got that way because they were shot. Most of them just sit back, live on SSI and go back to what they were doing before, stealing, doing drugs, scamming. I had to give up a lot of friends so I wouldn't go back to that. It's still hard for me sometimes."

Any advice for newbies?

"The same stuff is possible; physical fitness, relationships, fun. I tell people that life isn't over because you're in a chair. Concentrate on what makes you feel productive and good about yourself, like working or going to school or helping other people. There are programs such as Voc Rehab that can help if you're persistent and assertive and willing to go over people's heads. I tell them that I'm very satisfied with my life." ∎

Benj Anderson

"When I first got hurt I said I wasn't going to let this slow me down, that I was going to keep moving forward just as before."

Most everybody says that. Unlike most of them, Benj Anderson is one of those people who has managed to put these words into action. Benj (which he pronounces as Ben) may, in fact, be going faster than ever. OK; he's 26 and it's only been four years since he broke his neck in a rodeo accident, but I got tired just listening to all he's packed into that time.

Benj works at the Western Summit construction site at the Buford County water treatment plant, about 45 minutes northeast of Atlanta. This project is a work in progress. Once I got past the gate and followed the rutted-out makeshift dirt roads, I circled the perimeter, dodging dump trucks, construction equipment and workers until I found his van and several construction trailers, including one with a ramp.

In contrast to the controlled chaos outside, the trailers are quiet, warm and organized, with good lighting, walled offices, computers, copy machines, faxes; everything you'd expect in a permanent, brick and mortar office. These trailers house all the project engineers including Benj, a professional who happens to use a chair.

His entry level construction management job comes with a great deal of responsibility. After checking all submittals from vendors and subcontractors to insure that materials match the specifications, he then coordinates the material, equipment and schedule to insure everything is on site and on time. He questions blueprints and makes suggestions for modifications. He oversees the budget and makes sure all the subcontractors get paid. Any mistakes he makes cost the company substantial time and money. Listening to Benj describe his job, you wouldn't know he's only been on site for a few weeks or out of school a couple of months. He sounds like a very competent, experienced fortysomething, which goes a long way in explaining why he was hired.

He found his employer while still in college when, as part of his course work, he signed on with them for two internships. During that time he increased their productivity by developing a tracking system for all the concrete form work. Both he and the company liked what they saw and after graduation he hired on.

His 50- to 55-hour work week demands serious dedication, especially if he wants to reach his goal of rapid promotion and becoming a project manager by age 35.

"It's a good fit for both the company and me," Benj says. "This is what I've always wanted to do. It's challenging and different every day. I have to work, both for the money and because I'd go crazy doing nothing. I wouldn't want to be doing anything else."

Several months after we met, Benj became the full-time scheduler at a different treatment plant project near Atlanta, where he also has some engineering and payroll duties. The company modified a John Deere Gator ATV for him, complete with a lowered seat, hand controls, a Bruno arm to load his chair and a siren to warn off heavy equipment. With it, he has full access to the construction site.

Living alone, he does his own cleaning and cooking. "At one time," he says, "my mom and grandma were both home economics teachers and I learned from them. I can cook pretty good." He uses a standing frame for an hour each night, watches a bit of TV, calls friends and then sacks out. He's up at 5 am and at work by 7.

Rodeo Rehab

Benj was riding bareback bronco in a rodeo in 1999 when his horse threw him, dislocating his neck at C6-7. He was rushed to a local hospital in Bismarck, ND, and placed in traction. When that didn't do the trick he went to surgery for a C5-7 fusion. Rehab in Fargo was a disaster; he was the only person with SCI on a floor of seniors. The place was filled with elevator music, bingo and patients with an average age of about 80. After some fighting and maneuvering, his parents eventually got him transferred to Craig Hospital in Englewood, Colo.

"That made a huge difference," he says. "Most of the people were my age, between 18 and 25. My cowboy/rodeo mentality kicked in—never quit, give 110 percent, get back on track with that one good ride. The PTs and wheelchair endurance runs sucked bad and kicked my butt. I ran with a lot of the big-dog paras and still have contact with friends I made there. It was fun."

Benj began experimenting and problem solving while he was still in rehab. Because of his interest in sports, he went to a rugby demonstration and liked what he saw, even though he remembers that it was a bit intimidating.

"I was scared of getting knocked out of my chair at first, but as soon as I got in there I was banging and crashing like everyone else," he says.

His incomplete injury gives him nearly the function of a high para, except for his left hand, which doesn't work very well. Expressing gratitude for what he can do, he calls his good fortune the luck of the draw. Watching the level of independence people with more severe injuries gained was all the motivation Benj needed in rehab, and he quickly set out to learn to do as much as possible. He vowed not slow down, stuck with old dreams and committed to some new ones.

"I saw people with less function and people with more," he says. "There was a woman quad who complained every day, even though she ended up walking out of the hospital. I didn't want to be like that."

The Winning Ingredients

After his accident, Benj's parents, both university construction management professors, assured him he could still go after a career in construction. Western Summit thought so too, and because he had proven himself through his pre-injury internships, they stuck with him so he could continue his field work for credit. His parents helped him secure benefits such as VR, SSI, a PASS plan and Pell grants, and both Western Summit and Craig Hospital chipped in with scholarships.

"If my parents hadn't taken care of all the benefits stuff so I could focus on school it would have taken me twice as long," he remembers. "I couldn't have done it without them."

Benj returned to school quickly after injury, first to North Dakota State and then to Minnesota State University in Moorhead. Getting back to school so quickly helped.

His interests go beyond school and work. His assertiveness in securing VR benefits generated an invitation to serve on the Governor's Vocational Rehabilitation Council. When he was only six months post-injury, a friend asked him to chaperone a Special Olympics state bowling tournament. He fell in love with the athletes and went on to coach them in basketball, handball and soccer. When a friend's dad helped him modify a saddle with a solid back using rods, metal plates and plastic ties so he could strap himself in, he was back to rodeo.

"Friends toss me up there, get me situated and off I go," he says. He does team penning, an event that requires him to ride and sort cattle. Competitions, he says, give him a chance to travel and see old friends.

Basketball, rugby and skiing all helped him build his strength, which still continues to grow. Since moving to Georgia he's right back into rugby, commuting to Shepherd Center in nearby Atlanta a couple of times a week to practice and play in matches and tournaments, both local and on the road.

Swing dancing was a big deal for Benj before injury and it didn't take long post-injury before he began working with the top instructor in North Dakota. After a few stylistic adjustments, he focused on three or four solid moves and was back on the floor.

"I only use one hand instead of two and can't do any flips, but I still have a lot of fun," he says. "I like to surprise people who can't imagine someone in a chair swing dancing. Now I just have to get over being shy."

Rebuilding after SCI can be a continuing education in life and Benj says he's learned from everything he's done since his injury. Special Olympics taught him he could still teach and be productive. Rugby, dancing and riding all taught him confidence. Continuing his construction major and on-the-job internships kept him moving forward while he got down to the real work of life on wheels. Exercising the creativity and motivation he needed to accomplish those goals taught him that he can do almost anything else he sets his mind to. He's learned that there is life after SCI. He got his back through family support, creativity, a pledge to not slow down and his rodeo mentality.

"The chair is more an ongoing consideration than a major obstacle," he says. "I have to plan and think about things in advance more now, but I have the same goals. I'm still learning how to deal with people and their assumptions about me, like that I have mental problems. And I still hate people staring at me, even though I remember doing the same thing before I got hurt. Every day is still rehab for me.

"I remember my mom saying 'We are all going to fight to turn this into something positive for you and our family.' We've been able to do that. I got hurt doing something I love and if I had to trade all my rodeo experiences in order to walk again, I wouldn't do it. Those memories and experiences are priceless and I wouldn't trade them for anything. There are things more important than walking. I'm doing what I want to do. I'm happy." ■

Patricia Rivas

"I tell myself, 'Patty, you're halfway there.' Seeing how far I've come motivates me to keep trying."

That's how Patricia Rivas describes her life seven years after a drive-by shooting in 1995. She got enough return from the C6 incomplete injury that she's occasionally able to use a walker or a quad cane. Getting 'all the way there' to her would be not using her chair at all.

She was 18 and in the first semester of college when the bullet intended for her date took her down. Following 11 days in acute care near her home in Rockville, Md., she spent three months in the National Rehabilitation Hospital (NRH) in Washington, D.C. learning her new body.

After about a month or so of rehab, Patty began to regain some leg mobility. Functional return continued throughout her stay, so much so that she progressed from a walker to a quad cane to a straight cane over the next three years.

"They told me it could be up to three weeks for the swelling in the cord to go down, so I figured that's when I would walk out," she says. "I've been fortunate, but I wasn't that lucky. I guess I didn't have time to get really down and totally depressed after this happened because I had things to do, things to accomplish. I enjoy life too much to be down."

Returning to school cut deeply into Patty's walking time, but didn't stop her from getting more return. Having nearly full use of her upper body makes using a walker at the mall possible, though her balance remains a constant concern. She knows it could have turned out differently.

"I always assume that good things will happen to me," she says, "so when I started getting the functional return it wasn't a total surprise. Getting this much back has made life so much easier. I know this doesn't happen for most people and I'm very grateful."

Grounded in Family

These days, Patty is finishing up her first year of graduate school in social work, preparing for a career she's wanted since the sixth grade. She's grateful and proud to have held onto her dreams.

She says her disability has brought her more opportunity than prejudice, and she's found ample programs for people with disabilities, some of which provide financial help. Tuition waivers for disabled residents covered her community college undergraduate work, she draws SSI benefits, and got help from Voc Rehab to pay for a driving evaluation and hand controls. MetroAccess remains her primary mode of transportation and gets her wherever conventional public transportation goes throughout the D.C. area. "These programs are there so why not use them and take advantage of my disadvantage?" she asks. "They can make things happen for me."

Programs unrelated to disability have helped as well. When Patty began graduate school at the University of Maryland, she learned of a Child Welfare program that would pay her tuition, $4,400 a year, in exchange for her pledge to work at least a year in the child welfare field.

Grad school's been stressful and something of an eye-opener. Social work usually requires visiting clients in their homes, and in D.C. that often means facing the hassles of inaccessible homes and the safety issues of visiting dangerous parts of town. Some of her coursework involves activity outside the classroom, and many in-class activities such as role playing demand that she move around in crowds. Even her first internship, a school-based program, has been something of an accessibility challenge.

Most of her clients are from Central America and come to her seeking assistance with legal, financial and language problems, so being bi-lingual is a big plus. Initially families expressed some reluctance because of her chair.

"It stopped being an issue when they saw my work was the same as everyone else's," she says.

Patty's enjoyed strong family support from day one. Her parents, though divorced, divided transportation duties early on. Her father drove her to NRH for morning therapy, her mom took her home before leaving for work in the afternoon. Sometimes her mom, like most parents, worries about her too much, and occasionally she finds her entire extended family overprotective. As a result, she says, assertiveness training with her family is on her agenda.

"My family is the most important thing in my life. They help keep me grounded but I think they also hold me back some," she says, sounding like many young people with disabilities who live with their parents. "I'm 26 years old and they know every scratch and bruise on my body. I know lots of people who live on their own, though I'm still not sure I can do it. I need to convince myself and my mom that that's possible."

Beyond Ambivalence

She concedes that some of her conflicted feelings are culturally influenced.

"The Latin culture sometimes confuses pity with empathy," she says. "When I go to Nicaragua to visit family, the expectations

for people with disabilities are very low because of all the poverty and lack of equipment like wheelchairs. It's not that bad here in the States, but I've seen some here, too."

She's been blessed with great friends who include her in their activities, which means going out to clubs, bars, movies and dinner, so much so that she says it's hard for her to feel bad. I suspect one of the reasons they've all stuck around is because she's so open, optimistic and positive. Still, her friends sometimes display the same kind of overprotectiveness her family does and become upset with the way some people react to wheelers and their chairs.

Her adjustment to life on wheels is ongoing. Walking remains important enough to her that she continues to work on it, but some of that need may stem from pressure from family and friends who constantly push her to never let up. For her own part, she feels she has to give walking her best shot and isn't totally convinced she can be successful if she doesn't lose the chair.

"I've felt okay with myself this way for the past three years," she says. "So even if it doesn't work out and I stay in the chair, I don't think it will be the worst thing or the end of the world. I think I'm still improving and I know that most people don't. I've been very fortunate, but I still have to try."

Like most of us, Patty is a mix of ambivalence and contradiction about both life and disability. Even though she's had her driver's license for a year and drove throughout D.C. before her injury, the thought of driving around the city intimidated her for a time. Even though she has flown to Nicaragua numerous times, often alone and for up to three weeks at a time, she's reluctant to leave her family's home. Even though marriage and children remain her dream, she's not sure she could choose between walking and having a family. And even though she often speaks with encouragement to people with new injuries, she says she feels no particular connection to people with disabilities.

"I don't know if it's the right thing to say, but I don't think of myself as disabled," she says. "Most people I know with disabilities were born that way and a lot of them are very lonely. That hasn't been my experience and it's not who I am. I'm the same as before; I have the same friends and do the same things as before."

If Patty is unconsciously denying her disability or unintentionally stereotyping others with disabilities, she's far from being alone. It takes awhile to feel comfortable with so many changes, and she's only one example of what many of us have done and sometimes continue to do. It's one of those things that tends to change over time.

With one year remaining in her master's program, Patty thinks a lot about working. Where does she want to be in five years?

"I hope I'm married and working and living in my own place. I hope I'm good at what I do. I'd like to have children.

"I think people are born with a destiny, that God has plans for people. I hope that what I want and His plan are the same. There's a purpose for all the obstacles, big and small, that we have to deal with every day. Maybe my purpose is to move on and show others life can be okay even after they're injured." ∎

Charmaine G. Brown, A *Royal Flush*

CHAPTER TWO
The First Years

It's discharge time, or maybe a month or two afterward. Novelty is wearing off, reality is setting in and you're realizing just how hard all this is. There are so many adjustments to make; so much to learn, so much to get used to, so much to fear.

Q: What were your biggest fears during that first year or so?

- "What about dating, marriage, having sex, kids?"
- "I wasn't sure life would have any meaning, that maybe this was a fate worse than death."
- "Will I be able to work and support myself and my family?"
- "Can I survive and live independently?"
- "I was afraid of falling out of my chair."
- "How will others react?"
- "What if I have a bowel or bladder accident in public?"
- "Will I be alone forever?"

If you're new to SCI, these fears all probably sound familiar. So many questions, so few answers. And the fears, clearly, haven't changed a lot since before discharge. A lot of the ignorance might be gone, but the problems remain.

Relationships and sex, self-support and living independently topped nearly everyone's list of major concerns. If you feel terrified about what's happened and about what might happen, you're in good company. Most of this group spoke of their first year as being their hardest. But the good news here is that they eventually resolved many of their problems. You can, too.

First, let's look at the fears, one by one, then how people tackled them.

Dating, marriage, sex, kids

Attracting a partner, enjoying sex, getting married and having and raising kids remain the great unknowns for SCI newbies. All that is hard to imagine if you're newly injured.

This group says it took time to build the social confidence they needed. They say it also took accommodating a new body and getting out and meeting people. Yet, nearly half, 24 of 53, now live with a spouse or significant other. Eleven are parents, 10 the old-fashioned way and one through adoption. Most who are single date at least occasionally and all but five have been sexually active since injury. None of those things has to be out the window. For now, know that most worries about sex and relationships after SCI are paper tigers.

Working, supporting self and family

Worried about working? Wondering how you're going to support yourself or your family? So was this group. For many, this concern topped the list. For most, finding work meant getting an education to make themselves employable, and the vast majority got help from one or more government benefits programs. Schooling and eventually working have been very important for them.

Most who wanted to work found jobs and worked for at least a time after their injuries. Over half worked full time and fully supported themselves. Three-quarters have done volunteer work.

Living independently

Early on, everyone in this group worried about whether they would need physical assistance or, if they did, how they would find the help they needed to live. They worried that accepting help would mean they were no longer independent people. It was an overriding concern for them.

Now they are loud and clear in saying that independence is possible after SCI. Independence, most insist, is about control and making decisions, not about physically doing everything without help.

And those other fears? Most in this group manage to keep bowel and bladder accidents to a minimum and seldom fall out of their chairs. They've found solutions to their SCI-specific fears through a process of trial and error and taking the time to gain experience and confidence. And by going out and living they've overcome other fears about interacting with nondisabled people. They say their lives have meaning and are hardly "worse than death."

Q: How long did it take to get past those early fears?

"Look," you say, "I know what I'm afraid of. What I need to know is how long it's going to take me to get past all this."

About two-thirds of this group felt they were at least on their way past those early fears within two years. For some who took longer, it was a matter of finishing college and getting out into the world. Almost all were back on track, or at least getting past some of their initial fears, within three or four years.

"The first year was the hardest" is a nearly universal sentiment. No one suggested their first year was easy; no one tried to downplay its difficulty. Most said it was filled with doubts, frustrations, anger and depression. A few stumbled and struggled for years before finding their way. They denied the permanence of their paralysis or refused to believe they were anything like those other crips they occasionally saw on the street, in the classroom or at the hospital. Some just couldn't believe that life had anything left to offer. Several partied hard until their parents kicked them out of the house, others got lost in alcohol or drugs, a couple of gang members went back to the old life for a while. Two people attempted suicide.

This is hard stuff, serious business. It takes time to resolve. Nearly everyone says getting past those early fears was a gradual,

step-by-step process. But rather than *how long* it took, most say the more important question is *how* they did it.

Q: How did you get past those early fears?

There is a lot of agreement here and essentially their advice is to keep moving, trying, pushing, doing. Here's what they say helped most:

- Getting out, being active through school, work or sports
- Learning from peers
- Facing fears and testing boundaries
- Building step by step on accomplishments
- Support from family
- Support from friends

While sex might have been their biggest initial fear, most of these people first tackled the basic issues of living independently and learning self-care.

Living Independently Revisited

Nearly half this group required assistance at some point after injury and those who eventually achieved physical independence usually did so in slow steps. Brian Johnston and George Taborsky, C5-6 and C6 quads, respectively, got there out of necessity. Brian learned his skills when he began living alone. George lost his in-home health assistance when he returned to full-time work.

Many who have higher injuries and still need assistance, like Steve Ferguson and Donald Collier, insist on doing as much as possible for themselves. They know and understand their care so fully they can teach it to others and properly supervise them. They have gadgets that help them use phones or operate garage doors, voice recognition so they can use computers, water bottles with long straws mounted on their chairs. They do what they can for themselves so they don't burn out their caregivers or become overdependent on them, and so their helpers don't become overprotective.

"Don't be dependent or rely on people for more help than you need," advises

Glenford Hibbert. "I did that and it cost me my marriage."

At the end of the day, here's what independence means to them:

Pat McGowan, a C5 quad who needs daily help and lives alone in Manhattan: "Independence is managing life on your own. One of the most independent guys I ever met was a complete C5 who needed daily care. Independence is being in control."

Anne Herman: "Being in control and in charge and managing the people who help you is being independent."

Audrey Begay, who has in-home help every day: "Before I was injured, I was emotionally dependent on people. I feel more independent now because I'm making all the decisions."

Those who didn't need assistance still had things to learn about living independently. They began by learning to manage their bodies, which gave them the confidence to go out and start doing more. It was, once again, that process of first things first.

"You learn your body and the signs," says Susan Douglas. "You learn to deal with some of the differences, like everything taking so long and always being late."

They used different approaches to body management. Some were obsessively vigilant for signs of trouble, others committed themselves to rigid routines, a few tinkered with diet. Some relied on regular exercise while others experimented with meditation or biofeedback.

"In the beginning everything—transferring, dressing, driving—was such a big deal," says Gretchen Schaper. "Over time it all gets easier."

With the basics out of the way, most of this group were able to get down to the business of living life.

Getting out, being active through school, work or sports

Moving through those early years, this group says, is a matter of getting out, interacting with people and doing things that help them feel productive, useful and having fun.

Many started moving forward by going to school, which for some meant returning to high school, and for the majority meant either returning to college or starting it. Others began working within a year or two, even if only part time. Some volunteered.

Robert Statam takes continuing education computer classes. "School really helps," he says. "It gives me some structure, helps me manage my time, and I'm learning."

Both Jason Graber and Phillip Mann were antsy after injury. Wanting to fill time and do something useful, they went right to work. Jason did part-time tech-support phone work within six months of discharge. "Getting up, going to work, coming home, hanging out—it gave me a normal routine," he says. Phillip returned to police work. "Going back was the best thing I ever did," he remembers. "It was great. I had a schedule, felt productive and had fun."

George Taborsky volunteered, putting in unpaid time at his old job before returning full time for pay. Wardell Kyles, Charlotte Heppner and Joel Irizarry all volunteered at their rehab hospitals. Fred Fay joined with others in advocating to make the Washington, D.C. subway system accessible. Gretchen Schaper volunteered with kids in an after-school crafts program. "It felt so good to do things for others," she says. "I was giving back and could be the teacher. That was very helpful."

Some got physical, regaining identity through sports. Anne Herman quickly started swimming again. "Meeting wheelchair athletes who had lives was very helpful," she says. When she returned to college she realized dating was possible too. Basketball helped Don Dawkins get past a lot of sadness, fear and denial. "I lost my identity as an athlete when I got hurt," he recalls. "It took me years to get it back through wheelchair sports."

Others just tried to stay busy with something, *anything*. Greg Adcock was afraid to do anything on his own after breaking his back, but then he weaned himself. "I just started doing things," he says. "I began by mowing the lawn, then went camping on my own. I just kept trying things until I figured I could do most anything. It took me about five years." Joel Lorentz discovered most of his fears were without substance, especially fears about how others would react. "I got out meeting people right away and that helped work them out."

Taking one day at a time seems to have worked for some. Ryan Odens: "I was pretty afraid of everything, so I hung around with other patients a lot and tried not to think about much." Kevin Wolitzky: "I just stayed busy so I wouldn't worry." James Turner: "Mostly I approached things day to day." James tried not to think too far into the future and instead dealt with whatever came up, focusing on small improvements along the way.

But what about specifics? How did they address those biggest fears and problems?

Dating, marriage, sex and kids revisited
Most people started edging past their fears by talking to someone in rehab, a doctor maybe, or a nurse or counselor. Next they found an experienced wheeler for some firsthand information. Then they went and found out for themselves.

"I was afraid of sex and how women would react, so I talked to someone while I was still in rehab," Juan Garibay recalls. "He told me about options for sex—Viagra, shots and stuff. It wasn't as scary as I thought and I had a girlfriend by the time I was discharged."

"I couldn't believe that women I didn't know could be attracted to me," says Dennis Bossman. "You just gotta go for that."

"Dating after SCI was easy, actually," Bobbie Humphreys remembers. "I met a guy when I was in the ICU and we started dating."

"I don't know why, but meeting women just isn't a problem," says Wardell Kyles. "Sex was trial and error for me. I tried Viagra. I tried the pump. I talked to a lot of other guys."

Where did they go to find partners? Everywhere, just as ABs do. Susan Douglas was dating in med school less than a year after her injury. Gretchen Schaper met her guy in a store. Kevin Wolitzky met his wife through a friend at work. Joe Jeremias married his rugby coach. Anne and Paul Herman met through wheelchair sports. Some married their nurses, attendants or physical therapists. A few met in bars or on the Internet. Mark Bussinger meets women everywhere, including on elevators.

Was the chair a turn-off to potential partners? Usually not.

"I thought about the chair a little when we first met," says Gretchen's partner Peter, "but there were too many other things to think about—she's an artist and a mountain biker and a beautiful blonde. I'm not with someone in a chair, I'm with Gretchen."

Dale Green, Cathy Green's husband, says "I don't think of myself as being married to a woman in a chair; I'm married to my wife."

Dating's not necessarily easy and many say it reminded them of being fumbling teenagers again, or worse. Bobbie Humphreys set out to lose her virginity and lost her catheter instead. Audrey Begay recalled being self-conscious about spasms, legbags and paralysis. Donald Collier struggled to get women to see him as separate from his chair. Yet the addition of wheels made many approach dating more maturely. Several said that dating became more about getting to know and become intimate with someone than about sex or partying.

Crossing the line from friendship to relationship and sex may require some changes. This group emphasizes communication and trust, especially in starting relationships with new partners. When I asked people about sex, their replies focused as much on emotional intimacy as on physical pleasure.

"It's about intimacy, honesty and openness," says Patty Rivas. Juan Garibay concurs, saying "It's much more about intimacy for me now."

Most experimented, both alone and with partners, until they found ways that worked. And most tried different ways of self-stimulation, either manually or with vibrators or other devices. Several spent months and even years discovering what felt good and what gave them pleasure.

They say you have to know what works and what makes you feel good before you can communicate it to a partner.

Glenford Hibbert: "Before I could enjoy myself, I had to find out what gave me pleasure. Then I had to tell the person I was with. You have to be able to talk and communicate." Mark Bussinger: "I had to learn to be open in my communications and explain about the mechanics of everything." Don Dawkins: "It's not what I thought it would be in rehab. It's way more satisfying than I imagined, but it takes work and communication and time."

Many talk about how much pleasure they got from satisfying their partners, a taste that took them some time to acquire. Some had to get beyond erections and orgasms as sole standards of sexual pleasure. For some, sex proved to be both a validation and turning point.

James Turner: "It's about getting and giving pleasure. It's right up there with recreation. Maybe it *is* recreation." Keith Davis: "Not having function doesn't have to mean you're not a man. You can re-define sex, act more like a woman and get into foreplay and caressing and going slower and being vulnerable. You can drive women crazy doing that." Jamie Peterson: "Being intimate was a big help to my self-image and self-esteem. It helped make me feel whole again."

Angel Watson offers an important consideration for women: "We're more vulnerable physically and there are some men who like women who can't run away. I think it's important to avoid being alone in situations early. I call it the broken-doll syndrome; some men want to fix us." She likes using the Internet as a screening tool: "It lets you get some stuff out of the way without meeting. You can exchange pictures, and instant messaging can tell you a lot about a person."

Several women say that while sex is still important, it isn't always as enjoyable as before injury, usually because it now causes some physical discomfort.

Some in this group still struggle to bring relationships and sex back into their lives. A few of the younger people either haven't done much dating or remain sexually inactive. Others have decided, at least for now, to stick to connecting with other people on a social level. Benj Anderson looks for dance partners. Steve Ferguson concentrates on friendships with women instead of romance. A few who divorced or ended relationships after injury remain unattached. Relationships and sex are big and scary adjustments. Jason Regier: "It was one of the tougher aspects for me. I went from a walking hard-on to 'what's going on?' I had to learn that sex is only part of a relationship and has a deeper meaning, not an easy thing to teach a young male."

After 48 years Wally Dutcher might have the best advice: "Suspend judgment so you can go on a mental journey to explore and experiment with what gives you pleasure."

Working, supporting self and family revisited

This group gets uneasy doing nothing and most feel they regained self-esteem and a sense of identity by staying active and making contributions.

Their careers are as varied as they themselves are—executives, teachers, customer service representatives, sales people, engineers, a real estate agent, social workers, a TV repairman, a music producer, a high school yearbook company representative, doctors, a lawyer, technicians, a public speaker and advocates for people with disabilities. Money is an important motivator for many of them, either to meet the high costs of disability or to prove they can do something important and valuable.

James Turner, who works for the USDA: "I like my job and I'm proud of doing it. I make a difference by helping people."

Juan Garibay: "I love going to work. It gives me purpose. I'm contributing to society and influencing kids and making money."

Marina Conner: "For me, it's survival. I have to work."

Pat McGowan: "I needed a job that would give me the extra $15,000 per year to pay for attendant care."

Many see work as a valuable way to stay connected to people and the larger world.

Some say work keeps them occupied, fills their time and helps them steer clear of temptation and trouble. They appreciate the structure a job imposes on their lives.

"Working got me back on track," says Joel Lorentz, a police dispatcher. "It keeps me busy and gives me some purpose."

Just as with relationships, people found work in any number of ways. Some, like Joel Irizarry and Steve Ferguson, began with volunteer positions that turned into paid ones. James Lilly spoke to a high school class as a favor to a friend and turned it into a profession. Cathy Green volunteered at the local unemployment office and got first dibs when a good paying job came up. Dennis Bossman went shopping for medical supplies and picked up a job at the store. Others found jobs through connections they'd kept up over the years. A few, like Michael Slaughter and Glenford Hibbert, started their own businesses.

When I asked people just how important work was to them and where it fit into their lives, they responded as follows:

- "Work gives me my identity, self-esteem, self-worth; it's independence.
- "Working is making a contribution, being productive, giving back."
- "Making money is important and necessary."
- "It's important to be out and part of the world."
- "Work provides social connection and interaction."
- "Employment provides structure and fills time."

Learning from peers.
Almost everyone in the group took advantage of peer support and learning from the example and experience of seasoned wheelers helped some as much as staying busy. It was especially important for those late bloomers who took longer to gain perspective or get beyond self-pity.

Old-timers had the information these people needed and often were helpful in getting them to understand that what they were feeling was normal. One such experience stands out for Eric Gibson: "The first time I saw a well-dressed African-American man using a chair, he was with a good-looking woman, had a nice set of wheels and looked like he had a good job. I knew I had to be talking to him because I couldn't stop talking about him."

Talking to veteran wheelers helped them build confidence and the more they saw successful wheelers, the more they thought they could succeed themselves. Felipe Antonio remembers the impact of getting into wheelchair sports: "When I got involved in sports, I looked at the guys I played with and thought, 'I want to be like them.' I got strong and I got some social skills. I learned how to solve problems, too."

A Parable

A guy's wheeling down the street past a construction site. He's not paying close enough attention and rolls down into the basement. He's stuck down there, can't get out and starts calling for help. Pretty soon a doctor walks by and the guy shouts up to him, "Hey doc, I'm stuck down here. Give me a hand, will ya?" The doctor writes him a prescription, tosses it down to him and walks on. A little later a priest walks by and the guy shouts up to him, "Hey Father, I'm stuck down here, give me a hand please." The priest says a prayer, blesses the guy and walks on. After a while the guy sees another wheeler. He shouts up for help, and asks this other wheeler to go get someone. Instead, the wheeler rolls down into the hole with him. "What did you do that for? Now we're both stuck!" "It's okay," the second guy says. "I've been down here before and I know the way out. Follow me."

Peer support is no joke. People use it because it works.

Experienced wheelers weren't hard to find. Donald Collier, Dan Wilkins and Glenford Hibbert ran into them at independent living centers. Joel Irizarry,

Wardell Kyles and Jason Regier hooked up through peer counseling groups and sports. Many, like Don Dawkins, met wheelers in college.

Peer support may be even more important today than it was when this group was starting out. As hospital and rehab stays get shorter and people are discharged with fewer skills and less information, more of the needed support must come from peers, the Internet and the community. Peer support has a long and successful history, from 12-step programs to cancer support to simple social contact. We all know it's impossible to understand rape, disease, drug addiction or the painful joy of childbirth without personal experience of them. Spinal cord injury is no exception.

Pat McGowan compares the isolation of early disability to being lost in a foreign land, unable to speak the language. Experienced wheelers can be your tour guides and translators. You don't need to reinvent the wheel, you need to learn how to use the ones you've already got.

Facing fears and testing boundaries

Afraid of everything? Not sure of your limits? Don't know how far you can push yourself? You're not alone. Everyone in this group admits to having fears early on. In fact, most say they were terrified. Of what? Of falling out of their chairs, of bowel and bladder accidents, of being alone, of being stared at, of being rejected, of not being able to make their own way.

For many, the best way past those fears was facing them head-on. That's how Anne Marie Hochhalter broke out of her isolation and depression. "I forced myself to do things," she says, "and I tried not to think of what might happen. If I didn't try, what was the point?"

Keith Davis's fears may have been different, but his approach was the same. "I had fears about girls and sports and all that I had lost," he recalls. "I got over them by doing." It was a similar story for Mark Bussinger. "My biggest fears had to do with relationships and attendant care. About a year out of the hospital I got sex taken care of." Building a network of reliable aides

happened later, when his sink-or-swim approach left him with no choice—he moved out on his own and had to find help.

Curtis Lovejoy worried about women and what they might think of him on crutches or using his chair. "I spent a lot of time grooming and making sure I looked good," he says. "That put me at ease and let me feel good about myself. Then I went to the mall and forced myself to talk to people."

Not long after injury Michael Slaughter sensed his marriage was on the rocks so he began preparing in case he had to take care of himself. "I got into a survival mode and started learning everything I could. I can't explain how, but I just did it."

Building step by step on accomplishments

If confronting fears head-on or using a sink-or-swim approach isn't your style, slow and steady can also win you the race. Many people succeeded with a step-by-step process, starting with the basics and moving up that ladder of needs.

A high number in this group stayed focused on the basic, day-to-day stuff and were soon amazed at how each step led to another, bigger one until they'd gone much further than they thought possible.

Once Robert Statam learned his self-care, he began hanging out at the VA Center. Then he learned to use public transportation and went out more, which led to computer classes. Then he got involved with the tenant committee in his building, and became an officer in his local PVA. His take on it now? "Well hell, nothing's impossible."

Richard Famiglietti earned a degree after learning his self-care. Then, when he couldn't get a job without losing Medicaid, he worked to change the law. Along the way he organized a rugby team and found sponsors for it. Audrey Begay started by getting out with her brother. Then she began dating. She found Section 8 housing and got her own place. She found a guy and now she's a mom.

After Joel Irizarry learned his self-care, his mom set him up in a basement apartment where he learned to cook and clean for himself. Then he checked out peer counseling and went to college. When money ran short he found a full-time job.

Jason Regier describes this step-by-step process best: "It's pretty amazing how all these little things—getting out, working some, learning independence, traveling— build on one another until one day you look around and realize, 'Hey, I've got a life!'"

Support from family

Family, this group says, can be your best ally. Almost everyone talks about the help they got from family and many said they would have been lost without it. They counted on family to do the legwork and paperwork for SSI, Medicaid, Voc Rehab and all their other benefits and insurance issues. Many relied on family for basic housing and for their personal care early on until they learned to do it themselves. People felt grounded by their families.

Most family members will be there for support when times are tough and they'll usually give whatever it takes. But they're a resource that shouldn't be squandered. Eventually they need to get something back in the way of genuine appreciation, strong effort and good humor. In the face of persistent negativity—rage, depression, indifference, inaction—even the most devoted family members may give up. Your positive attitude and best efforts can go a long way, especially during those first few months when everyone is hurting and mutual support is critical.

Spinal cord injury didn't just happen to you. It happened to your entire family. Their support is crucial, but there are dangers, too, both for them and for you.

Sometimes it's harder for your parents or siblings than for you. Siblings may feel lost when all the attention focuses elsewhere. Parents often become overprotective and everyone in the family can feel over- whelmed and burned out.

"This was a trauma for my entire family," says Mark Bussinger. "I think I became the focus, much to the detriment of my siblings." Ryan McLean remembers how hard her injury was for her mom and sister: "My sister has struggled a lot with my

accident, more than me. This has been very hard on them, and that's been hard on me."

Joel Irizarry knew he had to be strong because he could hear his mom crying every night after he went to bed. Gretchen Shaper saw the toll her injury took on her parents: "I know my dad feels guilty that he didn't tell me more about Jeeps being dangerous. Both my parents still struggle with my chair and I know they don't let me see all their pain."

"My mom took my accident harder than me," says Jason Graber. "When she was a rehab nurse, she had no patience with whiners."

Parents want the best for their children and don't want to see them suffer. But their desire to help and make things better can be more seductive than helpful.

"It gets real easy sometimes when there's someone there to do everything for you," Dan Wilkins says. "You forget how independent you were." Wardell Kyles agrees: "They can make you lazy and more dependent, because sometimes they want to do too much."

The desire to hold on is especially strong—and troublesome—as kids become young adults. "My parents have been supportive to the point of being intrusive," says Karen Hwang, who was 21 at injury. "They've given me all I need, and I'm very grateful for that, but sometimes they want to micromanage everything." Patty Rivas can relate: "I'm 26 years old and they know every scratch and bruise on my body. That bothers me sometimes."

Pat McGowan, who was 23 when he was injured, says it's hard to balance love, help and the need for some personal space. "You can't let them treat you like a child," he says. "You have to maintain your boundaries."

And sometimes parents or other family members can want to help too much for their own good and just get burned out. "You have to be careful not to put too much on family," says James Lilly, who relied heavily on his family, especially his mom, when he was hurt at 15. "They're doing so much for you and it's so hard on them." Glenford Hibbert was angry, depressed and scared when he went home from rehab.

Even though he was a para, he expected his wife to do everything for him. "She got burned out and left," he says.

Most of this group expresses a deep and lasting gratitude when they talk about the support they received from family, often rolling their eyes in wonder that that they made it through and their families put up with them. They also speak of how complicated all this can be and how much attention and work it takes to keep things on an even keel. Some don't want to speculate as to what might have happened without family help: "If it hadn't been for my parents … ."

Support from friends

Many people lean on friends as heavily as they lean on family. Some say they wouldn't have survived their early years of SCI without their friends, and others regret having shut them out. Most learned who their real friends were. Friends can lend support, companionship and advice, serve as sounding boards and provide connections to the larger world. They can help you make that transition from the old life to the new.

Joe Jeremias says you can be more honest with friends. Jamie Peterson says friends help him decompress. And Audrey Begay says "you lose some, you gain some and you use the chair to filter out the assholes."

Amit Jha needed physical help to go anywhere after his injury. "Without friends," he says, "I may not have gone out at all." Don Dawkins says his high school friends simply refused to abandon him. "They were my rock," he says. "They'd take my bedroom door off the hinges to get in and take me out. We went everywhere." I asked one of Don's friends about why they'd stayed so loyal. "Don didn't want any special treatment," his friend Dan said, "and in return we only saw him and not the chair." Richard Famiglietti says his friends saved his life and never wavered. "They would drag me out of bed," he remembers. "Before I learned to cath myself, they would do that for me. We were puppies together. Friendships are priceless."

You may need to spend some time putting friends at ease and helping them feel comfortable. "Some of my old friends were uncertain about how I'd be or react to things," Dennis Bossman says. "It took a while for them to warm up. Once we went rafting together and they saw I was the same, then everything was OK."

Sometimes old friends and lifestyles aren't compatible with new realities, and the only way to move forward is to cut them loose. Robert Statam says that when he decided to get clean and sober he had to give up many friends. Dropping buddies was agonizing for Joel Lorentz: "My two best friends, the ones who never left and were most supportive after I got hurt, were also my two drug buddies. I felt bad because they were always there for me, but I knew if I wanted to be sober, I had to give them up."

Most of Juan Garibay's gang friends saw his chair as too much trouble, so they gave up on him. In some ways they were all he had, yet he knew he had to steer clear of them if he wanted a life so he did. James Lilly took nearly five years to break away from his old gang friends. Juan and James both had to cut old ties to make new lives.

Friendships, like family relationships, can be abused. By all means lean on your friends but make sure they can lean on you, too. Some in this group express gratitude to friends 10, 20, even 30 years later.

Dennis Bossman still speaks warmly of a friend who housed him and got him started after his injury 20 years ago. "Needless to say," he says, "whenever Butch calls, he gets whatever he wants." ∎

Peer Support

A peer support group helped Don Dawkins realize something important: "I didn't survive so I could be miserable," he says. "The support group forced me to deal with my denial." That's when things began to change for him.

When Eric Gibson checked out a local chapter of the National Spinal Cord Injury Association (NSCIA), he met a group of wheelers who were positive and doing well. They knew the ropes and were willing to help him turn the corner.

Robert Statam was lost and unsure of himself until he hooked up with a local PVA group. "I thought I should be able to deal with all this on my own when all the time there were other veterans around with answers to my questions," he says. "They showed me I could do things and taught me I didn't need to be ashamed or embarrassed. They helped me deal with sexual dysfunction and bowel and bladder stuff."

Peer counseling works. It has a track record of benefits that comes from people who have lived through similar situations and are willing to share their experience and knowledge with others. Peer counseling programs offered in rehab and by independent living centers give newbies a way to get answers and support.

These programs can shed light on relationships, working, attendant care and recreation, whatever seems murky to you now. Some feature guest speakers from Voc Rehab and Social Security, or experts on sexuality, pain management, travel or gear for living on wheels. They connect you with other wheelers so you can compare notes and gauge your progress. Some centers offer mobility training, weight training or informal OT and PT programs. Others teach practical skills like using computers. Some women's groups focus on relationships, pregnancy, parenting, social stigma, personal grooming, self-defense and other issues not often addressed in rehab. Other programs emphasize assertiveness, taking risks, building self-esteem and maintaining a social support system. Family support groups provide peer support to parents new to SCI. Some meetings are informational, others more for emotional support. All offer the inestimable gift of shared experience.

Several centers throughout the country offer the *Disabling Bullet* program, connecting people injured through violence to others similarly injured. Experienced wheelers tell newbies about their lives, how they put them back together, what's possible afterward. Peers have a chance to ask questions and voice their concerns.

For the physically active set, there are programs designed to test physical and mental limits through sports like skiing, sky diving or whitewater rafting. Many participants come away feeling they can do anything. City park and recreation departments sponsor sports programs. Many large ski areas offer disabled ski programs. The point of all these programs is to connect with other wheelers.

The true value of peer support comes in the camaraderie, not the program or specific activity. If inadequate rehab has left you scared and isolated and needing skills and information, peer support is a way to fill some of that gap. Look to old-timers for tips on everyday living skills, applying for government benefits, finding recreation programs or financing a van. If you can't find a good support group in your area, find one online. If you don't have a computer, go to the library and use theirs. See the appendices for places to start. Veteran wheelers have been there and done that, they can tell you how to go there and do the same. And once you've benefited from their experience? Consider becoming a peer counselor yourself. ∎

Clockwise from top: Jason Regier, Pat McGowan, Michael Slaughter, Jason Graber, George Taborsky, Joel Lorentz, Matthew Seals & kids, Joel Irizarry, Felipe Antonio; Ryan McLean (middle).

Joel Irizarry

I find Joel Irizarry, first by phone and then in person, about four years after his injury. What comes through loud and clear in our phone conversations is Joel's optimism. He's got *total* confidence in the future, sure that nothing will get in his way on the path to success and the goals he sets, whether they are good health, marriage, a good job or simply having fun.

I ask him where he gets that confidence.

"By keeping a positive attitude and staying around positive people," he says. "I've been blessed with a really strong support system of my family, my mom and my friends."

We meet in Chicago, in the lobby of the Schwab Rehabilitation Center, where he's mentoring a new wheeler. He'd told me he was good-looking and he wasn't lying. After greeting me with a big smile and leading me through some corridors, he introduces me to a couple of rehab counselors he works with. They clearly hold him in high regard. This is a young guy who's comfortable with himself and where he's headed.

In 1999 Joel was 17, a senior in high school and trying to straighten out his life. He'd been running with the wrong crowd and it was getting him into trouble regularly. He saw what was happening to some of his friends, decided that wasn't what he wanted, and figured it was time to distance himself from the gang he hung with in Chicago. Like most of us when it comes to change, he waited a bit too long.

While he was trying to drive away from a sticky situation, a bullet left him with a T11 complete injury. Acute care at Cook County Hospital—no windows, no privacy, no fun—then to rehab at Schwab only five days later. It was quick and rough.

"I cried some when they told me I wouldn't walk again," he says, "but my mom and girlfriend wouldn't let me get down. When someone told me I couldn't have kids, I got scared but got that cleared up real fast by talking to a real doc. I never really got too depressed; I've always been pretty optimistic."

Though he felt pretty lost, he spent most of his six weeks at Schwab learning his self-care and getting used to the chair. With the help of a tutor, he also finished his high school requirements. What helped him the most in rehab, Joel says, was meeting someone who had used a chair all his life and told him how independent he was, what he could do, what was possible.

"Rehab was good and I learned a lot about being independent," he says. "I see a lot of guys in chairs who can't do what us Schwabies can do."

After rehab he went home to an inaccessible apartment—a five step entrance, a bathroom he couldn't get into and a landlord unwilling to make modifications. He could hear his mother crying every night. Perhaps it was for her that he began sucking it up and getting strong and positive. The inaccessibility and landlord problems were solved when his mom bought a house and modified a basement apartment for him, which he now rents from her. Even though she lives upstairs, he's on his own and comes and goes as he pleases.

Mentee to Mentor

Joel spent that first summer getting acclimated to life on wheels. Going out with his friends helped him get comfortable in public.

"My friends were pretty goofy," he recalls. "If people stared at me, they'd all stare back. That stuff's not an issue any more."

When his rehab caseworker steered him to ORS (Illinois's Office of Rehabilitation Services), Joel got them to pay for most of his school tuition. Within a year, he'd begun classes at Devry University. He wasted no time getting on with life.

Today, four years later, he's got a part-time job at Schwab as a peer mentor, working primarily with people who were injured through violence and are under 30. Now he's that guy in a chair telling others about his life, what he used to be like, showing them what he can do and what he's finding out is possible. "When I was offered the mentoring job, I thought it was cool because I like helping other people," he says.

He also spends a day a week working in a youth diversion/violence prevention program called "In My Shoes" for kids doing community service. He tells them about the consequences of SCI and brain injury.

"I don't sugarcoat anything in either program. I tell it like it is. This is the kind of program I could have used before I got shot."

School's going well and he's maintaining a high GPA. Because Devry is small and accessible, he knows almost everyone, socializes a lot and is treated the same as everyone else. He plans to finish his course work in computer information systems by the fall of 2003. [See update.]

His reason for studying computers is simple. Entry level salaries average about $45,000, and climb into six digits within four or five years. For now, he's getting by with SSI and Medicaid, money from his

mentoring, and help from voc rehab for his schooling. A big part of why he's doing so well, he says, is that he's afraid of failing and having to depend on SSI for the rest of his life.

"When I was at Schwab I learned a lot about what the system has to offer—Voc Rehab, SSI, Medicaid, parking perks. I use all these things to my advantage. For example, because I'm a full-time student under 22, SSI can't touch any of the money I make. That's the kind of information I pass along to the people I mentor. I think everyone has to find a way to use the system in order to get ahead and be successful. The system isn't always easy but it's there."

There's more that's not easy. Three times a week he's up by 5 a.m. in order to get the necessaries done before classes, and is out the door by 7. He's at school all morning four days a week, and spends Thursday afternoon and all day Friday at Schwab either speaking or mentoring.

Being treated as "special" isn't easy. Winter isn't easy. On the hassle scale, Joel rates snow right up there with stairs.

His compensations are clubbing with his girlfriend and other friends, going to sporting events, an occasional trip to an amusement park, keeping tabs on the people he mentors. Sports are especially important to him. He plays football with the local PVA chapter and has traveled the country with them going to competitions. He's living his opening mantra: Stay busy, keep a positive attitude and hang out with positive people.

Reacting to change

How does Joel define success?

"I'm working, I'm going to school, I'm active, I stay busy and productive," he says. "I'm not locked up in that basement apartment. I'm positive and not depressed. I'm healthy and taking care of myself. That's what I look for in the people I mentor. Hey, I've seen what's happened to some people. I've seen some get shot *again*, or not take care of themselves, get a sore and lose a leg or die. I've seen the photos of bad skin sores and don't need to have that kind of Kodak moment."

What's helped him the most?

"Strong support from my mom, my girlfriend and some friends. I think my girlfriend is the single most influential person in my life. Playing basketball at Schwab is very cool and helped me a lot. Things could be a lot worse, and every time I'm at the hospital working I'm reminded of that. I'm grateful for life. My faith in God tells me He won't give me more than I can handle. That helps me from getting overwhelmed. I believe that most things happen for a reason."

And that would be?

"So I can help others. So I can be a role model. Helping others helps me and makes me feel good about myself. Sometimes I think all this might be a test for me so that I can figure out how to do things differently and see how strong I am."

Has he changed?

"I'm pretty much the same guy I was before I got shot, maybe a little smarter and more experienced. I may be a little less spontaneous and plan ahead more, but I've also straightened out my life. Hey, I'm going to college and doing what needs to be done to make all these things happen."

The future?

Joel wants the American Dream—a good job, a very fast car, marriage, kids, a house, preferably in the sun and sand of Florida, and living happily ever after—and he wants it all in the next five years or so.

Where won't he live?

"Any place with snow."

Update: Remember that SSI deal that didn't limit Joel's income because he was under 22? Well, he had a birthday, his SSI check dropped to $50 a month and he couldn't pay his bills. His solution was to work full time at Schwab doing recruiting, tracking and follow-up for a major research study on skin.

"I'm also a mentor slash counselor slash translator," he says. "I had to drop out of school last semester after making the honor roll for my grades because tuition went way up and I didn't have the money. But now I'll keep working full time and in the fall, when I can get some more help from ORS and Financial Aid, I'll go to the community college by my house at night and get some more credits. When my benefits kick in at Schwab, I can get the new chair I need. I'm going to Vegas this spring to play football in the Extreme Bowl. That should be fun. Things will work out."

Confidence. Confidence to burn. ■

Charmaine G. Brown, *A Royal Flush*

Jason Regier

Jason Regier was one semester shy of a degree at Oregon State when he drifted off the road while changing radio stations. When he tried to get the car back on the highway, he over-compensated and rolled it. A very complete C5-6 injury, acute care at Latter Day Saints Hospital in Salt Lake City, two fusion surgeries to repair shattered vertebrae, then back home to Denver for rehab at Craig Hospital.

He finished his school work by correspondence while in rehab and received a bachelor's degree in philosophy at 21.

"Spinal cord injury is a crash course in life," Jason says. "I had to focus on some real-life issues like, 'What's my life going to be about?' I had to grow up in a hurry, but I think injury can be a catalyst for change and self-evaluation. It's sort of like having a midlife crisis in your early twenties. But that's OK; I don't want to have to figure it out when I'm 50."

That crash course in life began when he left rehab. Here are some of his curricular goals: Learn independence. Find passion in life. Find pay-offs through patience and persistence. Discover himself. Develop the courage to accomplish goals. Choose his own way to react to life on wheels.

His best teachers have been long-term SCI survivors, quad rugby teammates, paralyzed vets, rehab pros and lots of self-directed study.

Initially not much seemed possible to Jason, and the scope of his injury overwhelmed him. Like many, he learned through a series of baby steps, beginning with the basics such as feeding himself, driving, dressing, transferring and pushing his chair.

Still weak when discharged, he was barely able to push a half block of flat terrain. Once he regained some strength and got a van he began venturing out alone more, though it took a year before he popped a wheelie over the threshold of the front door and got out of the house by himself.

"I tend to forget how hard it was in the beginning," he says. "It was two months before I was able to move my arms, at least 18 months until I was able to wheel a mile. This is probably the hardest thing people ever go through. Everything takes longer, not just the physical stuff but school, work, benefits applications. It takes a huge effort to get back out there because it's such a mental challenge."

Jason took on the challenge. He called for informational job interviews, went out on trips alone, coached a soccer team and began asking women out.

Recently laid off from a corporate training job, he's now in graduate school working on a double masters (MBA and Marketing) and financing it with a combination of self-pay, Pell Grants, scholarships and, he hopes, help from Voc Rehab.

Because his studies require him to do an internship, he's now trying to combine school, pleasure and possible future employment. He works with a local video production company on producing a feature length video on quad rugby. Because the company is still getting off the ground, it benefits from his help with marketing while he furthers his education.

The video stuff isn't new. He has worked with the local PBS station covering the quad rugby Nationals and done promos for his rugby club. He also does a bit of website development and volunteering at Craig Hospital.

"The single most important factor ..."

Remember the second goal in Jason's self-directed curriculum? Quad rugby has become his passion. He describes the game as basketball meets football meets rollerball, plus a lot of strategy. Rugby has taken him to Canada and both coasts, and will, he hopes, take him to future world competitions in Greece and New Zealand. In many ways quad rugby has served as a rehab surrogate.

"More than anything else, rugby has really shaped who I am," he says. "I learned to overcome obstacles. I got out and began meeting other people. I've had a chance to

51

travel alone with minimal help and learn something new each trip. I'm stronger and more independent. Rugby's been the single most important factor in helping me deal with the mental aspects of being in a chair and interacting with other people."

Jason's .5 classification means he's the most severely disabled athlete on the court. He's serious enough about rugby to train five or six days a week with weights, sprints, ball work or endurance runs, and often wheels three or four miles daily. His on-court performance earned him invitations to the World Wheelchair Games and the Paralympic tryouts.

Rugby's not a cheap sport. An out-of-town tournament can easily cost a player $500 and it's easy to spend up to $7,000 a year. He began by borrowing hand-me-down chairs until he could afford a used one. When United Airlines broke that chair, they bought him a new one. But meeting the costs takes sacrifices.

"A lot of players are living on SSI and Medicaid and are still very active in rugby," Jason notes. "That speaks to how important it is to them."

Trade-Offs for Independence

I visit Jason in the modest home he shares with his dad in southeast Denver where, after I wheel up his long, steep ramp, his service dog Newlie greets me at the door. The house is open; the living room, dining room and kitchen all run together, with hardwood floors throughout. The dining room table overflows with benefits information, insurance claims, correspondence and rugby stuff. A standing frame and a big dog carrier sit in the living room. The bookcase holds text books and self-help treatises, plus Hockenberry's *Moving Violations* and Viktor Frankl's *Man's Search for Meaning.*

Newlie is a big part of Jason's life, helping him to be far more independent than his injury would normally allow. Newlie will pull him up to sitting in bed or offer his body for balance during transfers. He picks things up from the floor and at bedtime helps Jason get his pants off. The dog is a constant companion at tournaments

or Avalanche hockey games, and pulls him around when he's tired or sick or it's very cold outside.

"Having a service dog is pretty special, gives me a lot of companionship and more or less replaces the dog I had before I got hurt," Jason says. "He's an icebreaker for meeting new people."

Jason's life hasn't been all sports and school. He got his feet into the employment pool during his first summer on wheels when, with the help of a church friend, he began an internship with a teletech firm. Initially he worked a day or two a week from a power chair. After three months in recruitment and six months in corporate training with a number of Fortune 500 companies, he went to full-time work. He taught management skills for 18 months before being laid off and beginning grad school.

Bringing home paychecks for a couple of years taught him that he wanted to work, get off benefits, be productive, pay taxes and hang out in the business world. He also learned that work needs to be something he loves, and right now that means video production. The challenge of work is finding the energy to do it full time.

"It all comes down to energy, and to me the trade-off for work is accepting help," he says. "If taking help will save me energy and 30 minutes of my time so I can work, I'll take the help. The young independent male butt-head in me is gone."

Though he continues to use an attendant for help with some transferring and dressing, not working gives him time to see if he can go it alone. He sees independence as a mindset and the assistance he receives merely as a means to such ends as work, school and rugby.

Like most men his age, Jason worried about what women were thinking, how they'd react to the chair or if anyone could be attracted to him. He struggled with his doubts until he realized that women were probably just as nervous about the whole thing as he was. At that point he stopped trying to figure out the difference between early dating anxiety and chair issues. More relaxed and sure of himself now, he relies on his 'let's just see what happens' attitude.

"It's pretty amazing how all these little things—getting out, working some, learning independence, traveling—build on one another until one day you look around and realize, 'Hey, I've got a life!' After about a year I was able to get past all the 'I can't do this or that' and start focusing on what I was still able to do. A couple years after that I was able to say 'Hey, I'm okay with this.'"

Choosing the Big Picture

Jason seems way too bright to be only 27 and just six years post-injury. Maybe it's the degree in philosophy; perhaps it's all the introspection; it could be that he makes a conscious choice to do things even when he's afraid.

Maybe what's helped him most is his ability to place things in perspective. He's a big-picture kind of guy and makes a conscious effort to remember just how dismal those first few days and weeks following injury were. He doesn't want to forget how far he's come, how much progress he's made. He works to stay aware of his present and past good fortune: good rehab, a great support system, a van, a state-of-the-art chair and living in the USA as opposed to, say, Bosnia.

"You know, SCI is pretty tough, but it's also an opportunity to reevaluate and see where you are in life," he says. "It can have a huge negative impact on your life, or you can find ways to continue doing the same things you've always done. If you do that, go back to those old things, they're worth more because they take so much more effort.

"Hey, I still have my days where the chair sucks. The bowel and bladder and sex stuff are the big things, and sometimes it's hard to refocus away from those things, but you must. I can choose to blame the injury for things but I don't go there anymore. Maybe that's denial or a survival mode, but it's better for me when I don't.

"I can focus on the things I can't do, or on the things I can. The bottom line is that even if I was ablebodied I know I'd never be able to do all I'd like to do. I can still do most of what I want and love to do—ski, sail, run a business—and I think many of my limits are self-imposed. I can still choose how to react and be optimistic."

This guy's wide-eyed excitement for life is pretty contagious. I can't help but believe him when he smiles and says: "I'm amazed by all this, especially seeing all those clichés about hard work and persistence coming to life. When I got to rehab I couldn't move my arms at all, yet here I am now, right where I imagined I could be. To me, that's pretty amazing." ∎

Felipe Antonio

I found Felipe Antonio at Homeboys Industries, a nonprofit organization in Los Angeles. Felipe is a former gangbanger; Homeboys is a nonprofit organization in Los Angeles that offers job placement, tattoo removal, counseling, community service opportunities and case management services for former gang members. Its motto is, "Nothing Stops a Bullet Like a Job." After Felipe stopped a bullet, Homeboys gave him a job.

Homeboys is about two miles east of downtown L.A., housed in an old storefront. I park down the street a couple of hundred yards and wheel back on the cracked, uneven sidewalk. Not the greatest part of town. But it's a different story inside. The building's been gutted and redone, and is now open, clean, bright, organized, warm and *busy*. Glass-walled offices, accessible by ramps, overlook the common space housing reception and waiting areas along with a group of employees at work on phones or computers.

Most everyone here is in their twenties or younger, almost all are people of color and a few are in wheelchairs. Being very white and approaching the far side of middle age, I stand out here, making it easy for Felipe, a 23-year-old T5, to quickly identify me. He's well groomed, impeccably dressed and has the professional appearance of a 9 to 5 office worker. His chair is clean and almost gleaming. Once we settle in a vacant office, I comment on his appearance.

"It's part of how I know I'm doing OK," he says. "I see guys in chairs who don't care. They wear dirty clothes or sometimes smell like urine. I don't want to be like that. I've got my pride and want to be a responsible person. I feel good when people notice and tell me I'm doing well. That's important to me."

It's summer, so he's working full time answering phones, taking messages and keeping track of all the charitable donations Homeboys receives. He likes the environment and the people he works with, many of whom, like him, are former gangbangers who had a hard time finding work. He likes that his job gives him some purpose, he tells me, and he enjoys all the contact he has with people throughout the day. And of course there's the money.

"I needed a job," he says. "I was going to school and my family was supporting me. My doctor told me about this place. I came down and Father Boyle, the director, hired me on the spot. I thought I'd be a janitor or something, but he put me in charge of the donor database."

Felipe's up each day by 6:30 to shower, dress and eat so he can do his 9 to 5. Once college is back in session, he'll return to part-time work. I suggest that 9 to 5 office work sounds downright boring compared to running with a gang.

"Hey, I need money to support myself just like everyone else," he says. "I can't bang from a chair and besides, it's too boring if I don't have something to do. I like having a normal life like everyone else. Staying busy and being productive, life is better this way."

The Inventive Spirit

Six years ago, when Felipe was in his last year of high school and hanging out on the edges of gang life, he was shot in his car while parked in an alley. He spent a month in a general hospital, had surgery to repair his esophagus and spent most of his energy in acute care just getting through the days. During his six weeks at Rancho Los Amigos in Downey, Calif., he was surrounded by friends who ditched school to visit. Once he figured out the permanence of the paralysis, he quickly learned the necessary skills and left independent. He says rehab was fun.

Four days after discharge he was back in high school. That was less fun. He was the only person there using a chair, and he felt embarrassed and self-conscious. Class changes were a nightmare but his friends were there, always wanting to help. School filled time, got him back out with people and helped him get through that first year.

Since Felipe's discharge, home has been a garage apartment adjacent to his sister and her husband in Compton. The situation works, letting him come and go as he pleases, and he enjoys spending time with his nephews and niece, helping them with homework and setting an avuncular example.

Now the chair is just part of life. "It's my legs, a way to get around," he says. "I don't think about it much. Why should I worry about what other people think?"

Initially dating made him nervous, but not anymore. "I lost a girlfriend when I was in rehab because I was so focused on myself, but got interested again when I went back to high school. Dating's not that hard. If someone turns you down, you ask someone else. Sex is different because you have to trust the other person more."

Felipe has found that resourcefulness is a big part of having a disability. "When you

don't have money to buy things, you do something else." Like fabricating shocks for your casters out of old springs or customizing the tubing of your chair with steering wheel covers or making your own hand controls out of wheelie bars. "Why should I buy something if I can make it?"

Well, safety comes to mind.

"Never had a problem with those hand controls in five years," he says proudly. "I drove with a broomstick once. A friend of mine drove around on the freeways using a hockey stick. I was like, damn!" he says with a big grin. Privately I'm thinking of car ad disclaimers on television: "Professional Driver, Closed Course, Don't Try This at Home."

When he's not driving, he's using the subway and city buses, though at first he was reluctant to try public transportation.

"I have friends in chairs who use public transportation, so I thought, 'Why not me?' Now it gets me to work and school, sometimes faster than if I was driving. People stare more on buses, but if I smile and say hi, they'll smile back."

This is only the second smile I've seen in a half hour. Is he always this serious? He quickly flashes some teeth again.

"I know how to have fun but you got to be serious about some stuff to have a decent life."

His game plan for that decent life is simple: take care of your health, be honest and hardworking, respect and be responsible for yourself, get out and meet people, and don't be afraid to try things because the risks are worth it.

The Helping Imperative

Felipe had seen basketball and tennis in rehab, but he was so sure he was going to walk out of there that he figured he didn't need them. The sports director at Rancho kept after him to give sports a try and two years later, when walking didn't seem so possible, he checked out a practice.

"These guys were good, but what really impressed me was that they had cars, jobs, women. They had regular lives. That opened my eyes some and I wanted to be like them. I've been playing about four years now and it's changed me. I'm more active and feel more normal."

The team is like a big family and that's allowed him to be himself. He plays basketball, football, tennis and hockey well enough to have been named Rancho's Athlete of the Year, and he welcomes the opportunity to be a role model to teammates.

"It's fun to help the younger kids. I tell them how I do things, about girls and life and working hard and taking care of themselves. Helping them makes me feel good."

Felipe likes this helping others business, and not just in sports or with his nieces and nephews. He's looking to make a career of it.

"There are lots of problems out there in the community and especially here in East L.A.," he says. "People need help, someone to talk to or give them advice. I want to be that person. I want to help single parents and those on drugs. I just want to help people."

He knows he needs an education in order to help others, so he's been taking classes at junior college for several years with an eye on social work. Rancho's sports director helped him sign up for community college and land a rehab sports scholarship to pay for his books. A state disability grant gets him a tuition fee waiver, which means free college. He's planning to transfer to a university soon.

Funny thing; while he was going to school so he could help people change their lives, school began to change him.

"I never thought much about the future and for sure I never thought college was possible," he says. "People there are different, more accepting of different cultures and more accepting of me in a chair. Their attitude becomes more positive when they get to know me and when their attitudes change, I get motivated to be more open-minded and less prejudiced about them and other people. College and the chair have opened me up."

It was enough to get him interested and curious about poetry and fiction, enough to become a Toni Morrison fan. But the changes are more than educational.

"People at college know more, are more interesting," Felipe says. "I like the challenge and the sophistication."

This isn't the same guy who was shot six years ago. He's doing good things. He's hanging with positive people. He's working and going to school. He likes his life and the future looks bright.

Five years from now? "I'll be with someone and have a family. I'll be out of college and working full time, counseling for a school or for the county." Until then, he'll stay with Homeboys. ∎

Matthew Seals

Matthew Seals is all about attitude and faith. For him, they're what make life livable.

"When I was first injured I was pretty emotionally helpless and prayed a great deal for guidance. I focused on what was still possible and that gave me peace and direction. It helped me realize that I could choose what my attitude was going to be. Believing God has a plan for us, though often the reason is beyond what we know, gives me hope."

I'd heard some real horror stories in the course of this project; love triangles gone bad, people injured by falling out of bed or lying undiscovered in a car for many hours. Then I met Matthew Seals.

When Matthew, then 30, heard the tornado warning in April of 1998, he did everything he was supposed to do. Having no basement in his home near Birmingham, Ala., he gathered the family in the center of the house and built a "shelter" of mattresses against an inside wall. When the Force 5 tornado hit with 300 mph winds, the house was thrown hundreds of feet into the nearby woods.

He lay in the woods with a T12 broken back for hours before he was found by rescue workers, who carried him to safety on a door they found in the wreckage. The tornado killed 34 people, including Matthew's 8-year-old son Nathan, who died from massive head injuries 10 days later.

"Losing Nathan was so hard," he says. "I thought of all the things we'd miss, like graduation and prom. We were buddies."

Because I don't use religion as a primary coping tool and don't see things like paralysis, famine and war as part of a divine design for the greater good, I usually find it easy to tune out people who say everything happens according to God's plan. But when Matthew tells me that, it rings absolutely and incredibly true. Not to listen would be a big mistake.

"I think maybe I'm in a chair to help other people," he says, "especially those who don't have what I have. I know I'm here to be a dad and to share my love and compassion with others. I expect God to take care of what I 'need' and I believe He will heal me, though it may not be in the time I want or in the way I want. I'm not a Bible thumper, but I do have a very strong faith in God. He helps me cope."

He's no Pollyanna and no religious fanatic. He quietly and confidently tells his truth as he sees it. When he does, I am a bit envious that I and many people I know don't share his high degree of peace and acceptance.

Matthew and I are spending a Saturday afternoon at the kitchen table of his double-wide while two of his children, John Michael, 7, and Margaret, 5, entertain themselves watching cartoons, eating pizza and playing together. Every so often they check in to make sure their dad is still there. Matthew is attentive and aware of what they're doing. He's easy with them, modeling gentleness and love. Their behavior and manner reflect it.

Unexpected Strength

The tornado banged him up pretty badly and kept him in acute care for nearly four weeks. He went to Spain Rehabilitation Center in Birmingham, but was released to a nursing home within a week because the cast on his right arm interfered with rehab. Once his arm healed, he returned to Spain for about three weeks of very intense work.

"It was like boot camp," he says. "They worked me hard and I liked it. I decided to learn to do as much as possible. I got strong and when I left I was fairly independent. The biggest help was talking to someone already in a chair who was making it. I figured if he could do it, so could I. Peers made a huge impact on me. Seeing positive people who are doing well is so important those first few weeks. I kept working on my attitude and choosing to be positive. My attitude surprised me some. I didn't anticipate I could be this strong."

Either paralysis or the death of a child can devastate people, but Matthew had to deal with both of these and divorce as well. Yet he was back on track within a year or so. How so fast?

"Well, I knew I was at the bottom and figured nothing much worse could happen. Life is going to throw you curve balls."

His wife wouldn't let him get close enough to help her and no longer wanted to be with him. He felt guilty and blamed himself for what had happened. Getting past the divorce, he says, was more a matter of time than attitude. Support from friends and family also helped.

"You know what? There was nothing I could do to change how she felt. The divorce was harder to deal with than not walking, but somehow I didn't want to feel sorry for myself. Depression can cloud your vision and bitterness is such a horrible waste of time and energy."

He found that sharing his story helped clear his vision, so he began speaking at churches and doing weather preparedness and injury prevention spots on local television. That helped him regain some sense of self-worth. Unable to go back to being an electrician, he got Voc Rehab to pay for two years of college. School got him outside himself, taught him how to maneuver in public, and gave him social experience.

"I never thought college was an option for me," he says, "but I had a 3.5 average and was running with the big boys. I found out I'm a pretty smart guy and education became much more important to me. I also found out I could still be a good dad."

Speaking, schooling, parenting and social interaction all boosted his confidence and moved him forward. Two years post-injury, the need for money and better health insurance forced him to look for work. Though he still wants that degree, he's happy and proud to have a job. He likes to feel productive.

He's up every day at 5 a.m. and at work by 8:15, where he is a customer service assistant for Blue Cross and Blue Shield of Alabama. That makes him the guy who pisses everyone off by telling them they're not covered for whatever they need.

"I'm the guy," he laughs. "I take the flak." The job is stressful, yet he loves it.

"When people call it's because they have problems and need help," he says. "They're upset and often fixing to pitch a fit, so I try to calm them down. This is very personal medical stuff and if I can help them it's fulfilling for me. I may only talk to them for a few minutes, but that call lasts lots longer for them. I know that when I give them bad news they're not mad at me. They don't know me from Adam's housecat.

"I know I'm in the right job because I'm talking to people all over the country and helping them. I'm sometimes making them smile or changing their attitudes a bit with kind words. Little things can make a big difference."

Walking the Talk

I ask him what else has helped him recover from loss, and he has a list for me. Being active and working with his hands, for example. He built a ramp and a big deck on his trailer, doing much of the work himself. Volunteering with Habitat for Humanity. "If you want to see something comical," he says, "watch a bunch of people with disabilities try to build a house."

Then there's water skiing, fishing and hunting, and receiving the support of family and friends in a church men's group. "We talk about what we're doing and feeling. We hold each other accountable. Who each of us is is about what we do and how we treat people, not about who we are physically."

And being open to people and their questions has helped. He puts them at ease by taking the initiative, by being personable and open and real. Because he's OK with the chair, most others are as well.

Like everyone else, he struggles with bowel programs ("Now *that's* fun") and is irritated by inaccessibility. He has had all the same fears about work, dating, being productive and falling out of his chair as the rest of us, and sorely misses working as an electrician.

Yet Matthew lives what he terms a normal life—working, raising his kids, maintaining a home, caring for a dog. He's an ordinary guy living an ordinary life under extraordinary circumstances.

A true Christian whose beliefs manifest in his day-to-day life, he walks the talk. I believe him when he says that his injury isn't the worst thing that ever happened to him. I believe him when he says he appreciates life more and thinks it is just as fulfilling as ever before. And I believe him when he says that a 35, he's found that most things are still possible.

And this News Flash: Matthew's married. "I met my fiancée Renée on the Internet," he tells me. "I came across her profile and decided to take a chance. I was thrilled when she wrote me back and wanted to go out with me. We conversed through e-mail for two or three weeks and then made a date. We hit it off great and we both knew that night that we were meant to be together. When God lets you know something, you know that you know. Neither of us ever believed in love at first sight until now. We tied the knot this past June. Woohoo!" ∎

Ryan McLean

Ryan McLean is a busy woman. She puts in a 20-hour work week doing medical billing for a couple of doctors. She carries a full class load at the University of Colorado at Denver, where she's finishing up her undergrad work, and has plans for graduate study toward a physician's assistant license. A T5 injury, she exercises for an hour most days at a local fitness club. Her social life is full of movies, clubs and dinner with friends. And somehow she fits in some peer counseling with newly injured patients at Craig Hospital in Englewood, Colo.

She also finds time to model for Quickie, appear on television and try her hand at hockey. Busy is how she likes it and she sees her goals and activities level as nothing out of the ordinary.

"Sometimes people are annoyingly proud of me but what I do isn't at all exceptional," Ryan says. "The general public doesn't have very high expectations for us, so they think anything we do is special. I don't want to be different or special. I don't feel like I am."

In February of 1997 Ryan was 16 and a junior in high school when the Suburban she was riding in crossed the highway median and into oncoming traffic. No one walked away unscathed; two of her friends sustained brain injuries, two others had broken bones and her boyfriend, along with one of the people in the oncoming car, were killed. When medical help arrived and Ryan was examined, the EMTs triaged her out, judging her a no-hoper because she had almost bled out and wasn't breathing. When something, possibly a moan, attracted their attention and they realized she was alive, she was rushed to the hospital.

She spent nearly two months in an ICU and then a multi-trauma unit, where she was stabilized and had rods inserted in both her back and legs. She had broken both wrists, required a number of skin grafts, was on a vent for two months and on oxygen for another month before getting to Craig for a very intense four weeks of rehab. When her

insurance maxed out, she got the boot and was sent home with a long list of instructions, even though she was still learning how to follow them.

"I think it helped that I was optimistic and never looked too far into the future," she says. "I never felt that I had to figure out how to do something right away if I didn't know how to do it. I figure things out when I have to."

On the day of her discharge, even before she went home, Ryan headed straight to the local swimming pool where she had competed on the club team for 4- to 18-year-olds before her injury. She quickly got involved in the administration of the league, began coaching the following summer and was soon the head coach, which she grew to love. Coaching gave her something to do with her competitiveness, let her share what she knew about swimming, allowed her to be a leader while giving back, and gave her feedback about the new Ryan from the kids she was coaching.

"Kids are brutally honest and not afraid to ask questions," she says. "They verbalize what lots of people are thinking. I really enjoy working with these kids and being part of their lives; I think coaching will probably always be a part of my life. Not everyone has that—something they like to do."

The Competitive Spirit

When she returned to high school six months post-injury, she was very self-conscious and the situation was, well, confusing. Some friends, not knowing what to say, didn't say anything; others, people she never really knew, began acting like old friends.

And because of that shortened stay in rehab, all her self-care, like spending 45 minutes in the restroom doing an intermittent catheterization, seemed to take forever.

"At that time, I was thinking, 'I'm doing it; this is great!' Looking back, it was pretty horrible."

Highly competitive and needing to see that she could still compete, Ryan rejoined her high school swim team her senior year. Even though it was very different and very difficult, swimming was a major help in getting her back on track and feeling comfortable in her high school environment.

That's the same competitive spirit that helped her keep up with others in rehab. She was always timing herself to see how long things like getting in and out of the car took. Though she calls herself the world's worst tranferer, she's in and out of her full-size Honda SUV several times a day and her transferring has gotten better and quicker as a matter of necessity.

"I think my competitiveness helps me out in most everything I do," she says. "My life is mostly competing with ablebodied people at work and in school, and the competition somehow helps me feel less disabled as well as happy, healthy and positive."

After high school graduation, Ryan worked for a week with a former Paralympic swimmer, began a rigorous training program and soon improved greatly. After making it through a qualifying meet in Arizona she competed in the 2000 Paralympic trials in Indianapolis. The training was grueling and demanding and just what she needed. She eventually advanced to the finals.

"It was a great experience," she says. "I competed against amputees, blind and deaf, stoke survivors and little people. I lost to an amputee. It was all very wonderful!"

Colorado State University in Fort Collins came next, when she was only 18 months post-injury and still learning all her self-care. School was good and occasionally, when she needed help with something, her boyfriend was around to lend a hand. She knew she needed to meet new people and by the second semester she was using her chair as an automatic conversation starter.

A skin breakdown and subsequent surgery brought Ryan back to Denver a couple of years later. Once she healed up, she found an apartment in the 'burbs and began taking classes at the University of Colorado's Denver campus, about 40 minutes from where she lives.

When someone at a local health club told her of a nearby medical billing firm that was looking for help, she quickly began working half time, taking care to stay below the earnings limit for SSI/SSDI recipients. She calls this her first "real" job and says she's learned a good deal about the games insurance companies and Medicare or Medicaid play to avoid or delay payments. Now she's learned how to be a player.

An Embracing Perspective

Ryan's had to grow up fast and in the process seems to have gained a lifetime of learning in just a few years. "I'm not necessarily a different person," she says, "but I think being in a chair has helped me grow into the person I want to be. This has been a humbling experience and sometimes it's put me in my place. But I can't imagine spending 24/7 wanting to be cured, consumed with being in a different place. You have to embrace yourself. My body's a house and I use it; I use my chair too, just like I use my heart and mind. But I don't have a disease that needs to be cured."

Some people find SCI to be much harder on their families than on themselves and that's been the case with Ryan. Shortly after she was injured, Ryan's mom began drinking heavily and Ryan found herself taking care of the entire family for several years until her mom sought treatment. Her younger sister became very depressed after the injury and was diagnosed as bipolar. Her sister's therapist attributed many of the problems to the impact of the SCI. Ryan found it difficult and confusing to see others struggle more than herself.

"I'm smart enough to know that none of this is my fault, but it's hard not to feel caught in the middle," she says. "After I got hurt, everything I needed from a mother I had to find somewhere else; now that she's sober I'm not sure where to put her in my life. To this day my sister is different around me, putting me on a pedestal like I'm perfect; I don't want to live up to that. This has been very hard on my family and seeing them struggle has been hard on me."

This steep learning curve has made Ryan more detail oriented, less apt to take things for granted, more observant and more in the moment. Still, she caught me by surprise when she said that the perspective she's gained outweighs any petty losses she's experienced.

Are you saying walking is petty?

"Oh, no!" she says, laughing. "But I have to make SCI a positive experience or I'd never leave home. I have to make myself believe I'm good and do good things. I have to make a conscious decision to find things that make me happy and then do them. If you put things off they may never happen.

"People get bogged down doing things they feel they have to do and don't pay enough attention to what makes them happy. I'm a bit more focused on being happy since I was injured. Why shouldn't I be happy?

"I think I react to things differently than my friends because I've learned so much, maybe even things I'm not aware I've learned. I notice more than my friends do, like seeing when people are happy or sad or troubled. It's cool because I feel more unique, like I have more of a reason to be here. It's also not so cool because sometimes I see or feel too much and then think, like, 'why can't I be more naïve?' Most of what I've learned I taught myself and sometimes it feels like everything I've learned about disability has been from doing it wrong."

Ryan's agenda for the future is as full as any young person's. She wants to travel outside the country. She looks forward to gaining her physician's assistant license. She sees marriage and children down the road. She just wants to be happy.

So what she wants is the American dream, like everyone else?

"Well yeah," she laughs; "is that okay?"

When we first spoke, she said she was probably the biggest fatalist I'd ever meet. What does that mean?

"I'm pretty convinced I was supposed to end up in a chair," she says. "I try not to look at this stuff too deeply. Things just happen the way they happen, for a reason. I can't say what the reason is, but I think I'm learning about it every day. I don't have any control over what happens to me, but I can control how I react. I think we all have these paths we're assigned; we can turn right or left at the forks, but eventually we end up at the same place."

All roads lead to Oz?

"In my world they do!" ∎

Joel Lorentz

Joel Lorentz is a good ole Kansas boy. He drives an SUV, his friends are cops and he watches NASCAR a lot. He likes to smile and to hear him tell it, breaking his back might just have been one of the better things he's done in his life.

"If this hadn't happened, something equally bad would have," he says. "I hate to say it, but I probably needed this to be a better person."

If you say that sounds like a pretty steep price, he'll simply smile and maybe point out that he likes his life much more now and knows much better who he is. He'll also tell you that despite the limitations that come with the chair, his life is way more positive than eight years ago when he fell at work and broke his back.

"This changed my life for the better," he says. "I was pretty miserable just before and after my injury. Now my life is pretty much straightened out."

In 1995, Joel was a "tankie," traveling from town to town painting the inside of water tanks. It's a job he calls one step up from being a carnival worker. While in Cherokee, Okla., painting a large tank with his boss, he was overcome by fumes, stumbled backwards and fell 97 feet down the shaft of the tower. He broke his back at T12/L1 and sustained massive internal injuries. About the only thing not beat up was his heart.

When the ground man heard Joel land, he ran out to the highway to get help. Because he looked like a Martian, still dressed in his painting gear and mask, it took an hour for him to flag someone down. Rescuers took another hour to lower ropes down the shaft, lift him off the ground enough to slide him out through the manway hole, and take him to a hospital about an hour away.

He spent five weeks in acute care, much of it in ICU with chest and feeding tubes and on a vent. He had surgery to repair a damaged intestine and fuse his spine, then went to Craig Hospital for rehab.

"I didn't talk at all for the first few weeks," he says. "I was so depressed that I figured my life was over. I just wanted to die. After a while in rehab, I began to accept that I wasn't going to walk again, and that's when I began working hard and learning what I had to do. From there it was back to Kansas to live with Mom and Dad."

It wasn't pretty. With too much time on his hands, living at home on Workers Comp, he fell into a funk. He had no interest in going to college. Instead, he partied hard with coke, meth and pot for three years, long enough to get him thinking about cleaning up and getting sober.

"Quitting was pretty easy once I made the decision to do it," he says. "The hard part was giving up my two best friends, the only two people who were always there for me, the only ones I ever called when things got really hard. I felt bad breaking ties with them, but I knew I had to let them go if I was going to stay clean."

"A real morale booster"

Looking for a fresh start, Joel called an old friend and asked for help finding a job. He was soon working in a different town, away from his best friends and worst habits, as a dispatcher with the Sheriff's office. That explains why he hangs with cops.

On the job, he takes 911 calls—everything from animal control calls to genuine crises. He monitors the whereabouts of all the patrol cars, and is also responsible for administrative calls and tasks. It can add up to more than 4,000 calls a month.

Answering 911 calls is all about taking information—the who, where, what, when and why—and relaying that information accurately to the officers in the field. He first worked in Erie, about 35 miles from his parents, then joined the Fort Scott Police Department. Within a year he was promoted to supervisor, training new hires and filing monthly reports. He was able to buy a small home. The main attraction of the job, he tells me, is seeing the motto, "To Serve and Protect," come to life.

"I'm helping people and I like that. I help the officers do their job by being their link to help and support. I watch their back."

"Working was my salvation, a complete turnaround," he says. "This job's been a real morale booster. I can't emphasize enough how beneficial my parents' support was through this ordeal, but now I'm independent from them, own a home and am doing something worthwhile. If I'm a cop I have to be clean of drugs. It's all or nothing; I can't backslide.

Up at 6 a.m., he's usually out the door by 7:30. The department accommodates his injury by letting him work an 8-hour shift rather than the normal 12, and he does some of his work from a standing frame he keeps there. More often than not he spends an hour or so in bed when he gets home each night to deal with ongoing skin issues, a remnant of his hard partying days. Then he'll fix dinner, hang out and watch the tube, play with his dog or go out with friends. A regular guy with a regular life, he spends weekends sleeping in, running errands, doing chores and watching NASCAR races with his friends.

With a good job, a nice house, unusually good function and great support from family and friends, he says it's hard to complain. His present life seemed more like a pipe dream than a possibility when he was in rehab.

Reasons and Acceptance

Making new friends has never been a problem for Joel, and he says meeting people is even easier now. He feels the chair opens people up and makes them curious. Meeting the right woman has been harder.

"I don't have trouble meeting them, but never the right one," he says, "including the one I married." He was married during a time of transformation. "Everything else in my life changed—I'd moved, started working, got off drugs—so I figured why not get married? But I did it for all the wrong reasons. I wanted to rescue her from a bad lifestyle and was afraid of not making it on my own and being alone for the rest of my life. We weren't in love and split up in less than a year. At least I was able to help her raise her kids. I liked being a dad."

Joel's certain his injury happened for a reason, though his rationale for thinking so is atypical. A few days prior to his injury, feeling unusually arrogant and cocky, he stood atop a water tower, shook his fist at the heavens and told God he didn't need Him.

Injury as divine retribution?

"I don't know," he admits. "It certainly woke me up and I'll never question God again. I could have worn a respirator and been more careful, so the fall and injury are on me. I needed to be taken down a notch."

In reaction to my skeptical look, he elaborates about how his life might have gone without his injury.

"I'd probably be the same arrogant, cocky guy I was 10 years ago. I was in a downward spiral and might be dead by now. Instead, I've got my life straightened out. I'm stronger than I thought and more patient, more ambitious, more humble. I wouldn't take the cure if it meant losing all I've learned."

The way Joel sees it, there are three kinds of crips in the world: those who stay at home filled with self-pity and misery, cure-seekers whose lives won't begin until they get the cure, and those who adapt, improvise, accept and move forward. That last group, he says, is where he wants to be.

"Life's not over until you want it to be over," he says. "At first, most of my fears were in my head. I was afraid of all the unknowns: could I support myself, live on my own, attract women? It took me three years to get a handle on all that. But I did it, especially after I started driving and getting out.

"Everyone gets disappointed. Everyone has problems. I expect those things to happen, because they're just part of life. When they do I try to stay in the game and not mope around.

"After I saw my X-rays I accepted that I wasn't going to walk again," he says. "That was pretty easy, partly because it was out of my control. I had to accept that reality if I wanted to grow."

What does he mean by acceptance?

"Acceptance is more than just moving on, it's also accepting that there are other ways to look at things, other ways to do them. It means appreciating the function and support I have and accepting that I have to work hard if I want to be successful and happy. Acceptance is being honest and true to myself about figuring out how to be happy and then taking responsibility for doing it." ∎

Charmaine G. Brown   *A Royal Flush*

65

George Taborsky

According to George Taborsky, 36, people living with quadriplegia have a choice. Either they can sit around doing nothing and getting depressed or they can go out, stay busy and find things that make them happy. Having tried both options over the last 10 years, he strongly suggests the second.

George grew up in Smithtown, N.Y. on Long Island, about an hour from New York City. Though he still lives there with his mom, he's rarely home. Between work, sports, travel, peer counseling and adventuring, he doesn't have much time to be a nester.

While horsing around at a college reunion in 1992, he lost his balance and fell into the shallow end of a pool. C6 broken neck. After two and one-half weeks of acute care, he spent several months at Burke Rehabilitation Hospital in White Plains, N.Y., about two hours from home.

Following rehab George lived with his girlfriend, but over the course of the next 18 months communication broke down between them as they each dealt with their individual stresses and the reality of the chair. Their breakup was sudden and abrupt. He took it hard and those first few years were pretty dark. That's when he moved back home.

Though he was always confident that things would eventually work out, distractions kept holding him back. During the first three years after injury, he lost his father, grandmother and a close uncle. Then his dog of 17 years died. He was plagued by health problems like pneumonia, back pain and blood clots.

"All of that was tough and hard to get past," George says. "The bottom sort of fell out and it took me some time before I was able to move on and get involved with other things."

Worrying, he wondered what kind of future he would have. How would his severely impaired finger dexterity limit his ability to use various tools on the job? Would he still be able to draw or boat or have fun at the beach? Could he have a family, get a job or even live independently? He was unsure about everything.

"I was pretty depressed for a couple of years," he recalls. "I never got into drugs or booze, but I began to understand how other people did."

Despite all the setbacks George slowly began getting back on track. Life started to become more about possibilities than losses when he looked for and found things that made him feel good. In the process, his attitude began to change, and when that happened everything else began to change. At first it was simply by getting out and around people. Outpatient therapy in Stonybrook, N.Y. and at Mount Sinai Rehabilitation Center in New York City got him on a functional electrical stimulation bike and that led to some peer counseling at

Mount Sinai. He started working with PTs there, demonstrating transfers and what are called ADLs in the rehab trade, activities of daily living. Next came volunteering at the Northport VA Medical Center repairing medical equipment, the job he did before injury.

"That was good and I enjoyed it," he says. "I was out of the house and feeling productive and better about myself. It got me thinking about going back to work and making some money to get the things I wanted."

But working full time would mean losing Medicaid and his personal care assistants, a tough proposition because he still needed daily help. Deciding to go back to work anyway, he got Voc Rehab to help him with van modifications so he could commute. Besides putting money in his pocket, working every day forced him to give up his home health care and gain independence. Through trial and error, he slowly learned to do it all — shower, bowel program, dressing. That's when things really started turning around.

Staying busy is important to him and the job helps to fill his days and add structure to his life. He enjoys feeling like he's part of the mainstream. The job and the daily contact with people are important enough to him that he's up by 5 each morning for bathroom duties before commuting 30 minutes to work and putting in his time from 8 till 4:30.

Work is a 40-hour week at the VA hospital, where his department services all the medical equipment there including vents and defibrillators, equipment that literally saves lives. George's job requires a great deal more fine motor function than he has, so work can get frustrating. He compensates with T-handled screwdrivers and Allen wrenches and a standing chair the hospital purchased for him. He calls hemostats his best friends.

"Saying that I work full time lets me feel like everybody else," George says. "I like having a routine and schedule and would probably still work at something even if I won the Lotto. You gotta keep that noodle workin'."

Back in the Game

Shortly after getting back on the job, he checked out quad rugby and life got a whole lot better again. Rugby's way more than just something for him to do. The practice, the competition and the commitment have become a lifestyle that's improved his conditioning enormously and put him in contact with other wheelers.

"I had a lot of sadness and loss in my life before I started playing," he says. "Rugby started to turn that around for me. It let me have fun and gave me something to excel at."

And it gave him something important enough that from October to April he spends three and one-half hours each Tuesday driving back and forth through New York traffic for practice.

As his play improved his floor time increased and he began going on road trips with the team all over the country. The traveling helped him gain confidence that he could take care of himself under most any circumstance.

"When we're on the road," George says, "there are never enough accessible rooms to go around so we have to make do with what we have. Sometimes that means taking bathroom doors off the hinges or using a coffee table as a slide board.

"I watched and asked guys how they did things and used their ways or created my own. I taught myself how to hold a pen by watching others. I kept trying to do new things like cooking or tying my shoes. Learning how to deal with all the frustrating or even trivial things felt great. Each one is like a test and each accomplishment— working, driving, cooking, cleaning, traveling, self-care—gets me more back in the game. Every time I'd do something, the next thing I tried, like shopping, going into the city or traveling on my own, got easier."

With no rugby in the summer, George turns to other outdoor adventures. He plays softball, kayaks using outriggers and likes to go camping. Each time he tries something new he comes up with creative solutions to obstacles, such as gripping a paddle, dropping a baseball bat after hitting the ball or doing a ground-to-chair transfer. When he got bored riding his bike in the same old places, he built a carrier for his van so he could explore new areas.

He got back to boating, going alone and doing everything by himself if necessary. He wants to travel more and get into whitewater rafting. Glider planes recently caught his eye and he says soaring, and a license, are probably in his future.

No Time, No Worries

George had a strong interest in the graphic arts prior to injury, and he's now trying to rekindle it. Computer graphics courses have given him a way to use his computer as a darkroom for altering photos and superimposing them on one another. He sees this as a hobby and a possible career change.

Some people throw themselves into things, taking huge chances along the way, while others are too timid to ever try anything. George's style is somewhere in the middle. He likes to slowly yet methodically solve small problems without having to take huge risks. That allows him to stay confident and safe while continuing to move forward and make good progress. Added up, these small steps amount to independence and a full life. Using each accomplishment as a building block gives him

the motivation to try yet another new thing. Bottom line is that he's found a way that works for him.

As we talk, he keeps going back to how getting out of the house opened doors for him.

"So many good things happened when I started getting out," he says. "I met people through work, sports, outpatient therapy or peer counseling. I've met people with Olympic medals through rugby and now I got a shot at winning one of my own. All kinds of opportunities. None of that would have happened if I was still sitting in my room."

George says he's learned that he can still be in control of his life even if that means asking for help. Independence, he believes, is more mental than physical. Too busy putting himself in good situations and watching opportunities show up, he's got no time for worrying about what he can't do.

"I can make my own luck by being positive and taking chances," George adds. "Getting out there is the key. Not much happens to people who are sad and depressed and stay home all the time. You gotta get out there and do it." ∎

Jason Graber

You might think he would be content now that he's got his college degree and a job in the media field. You might think that swimming and riding his handcycle would take up all his free time. You might think that chasing women and hanging out on the beach would be enough.

Nah. At 29, Jason Graber is hungry, curious and wanting more. Jason thinks large.

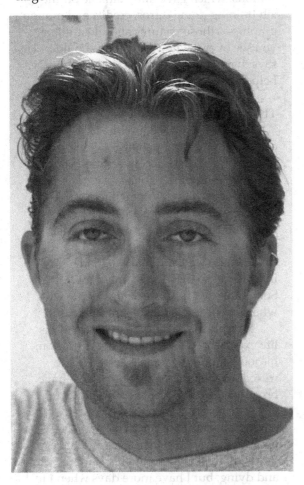

We're working on our tans in Encinitas, Calif., where Jason now lives. It's a sunny day in July, and he's telling me his story.

In the card game of life, he tells me, "I gotta play what I'm dealt because folding isn't an option. I'm betting on drawing the ace of spades."

Nine years ago he drew a T10 injury when, as a passenger, he was thrown from a car in a rollover accident. Before his accident, Jason had no real plans for his future, was getting high at lunch hour and needed an extra semester to finish high school. He wanted to pound nails for a living. Today it's a different story.

He's the director of media productions ("I gave myself the title. What do you think?") for a 500 employee company that produces newspaper, television and direct-mail advertising. If you live in the Midwest and have seen those ads that encourage you to dump cable in favor of satellite television, chances are you've seen Jason's work.

"Tired of cable? Call now and we'll send you a dish and receivers free," he says, mimicking the ad. "We say bad things about cable. The key word is free, though I haven't figured out just where the free is, but that's what they offer."

For now, Jason sees the job as a way to gain experience in his chosen field until something better comes along in video production. He's paying his dues and learning all he can.

"I just got out of school, I'm just starting out, and I have a job that gives me a lot of creative freedom," he says. "I like to evoke emotion and excitement and I can do that with video. I've got some great ideas and I need to put them into action."

Up by 5 each day so he can be on the job by 6, Jason's on his way home by 3:30. That schedule gives him plenty of time for swimming at the YMCA and riding his handcycle around the neighborhood.

On weekends, he's at the beach or out with friends looking for women. Meeting them, he says, doesn't seem to be a problem.

When Jason was hurt in 1994, he was living in Albuquerque with his mother. He was taken to the University of New Mexico Health Sciences Center, where his mom was a student nurse. Following surgery and two drug-fogged weeks, he traveled to Denver for 10 weeks of rehab at Craig Hospital. His response to his injury is as refreshing as it is atypical.

"I didn't have any image of what life in a chair might be like and thought of it as maybe a new beginning," he remembers. "I never went through any big depression during rehab or after, and never thought too far down the line. I took things day to day. I had a hairline fracture at C1-2 so I know how lucky I am to come away with all this function. I think about that every day."

Wheeling into Art

Back in Albuquerque after discharge and watching his mom struggle with his accident, he made a decision to push forward and focus on the positives. He found part-time work doing in customer service and technical support within six months, first for MCI and later for AOL.

"I wanted to get back to some kind of normal routine," he says. "You know, get up, go to work, come home, hang out. I tried to keep my life as much the same as possible with family and friends, too. Getting a car and not having to depend on others for transportation was big. "

He stayed in Albuquerque when his mom moved to Texas, but after two years of phone work he knew he wanted more. Then, when his mom moved to Denver, he joined her and enrolled in a community college graphic arts program. He was on his way.

He loved school even though he had to commute 76 miles every day, but when a blizzard left him housebound for three days during his second year of classes, he'd had enough of Colorado weather. When his dad suggested spending the summer with him in Southern California Jason jumped all over it. Once there, he took a junior college class and, liking what he saw, found a roommate and began classes in graphic arts at the Art Institute of California. He became active in student affairs by joining the Ambassador's Club, a group that gave voice to student complaints and concerns.

College wasn't just about classes and acquiring knowledge; he saw it as a big, fun, learning experience and an opportunity to make his own kind of art. Using his chair as a brush, he rolls over canvases with paint-soaked wheels, experimenting with different treads and levels of inflation to alter the effects. Some of it was for course work, some for the sheer joy of creating.

Nine years after taking that extra semester to finish high school, he graduated from college with honors, something he never envisioned when walking. The total cost of his schooling came in at about $45,000, but his share, mostly in student loans, amounted to less than a quarter of that. The rest came from state grants and disability related scholarships. As a student, he relied on SSI, Medicare and Medi-Cal.

While still in college, Jason did internships at the local PBS and FOX TV stations, which gave him valuable on-the-job training doing intros, credits and motion graphics—those pictures and illustrations you see over the news anchor's shoulder. He says that experience, along with his degree, helped him land work after graduation.

The Sum of All Experience

Jason seems to see his wheels as a catalyst for meeting people. "Often people will use the chair as a conversation starter," he says. "Everyone's got a story. Occasionally I'll offer my lap to a good-looking woman if there are no chairs around. I try to come across as a regular guy who happens to be sitting down. I try to treat people well and make a good impression so they'll remember me. Sometimes it's fun surprising people with what I do physically, like jumping curbs."

He feels that over time, the sum of his life experiences—his injury, his education, his job history, the people he's met, the recreational activities he's pursued—have broadened him and opened his mind.

"I've changed mentally, physically, emotionally and I'm on a different level now," he says. "I still struggle and have days when I feel like crawling under a rock and dying, but I have more days when I feel I'm on top of the world. Everybody's life can be a roller coaster, but now that I'm working and financially independent, life's more stable. I've got more respect for life. I know I'm way more mature and think I'm a better person because of dealing with the struggles we all go through. I've come a long way and I still have big plans. I'm not satisfied."

Now that he has some experience in production and voice-overs, those big plans include a shot at the big time in L.A.—directing, producing or possibly working in front of the camera.

"We need more wheelers on the screen," he says.

More wheelchair art is also in the picture, and maybe, way down the road, teaching.

"I want what everyone wants, to love and be loved. I don't need the million dollar mansion on the hill, but I wouldn't mind the million dollar bathroom."

I have to ask Jason how, after losing so much function, his dreams got bigger rather than smaller. It seems sort of backward.

"Actually, I think I've gained rather than lost from this. It gave me direction and some focus, sort of a nice kick in the ass from the subconscious or God or a past life. Getting hurt was pretty random. This is something that can happen to anyone so I don't think I was singled out. Now I have to find some meaning to it and make the best of it."

Advice?

"Do all that stuff they tell you in rehab. Stay active, maintain your body, take care of your health, do things to make you feel good about yourself. You can do pretty much whatever you want because there's modified stuff for everything. Life's not over and it can be pretty good."

Actually, he thinks his is just beginning.

"I got a second chance," he says. "I got my foot in the door. I see big things for myself."

Newsflash: Jason's cashed it in with Direct TV and is now working as a consultant with a publishing company that does high school yearbooks. He's traveling throughout Southern California and talking with principals, teachers and students and coming up with better ways for them to publish their yearbooks. ∎

Charmaine G. Brown,   *A Postcard Campaign, 2003*

Pat McGowan

The old saw that spinal cord injury is a life-altering experience is something Pat McGowan has taken to extremes. Since he broke his neck in a rock climbing fall in 1993, he's gone from ski bumming in the Colorado Rockies to making waves as an economist in New York's financial district. His simple formula for success? Focus on what you can control, go with your strengths and welcome opportunities to take risks.

"I think in practical terms and let go of what I can't control," he says. "That's what works for me."

Pat was 23 when he took a 40-foot leader fall. C5-6 injury. During his two weeks in nearby Boulder Community Hospital, where he had an initial surgery, he began to understand how serious his situation was. When he showed up at Craig Hospital [in Denver] for rehab, his entire right side was paralyzed. Most of his six-month stay there was consumed by getting medically stable. He wore a halo for 17 weeks, used a vent for two months and couldn't eat due to a torn esophagus. While he was at Craig, he had surgery for both his neck and to repair his esophagus. Percocet became his best friend.

When it became clear that no amount of PT would get him walking again, Pat decided to concentrate on gaining maximum physical function rather than waiting for the cure. Once past the medical complications, he spent the rest of that first year learning the basic independence skills of dressing and transferring.

After discharge, necessity dictated living with his parents for a time, but he knew that wouldn't be permanent. Within three months he was back in Colorado, living with his brother and figuring out his future.

His biggest concern the first couple of years was avoiding what he calls his worst-case scenario—living on public assistance and doing nothing productive. He knew it could happen. What he wanted was to pay his own way and do something worthwhile; what he didn't want was to be living in subsidized housing, collecting $550/month from SSI and relying on Medicaid when he was 40 years old.

Risky Business

As a climber and skier, Pat was used to taking calculated risks. When someone in rehab advised him to lose as many assistive devices as possible—chest strap, armrests, writing tools—he tried it and it worked.

"My father was always on me to wear a chest strap so I wouldn't fall out of my chair," he says. "I figured if I landed on the floor occasionally, so what? Most everything that's good in life requires taking risks. Being in a chair doesn't change that."

Though his life in college had been mostly sports and partying, Pat had always been a thinker and a reader as well. He saw that his cerebral nature would have to become a more dominant part of who he was, so he reassessed his life, decided what was most practical, and chose a career that made the best use of his strongest asset, his brain.

"I'm lucky enough to be pretty smart," he acknowledges, "so I figured I'd go with that."

He also realized that he had control of his attitude, and that a good one was more necessity than choice. And he knew he could control how he spent his time and energy, so he focused on education and finding a good job. That worst-case scenario was always in the back of his mind.

Since he was dependent on government programs until he could support himself, he used his smarts to navigate the benefits system. He saw it as a frustrating but necessary part-time job.

He found subsidized housing in both Boulder and Tucson, and used a PASS plan to help with the cost of college. When Social Security nixed the plan because he took a year off grad school, he appealed the decision. When the appeal was denied and he had to pay back the PASS money, he took out loans, sought tuition waivers and got a research assistant job to keep himself going. When he was finally working part time and feeling some confidence in his future, he gave up Section 8 housing for the chance to move into a nicer house. The risks paid off and he finished his degree.

"Grad school was probably the first time I really applied myself," he says. "Doing well gave me some direction."

Within a few months of graduating he got a job offer he couldn't refuse even though it meant moving to New York, a risk most people find intimidating even without the challenges that come with using a chair. Despite the astronomical cost of living in New York, the difficulty of finding reliable attendant care, the hassles of an inaccessible city, his need to rely on public transportation, and the chance that he could be stranded in New York if the job didn't work out, he took the gamble and the job offer. He's done well.

"Financially and professionally I had nothing so I didn't have much to lose," he says. "I ran through all the scenarios and realized the chance to go to New York was an opportunity of a lifetime. This—the job, a chance to work for a world-class organization and do something few people were doing, to experience New York—might seem like a big risk, but it was a no-brainer for me."

A Good Time to Be Disabled

Not all risks pay off. While still in school Pat developed a small skin sore. Though both he and professionals monitored it closely, he eventually had to take a semester off to let it heal. He's left with an extremely fragile scar that keeps him out of his chair and on his belly two days a week, and has forced him to change to a power chair for the pressure relief of tilt-in-space seating. Because his job is so computer-intensive, he can work at home during those two days he's flat.

"My employers and I agreed on this before I took the job and it's something I always brought up in interviews," he says. "With the 'Net and e-mail there are a lot of options for flexibility at a job, so it's a good time to be disabled."

Pat has worked in New York for four years now, analyzing advertising and marketing programs to determine how effective they are. He teaches companies how to market themselves by scrutinizing purchase patterns, then shows them how they can best meet consumer needs and make money. He enjoys the number-crunching aspect of the job, as well as the opportunity to interpret and explain to clients what the data mean.

One of the bigger challenges of living in New York has been finding reliable personal care. He had to hire an attendant over the phone prior to moving and went through a couple more once there. Eventually he found reliable help and uses networking and word of mouth for hiring new people.

"I'm very clear about what I need," he says, "and I try to be easy to work for. I think you get what you pay for in attendant care quality, so I pay a little more than is probably necessary, make it a point to be pleasant and try not to be too demanding."

Because work consumes so much of his life, Pat's serious about having and enjoying his free time. "I'd much rather go to a movie or be in Central Park on Saturdays than do laundry or grocery shopping. I'm not frivolous or wealthy, but I can afford to pay my attendants to do certain things for me. As long as I can, I will."

He sees health and conditioning as critical to quality of life so now that he has changed to a power chair to protect his skin, he lifts dumbbells three days a week to maintain strength and avoid future problems. To put some meat between his damaged skin and his bones, he uses a functional electrical stimulation program for building up his gluteal muscles and hamstrings. He regularly works from a PT mat at the office to cut down on his nearly constant pain.

"I've made changes in order to be happier," he says. "Using a power chair is more practical and less tiring. I feel better when I eat well and have lots more energy when I eat energy bars, so I try to do both."

The man knows how to focus on what he can control and it all seems to be working.

Translation, Versatility and Education

After taking up most of his Sunday afternoon, I asked Pat if we'd missed anything. He popped off a quick list of things, beginning with what most people in this book have in common.

"When I first got hurt it was like being in a foreign land and not speaking the language," he says. "Then I met Henry. He'd been in a chair awhile and he became my interpreter. He took me under his wing and showed me the ropes. He knew the system—Social Security, Medicaid, housing, parking, traveling and school—and he taught me.

"I decided in rehab that being a superquad wasn't worth the effort. The athletic stuff didn't look like fun and the adrenaline just wasn't there for me. I didn't have anything to prove to myself or others and I don't think that because I decided I didn't want to be a jock or go skiing again means I gave up. I accept the reality of my limitations and am versatile enough to find other things I enjoy doing."

He's unequivocal about what has helped him the most.

"Education. It's the single most important ingredient to staying clear of public assistance and reaching financial independence. Unless you're already wealthy, you have to work if you want something better out of life. Education or training is the way to get it. School is about more than just learning; you meet people, you learn how to think, you solve problems, you tap into resources. I needed a job that would give me the extra $15,000 per year to pay for attendant care. My education gave me that."

So, is success full-time employment?

"I don't think so. Success means moving forward in your life and being active. It means trying new and different things to make your life better. It means taking risks and finding out what gives you pleasure. Once you figure it out, you do it and have fun."

■

Michael Slaughter

At 39, Michael Slaughter seems to have it all. He has a great house—in Conyers, Ga., just outside of Atlanta—a solid job and a good marriage to a wife who happens to be an SCI rehab nurse.

That's certainly a far cry from 11 years ago, when he needed a nap just to recover from getting himself dressed. These days he spends eight to 13 hours in front of a computer each day buying and selling other computers. Michael's formula for getting here? Lots of hard work and a knack for problem solving.

To a casual observer, he's the example and the proof of two old bromides: If at first you don't succeed, try, try again. Don't be afraid of failure.

In 1993 Michael was rear-ended in the midst of a 16-car pile up on a Birmingham, Ala. freeway. His seat back collapsed on impact and he slid into the back seat, dislocating his neck. When he regained consciousness, he released his seatbelt and tried to get out of the car. Couldn't move. Broken neck, C5-7. That's when the fog set in.

"I just kept hoping I would wake up from this bad dream and find myself walking around," he says. When he woke up he was in rehab, but he wasn't walking. He's never walked again.

After he'd lived that bad dream for three months at Spain Rehabilitation in Birmingham, reality set in. Instead of snoozing he learned everything he could about SCI and becoming independent. It wasn't just for himself, but for his family. As with most of us, it was a long journey.

Mastering the basics of transferring and dressing, he moved on to driving and eventually became Mr. Mom, doing most of the cooking and shopping. He supervised his kids' homework and was a classroom dad. When problems came up, such as doing the laundry or fixing a flat, he solved them as they happened, putting his logic-oriented mind to work.

"I had to feel like I was pulling my own weight, being useful and productive," Michael says. "I had no choice because I know there's always a chance I could be totally on my own. I'm responsible for meeting my own needs so I was really doing this for me."

From Bad to Worse and Back

Despite his confidence in his employability he met obstacle after obstacle, mostly in the form of discrimination. Having worked in the auto repair field for a number of years, both selling parts and doing repairs, he figured he'd have no problem getting a job writing service orders or doing diagnostic work. But after months and months without finding work, he knew that his chair and fear of the ADA were at least part of the reason.

"I knew these people," he says. "I'd sold them parts and they knew my work was good. I'd always dealt with racial discrimination, but having to deal with it on a disability level as well has been a real challenge. I guess I thought I could open a shop and teach auto repair. My mind is what made me a good mechanic and I was still able to think."

Unemployed, Michael went to computer school for a year and a half until he hurt his shoulder and had to drop out. Income from Social Security was nowhere near enough to make ends meet. He was in a tight spot and pretty scared.

He had other problems. He and his wife had been married only a year before he was injured, and marriage to a quad wasn't on her dance card. In spite of his best efforts to reach independence and contribute to the household, they struggled to stay connected. He became angry, depressed and scared. Not sure he could make it on his own and convinced that his wife no longer cared, he made what he refers to as "a lame attempt at suicide with pills, a cry for attention really." His wife became even more distant.

And there were other signs that she was getting ready to bail, such as a separate checking account and a new car. One weekend while traveling with the local rugby team, he got a 'dear John' call. When he got home she and her things were gone.

Less than a year later, while he was still going to Spain Rehab for outpatient PT, a nurse there caught his eye. "Ernestine was always very nice, always friendly and I felt comfortable around her. One day I drove to her house and had my 10-year-old son knock on the door and ask her to come out. We talked, dated a year and then got married. I made the decision to make it work, but also stay independent in case I ever had to live on my own." Within a few years they moved to Atlanta and Ernestine took a job at Shepherd Center.

The Slaughters live about 25 miles southeast of Atlanta in a wooded and quiet neighborhood. After modifying existing house blueprints, Michael secured a contractor's loan and served as the general contractor for their home. They moved in about a year ago.

This house is a crip's dream and offers him total independence: front loading washer and dryer, kitchen with a roll-under sink, a track lift from the bedroom to the bathroom, a big accessible deck out back complete with a hot tub. Open, roomy, easy to get around in. Judging from his garage, with unfinished projects everywhere and a power chair or two in the midst of repair, you know a mechanic lives here.

A Simple Machine

About three years post-injury, Michael bought a laptop with the intention of writing a book. After playing with the computer for a while and seeing all the things it could do—desktop publishing, wedding invitations, photo editing, business operations—he saw the light.

"I can make money with this."

He took an H&R Block course and began doing taxes, starting with about 25 clients and building up to about 400 within a few years. When the computer needed upgrading, this former mechanic opened it up, saw a simple machine inside and thought it was a piece of cake. Soon he was the computer fix-it guy for the neighborhood.

Computers are Michael's full-time job now. He buys them in large lots and then turns them over online to schools or companies. His hours are unpredictable, he says, often set to match his wife's shift schedule.

"Computers changed my life," he says. "I was in a survival mode, needing a way to make money when I realized I could do this. I borrowed off my house to start the business and began by buying and selling computers and parts. Almost everything is through eBay and I often find great deals from firms going out of business.

"I spend a lot of time on line, looking for deals, diagnosing problems. I might waste a day or two on dead ends, but one big sale can make a month. Before computers I was just filling time. Now I have something to do. This has really helped my self-esteem. I always felt I could make it, though I'm not really sure what I expected. Now my mind has given me a very good life."

His combined office and workroom, a converted spare bedroom, is lined by shelves filled with computer cases, hard drives, software and more. It is, by most standards, a mess. Three or four computers are up and running on the counter that fills one long wall and on the desk that wraps around the corner. He'll tell you there's order in the apparent chaos.

"Make sure you say I know where everything is," he tells me with a smile. "That it's set up so that I can find it all."

Any Way that Works

Over the years Michael has applied all his problem solving skills from his auto-mechanic days to his life on wheels. Part of his commitment to independence stems from not wanting to become unnecessarily dependent on loved ones and wearing them out in the process. He saw too much of that in rehab. But his drive for independence wasn't something new.

"When I was a kid my mom borrowed money from me," he says. "I had a yard business. I bought my own clothes, car, hunting and fishing stuff. That's what I wanted to teach my kids. I think I amaze them sometimes; I know I amaze myself."

Support from friends has helped as well. Early on his pastor called him every day to offer encouragement and hope and something to look forward to. Friends took him fishing and encouraged him to push his limits. He reciprocated. When others came to him with car repair problems, he lent them his tools and talked them through the repairs. They, in turn, would pay him for his expertise and time. He both taught and directed the construction of his deck and ramp. A little Tom Sawyer always helps.

"It's like I'm doing it myself," he says,

"so I enjoy building or fixing things with inexperienced people or with my kids because I love to teach."

Some of his success comes from trial and error; some comes from simply having no choice but to find solutions. Those solutions don't have to go by the book; he's more interested in getting things done, even if it's not the way he was taught to do them.

"You've got to take what you learn in rehab and mold it to fit you," he says. "I don't do transfers or bowel programs the way they taught me. I experimented and now I do what works for me."

His desire to share and give back has led him into peer counseling. Hearing things from others with SCI is more credible, he says; they know what's going on.

"I preach independence and relying on others as little as possible. You've got to contribute to the household, you've got to pull your own weight, you've got to ask questions and find your own answers. I feel like I've had a pretty full life and can keep on having one. This isn't what I would have chosen, but I *have* to believe I'm here to help people, that that's why I'm in a chair."

Michael's still a young man and he still has dreams. He wants to build and run a transitional home to teach people independence. He wants to drive around the country in a motor home meeting other people with SCI so he can share his knowledge and see how they do things.

I tell him that he dreams big.

"Small things are easy to accomplish. Ain't no sense in dreaming small." ∎

CHAPTER THREE
Changes, Obstacles, Solutions

If there's one thing that's clear, it's that a lot has changed. You can't do some things you once did. Maybe you lost your career or the hopes you had for one. Maybe you feel like you've lost your identity, along with everything else. What more can happen, what else can change?

Everyone in this group worried about becoming a different, lesser person. Many called it one of their major concerns. Looking back, they say those fears were unfounded.

Q: Are you different now than you were before injury?

- I like myself more because I'm more caring, more giving, softer, gentler, nicer. I'm more responsible, positive and grounded.
- I'm the same person, no different.
- I was so young when I was injured that any changes are due to maturation.

Phillip Mann says he's less self-centered. Curtis Lovejoy claims to be more relaxed and willing to help others. Cathy Green feels more positive now that she's embraced Christianity. Steve Ferguson says he's more humble and patient. About half of this group feels that if SCI changed them at all, it changed them for the better. Many find they like themselves more since injury.

"I wasn't a very nice person before I got hurt," says Audrey Begay. "I'm more laid back and get to know people better. I don't hate my life now." Jason Graber's gone through major changes as well. "I'm on a different level now," he says. "Mentally, emotionally, physically and spiritually, I think I'm a better person, more compassionate and understanding."

Eric Gibson and Matthew Seals say they're different too. "Most definitely I've changed," Eric says. "I've slowed down and now I think I'm more passionate, more caring and helpful to others." For Matthew the changes are more philosophical: "I'm much more appreciative of life now. It feels like there's more value to it for me."

Felipe Antonio sees unexpected changes: "I feel more tolerant and less prejudiced towards black people. I don't know why, but it's because of my injury." Robert Statam's process is still going on: "I'm becoming the person I should have been."

Some changes were more subtle. Ryan McLean was only 16 when she broke her back and thinks that while her personality remained intact, she's much more mature than her years: "I feel older than my friends … and maybe more humble." Joel Lorentz: "Thoughts and feelings-wise, I'm the same guy. Not much different, but I'm less cocky and arrogant."

A number of people say they're essentially the same, though few are as emphatic as Greg Adcock, who says "I'm the same damn dude!" James Turner and Kevin Wolitzky had a strong desire to stay the same: "One of my goals was not to change," Kevin says. "Any differences in me are because I've matured."

For Anne Herman, staying the same just happened: "I always wanted to be a social worker and I became one. I continued to be involved in sports and take risks. I'm still a people person. If there's a change, I'm more self-confident."

Not all change was positive or neutral. Patty Rivas finds herself a little less secure. Pat McGowan says he's more jaded, adding, "I'm also less tolerant of whining and the incompetence of other people."

With an average age of 21½ years at injury, most of this group had plenty of growing up to do. Quite a few find it hard to distinguish normal growing pains from adjustment to SCI. Kevin Williams says he was a typical 19-year-old college student when he was injured. "Now I'm a typical mid-30s lawyer."

Some, like Jason Regier, see it differently: "I don't think SCI changed me as much as it's shaped who I am. This is more like a second life." For Joe Jeremias, who was 15 when injured and spent much of his adolescence using a chair: "It's a little piece of who I am but it colors everything."

Nearly 50 years after injury, Wally Dutcher finds all this a non-issue: "I was so young, who the hell knows if I'm different?"

Did attitudes change after injury? Absolutely. Most went through a dramatic change, from hopeless and depressed that first year to hopeful and engaged as they grew into their injuries. They moved past early fears, gained self-confidence and watched their possibilities multiply, in some cases astronomically. Only two people out of more than 50 felt their possibilities had diminished, while more than half said their prospects had improved substantially. As prospects improved, so did attitudes.

Wardell Kyles: "At first, I was mad at the world, but not now." Donald Collier's experience with his C4 injury was similar: "That first year I thought this was the end of the world. Not any more." Paul Herman thought his life was over, but eventually he got it all—wife, job, family, adventure.

Time helped many see the possibilities that still existed. Joel Lorentz: "My outlook was pretty bleak those first couple years, then lots became possible." Pat McGowan, who went from self-described ski bum to Manhattan economist: "I would never have imagined I could have a job like the one I have now. I'm more convinced than ever that with enough effort most anything is possible."

Sometimes possibilities were seen, not as waxing or waning, but simply changing. George Taborsky: "I can't do all I used to do,

but now other doors have opened or I use other avenues."

Audrey Begay speaks for many when she says life is more gratifying than she anticipated or imagined possible: "I'm more satisfied with myself as a person." Robert Statam: "I like myself better and I take more initiative." Glenford Hibbert: "I never thought I could be this satisfied. My life turned out very good!"

Jason Graber likes the changes he's seen, but says he has further to go: "I want more. There's still lots I need to change."

Throughout these interviews people repeatedly use the word "normal" to describe themselves or their lives—as in, "I wanted to feel normal again," or "I wanted to be normal, just like everyone else." They're saying they wanted to fit in and feel ordinary and common, truly "just like everyone else." While acknowledging that they are forever changed by spinal cord injury, they also make quite clear that those changes have not left them feeling abnormal.

We're changed by widely varying events. Graduating from high school, moving out on our own, having our hearts broken, getting married or becoming a parent can all be transforming experiences. In the end those who had changed liked the changes and those who didn't want to change got their wish. Together as a group, most all say that over time, life satisfaction increased and personal growth occurred in good and unexpected ways. They changed their perceptions and expectations through action and initiative, by doing, taking risks and staying active. They changed by living.

This change didn't all come easily. If there's another thing everyone in this group knows, it's that even as life is improving, making it happen is hard work.

That hard work was in response to all the obstacles that accompany spinal cord injury, both initially and over the long haul. For most, the biggest problems took a while to emerge, but as time wore on and the process changed them, they became even more capable of facing and overcoming ever larger obstacles.

Q: What has been your biggest obstacle?

- Physical and attitudinal accessibility (access to buildings, low expectations, discrimination, repeated need to prove self)
- Emotional adjustment (frustration, anger, depression, denial)
- Physical/medical complications (bowel/bladder, pressure sores, chronic pain)
- Personal relationships (dating and sexual challenges, divorce, broken engagements)

They've all had their share of physical and medical complications and problems, and they've all struggled with learning to use a chair, get dressed and get through their days. For some it's been maddening and exhausting.

And they've seen trouble in personal relationships: marriages sputtered and failed, weddings were postponed and some old friends disappeared.

Yet most people in this group say these problems were small potatoes compared to the physical and attitudinal barriers they faced early after SCI. By more than two to one, they found dealing with ignorant attitudes and lack of physical access much more challenging than any of their own physical complaints. They say attitudes and physical accessibility were even harder to deal with than major life transitions like education, employment, financial hardship, failed relationships or deaths in the family.

Felipe Antonio says stairs and lack of ramps stymied him; Dan Wilkins struggled with low expectations, lack of access and finding a job. Donald Collier struggled with a need to constantly prove himself to others and show them they didn't have to take care of him. Charlotte Heppner spoke of discrimination, lack of public transportation and the public's overwhelmingly negative attitudes toward people with disabilities. Fred Fay, too, fought discriminatory attitudes, especially during the 1960s when he was injured. Richard Famiglietti sums it up: "Society's still not ready for people with disabilities."

Finding reliable attendant care and relying on others for transportation or care are constant demands for some. Kevin Williams points to finances as an on-going problem. Kevin Wolitzky scrambled to pay for attendant care when he first began working. Anne Marie Hochhalter faced the media attention of the Columbine shootings, her mom's death and then the isolation of living in a distant and unfamiliar town, all while trying to get used to severe nerve pain and being unable to drive. Amit Jha confronted the culturally conditioned challenges of his parents' lowered expectations. "It was hard for them to conceive of me being on my own or going back to college," he recalls.

While the emphasis on non-medical and even non-physical issues may seem surprising, it matches the findings of the World Health Organization, which found that the biggest roadblock to quality of life for people with disabilities is not medical difficulty or physical loss but gaining full access to all society has to offer.

Even though medical complications were mentioned less frequently than social attitudes, they were clearly challenges. Bowel and bladder management was a trial for both Gretchen Schaper and George Taborsky. Eric Gibson says getting used to how his body worked and learning its signs was hard. Skin problems continue to plague some and chronic pain dogs others.

Some problems were self-imposed. Cathy Green didn't want anyone seeing her dependent or using a chair. Don Dawkins struggled with his self-image and guilt about the pain he'd caused his family. Jason Regier wrestled with personal doubts: "My main obstacle was my own uncertainty and the mental challenge of doing what I wanted to do." Many stumbled over their self-pity.

Losing spouses or fiancées was a mountain for some. Curtis Lovejoy says his divorce was the worst single thing he faced, as does Michael Slaughter. Audrey Begay's worst experience during her first year was her fiancé leaving her four months after she broke her neck.

Joel Lorentz might have come up with the best advice: "Expect problems and expect to be discouraged." That and Gretchen Schaper's gut-felt answer to her self-posed question, "Can I take it?"

"Hell yes, I can take it!"

When people talked about getting past their fears, they usually spoke in general terms: "I went out and did things" or "I asked questions." They got more descriptive when talking about how to tackle specific obstacles, though they stuck to the same action-oriented approach.

Once you've identified obstacles, you have to develop a style for addressing them. Here's what some in this group did.

Q: How did you address these obstacles?

- Getting active
- Going to school, volunteering, working
- Problem solving
- Persistence over time

Getting active

This group started by opening the door and venturing forth. The operative word here is *action*. They all got out of the house and into the world, early and often.

Being around people helped them get over fears and misconceptions, and also gave them a start on dealing with inaccessibility, discrimination and the low expectations of nondisabled people. They found experienced wheelers and rehab professionals to help them secure necessary and essential government benefits. They did what was necessary to get home health care. They learned to use public transportation. And many of them did these things before the ADA brought widespread accessibility to the country.

Schooling

This is an educated bunch. Forty of the 53 interviewees have some post-high school education. Most went to college and a few went to trade school. Thirty-one earned two- or four-year degrees, and at press time seven were still attending classes.

But this is *not* an elite Ivy League crowd. Consider this: At least six had no interest in college at all before their accidents, and several others felt they weren't smart enough. Some former gang members saw only death or jail in their futures; higher education was not even on their radar screens. Yet most of these retired gang members went to college or attend now. Most all who attended college came away with a degree and all say they benefited from the experience, sometimes more from the social, personal or athletic opportunities than from what they learned in class.

After all the disruptions of her injury, Susan Douglas wanted some stability and getting back to school as quickly as possible gave it to her: "Having lots of day-to-day decisions made for me was useful. I had an automatic social group. I didn't need to use anything but my mind. It was great." Anne Herman: "Being with people was good and I felt normal again. Going away to school helped me get independent."

People found challenge, validation and empowerment on campus. Wanting to compete athletically on an elite level, Keith Davis found the best wheelchair athletic program in the country. As an electrician, Matthew Seals never thought about college before his injury, but he did much better than he thought possible: "I got good grades, made friends and was running with the big boys. School helped me a lot." When Amit Jha saw that his chosen medical school was holding up his application because of his disability, he regained some power by filing a discrimination suit. Many others also spoke of standing up for themselves to get past early obstacles.

And almost everyone who went to school found funding from Vocational Rehabilitation or some other agency that helped pay for tuition, books and transportation.

Volunteering, working

Seventy-five percent of this group have worked at least some since injury and 60 percent spent at least a year working full time. Many did volunteer work and several continue to do both. They followed the formula of living well by doing lots and few are showing signs of slowing down.

Angel Watson began by baking cakes and taking in sewing and laundry. Then she learned to drive. From there she moved to retail and office work. "Things were rarely as bad as I expected," she says. "I learned how people reacted, how to deal with them, how to be on time and do my job despite my problems. People didn't care that I was in a chair, they cared about service."

Bobbie Humphreys' first job was operating a switchboard by manually moving old-fashioned phone plugs in and out of jacks. An odd choice for a quad, perhaps, but she had her rationale: "My logic was to do a nearly impossible job first; anything after that would seem easy. I find my limits by taking on more than I can handle."

Early on, volunteering got almost three-quarters of this group out among people and feeling good about themselves. Volunteering led to jobs for Joel Irizarry, Cathy Green, Wardell Kyles and Steve Ferguson. Serving as a peer counselor in a support program helped Bobbie Humphreys and several others come to grips with their own disability issues. Others stayed busy in out-patient physical therapy, painting or writing, sports or just taking time to decide what might be best for them. Above all, they refused to sit still.

This group did everything imaginable to meet the world halfway. Each time they got out around people, disabled or nondisabled, they forged new connections. Each exposure was an opportunity to test limits, succeed and feel better about themselves.

Problem solving

Many people profited from their problem solving skills—learning, experimenting and trial and error. A former auto mechanic, Michael Slaughter worked his way through shopping, cooking, doing laundry or fixing a flat tire as needed, putting his logic-oriented mind to work. Then he became Mr. Mom, supervising his kids' homework, helping in the classroom and learning as he went. The more he did the better he felt.

Brian Johnston began by making a sandwich or cleaning up the apartment, then moved on to transfers and learning the rest of his self-care. "As I figured things out, I gained confidence and tried more," he says. "When I saw other wheelers doing things I thought, 'Why not me?' Trial and error teaches you your talents." Over time Brian, a complete C5 quad, mastered it all—transfers, dressing, external catheters and nightbags. "If I can do something once," he adds, "I can probably do it quicker the next time."

Persistence over time

Jason Regier found that as he learned skills—socializing, working, increased independence, traveling—they added up and built on one another. One day he realized he had a life: "After about a year I started focusing on what I was still able to do. A couple years after that I was able to say 'Hey, I'm okay with this.'"

Instead of tackling everything at once, Paul Herman spent a few years figuring things out: "I loved not having to think past tomorrow, just getting those checks from the VA every month and kicking back. All I had to do was learn to drive and be independent." When that got old and he wanted more, Paul took up sports and went to college.

Some found that their faith in God helped them cope; for others, it was sports that got them going. Driving was liberating for many. A number had to make difficult lifestyle changes such as giving up drugs or alcohol or breaking away from gang life before they could get past their personal obstacles. Many tailored their behavior specifically to what they saw as their primary problem, such as preserving skin, preventing UTIs or meeting people. Virtually all made a point of taking personal responsibility for improving their lives.

People were selected for this project because they're happy with their lives. But even though they see themselves as doing well now, few will tell you that dealing with their obstacles was easy, especially at first. Most still have very clear memories of their intense anxiety. They remember fighting their fears as they learned to use public transportation, drive or ask for help. They'll tell you that, initially, going out in public, returning to school, looking for work or asking for a date was very difficult.

They'll also tell you that those are the things you have to do. They'll say you get better and move forward by staying busy, interacting with others, pushing your limits and solving problems. They'll tell you these actions and interactions put you in places you can succeed, learn and be open to opportunity. They'll tell you staying active is one of the best known antidotes for depression. No wonder these people are happy campers. ∎

Optimism 101

Did that exploding legbag leave you frazzled? Things like that have a way of getting you down, to the point where you feel this chair life just isn't going to work. Part of how you feel about things is often the result of how you explain to yourself why they happened.

As a psychology student, Martin Seligman wanted to know why some people kept trying to solve unsolvable problems while most others threw in the towel. He began with a series of experiments, first with lab animals and later with people. When he placed either animals or people in situations that couldn't be solved, about two-thirds simply gave up. The other one-third continued to search for a solution.

The difference between people who give up and those who don't, says Seligman, lies in how they explain *why* bad things happen to them. People who keep trying—that's optimists like you and me—usually explain bad events as *temporary* ("I was having a bad day"), *specific* ("Spasms kept me from getting dressed quickly") or *external* ("The usher at the ball game was a total jerk"). They also find a way to focus on the positives around them rather than dwelling on their misfortune.

In contrast, pessimists see misfortune as *permanent* ("I'll never learn to button my shirt"), *universal* ("no place I want to go is accessible"), or *internal* ("I'm stupid"), which leaves them stuck with just how bad and unfair life can be and how inadequate they are to deal with it. Pessimists give up and tell themselves "I'm stupid and I'll never get this right." Optimists persevere and tell themselves "I made a mistake but can do better next time."

If how you think about things helps determine how you feel about them, Seligman reasons, then changing the way you think can change the way you feel. Because your feelings result from your thoughts, sometimes from thoughts outside your awareness, if you can slow down those automatic thoughts and gain some awareness of them, you can gain more control over the feelings they generate. And then, by thinking of challenges as temporary and specific, you can maintain optimism about the present and future.

If you read between the lines, you'll see that this group did much the same. Time and again when they approached obstacles—learning to dress, eat, transfer—they treated each one as separate and specific, and addressed each with a specific solution. They also saw obstacles as temporary, something to be taken one day at a time. They could have seen their obstacles as an unclimbable wall of unchanging and impossible tasks, but by seeing problems as specific and temporary, they maintained their optimism. Each problem solved made life incrementally better, and made the next problem easier to solve.

Seligman also notes that optimists don't dwell on misfortune but look for the positives. So did people in our group, who often said they chose to be happy or to focus on the positives. Anne Herman tells her women's support group they "need to celebrate any success, no matter how small." Others concentrated on what they could still do, rather than on what they'd lost.

Seligman offers a simple formula for what he calls "learned optimism." He says it's as simple as ABC ... and D and E. It's worth a short look. (For more details read *Learned Optimism*. See resources.)

Whenever we're confronted with *adversity* (*A*), we quickly form *beliefs* (*B*) about the misfortune. Our feelings about that adversity—how we interpret and explain it—are the *consequences* (*C*). If we believe the adversity is temporary and has specific causes—"Things will get better when I get this attendant care straightened out" or "My catheter only comes disconnected when I'm getting in the car"—then we have grounds for optimism. When we believe the adversity is permanent and its causes are universal, we feel depressed and helpless. The consequences can be either optimism or depression. By changing what you believe to be the cause of your misfortune, you can change how you *feel* when that misfortune occurs.

This doesn't mean you should rejoice over the cup of coffee you spilled on your lap or the fact that you still can't transfer, but if you can believe it's possible to learn how to drink coffee without spilling and that you can learn to transfer, you can stay optimistic. The trick, Seligman says, is to interrupt negative beliefs that fill the mind when bad things happen either by *distracting* (D) ourselves or by *disputing* (D) those beliefs. Either one can change your beliefs about the unwanted event, thereby changing the consequence from pessimism to optimism. Many in this group stayed distracted by staying busy, especially early on. In the long run, disputing the beliefs is a far more effective method than distraction. In the heat of the moment, you use what works. By slowing down, examining the situation and disputing the reasons we give ourselves for why an adverse event happened, we can avoid making the same mistake in the future. The last component of Seligman's formula is getting *energized* (E) for positive action. In the process of all this we build optimism.

So if the tubing to your catheter gets disconnected as you're transferring into the car today and your pants got soaked, you'd first look at the facts: "When I rush getting dressed, I sometimes don't fasten the connections tight enough." Then, you'd question just how bad things are: "I need to go change and call ahead to let people know I'm going to be late. But this hasn't happened in three weeks, which means I must be getting better at it." Then you'd get energized to look for other solutions: "If I take the extra minute to get the connections tight and make sure the tubing doesn't get kinked, this won't happen." Simple as ABCD and E.

You can stay more optimistic and hopeful when dealing with issues ranging from attendant care or Social Security to mastering bowel management by seeing each individual issue as a separate and temporary problem, each with its own solution. Focusing on the positives in your life while looking at the facts and disputing your negative beliefs about events and why they happened energizes you to find a solution. ∎

PROFILES III

Clockwise from top: Juan Garibay, Angel Watson, Amit Jha, Keith Davis, Curtis Lovejoy, Joe Jeremias, Karen Hwang, Kevin Wolitzky, Gretchen Schaper; middle: Eric Gibson, Greg Adcock

Gretchen Schaper

Gretchen Schaper is hard to miss. She's 27, talented, strikingly attractive and anything but dull. Her résumé includes a fine arts degree with high honors, art exhibitions, off-road wheelchair racing and motorcycle riding. And now, when she speaks of her 11 years of paralysis, she's refreshingly honest and wise.

"I've been adventurous, taken risks, trusted what's been created in my life and dealt with it. My disability really sets me apart and gets me attention, good or bad. More people talk to me and I know that some galleries have accepted my art because I'm in a chair. I try to turn my disability into a positive wherever I can."

The three Chihuahuas that greet me at Gretchen's gate are so loud and hyper in her quiet North Hollywood neighborhood that I'm thinking they might be on speed. Gretchen quickly hushes them and leads me up the walk, into her home and down the hardwood hallway. We settle in her sparsely furnished living room and talk the afternoon away.

I first saw Gretchen riding a Harley in a wheelchair ad. Later I heard her name connected with off-road wheelchair racing. Then I came across a magazine article documenting her honors thesis project, for which she spent a day out of her chair and crawling from class to class at the University of Colorado in Boulder.

"That project was about the unexpected," she says. "It was about speed, height, disability, endurance, strangers, pain and the human condition. Wheelchair girls are supposed to stay in their wheelchairs. I wanted to explore my disability in full."

A career in art has been her goal since childhood and she began showing her work in high school as part of a young artist group in Boulder. Since moving to the L.A. area four years ago, she's been paying some bills with illustrations, child portraits and an occasional commission. She has also used self-portraits, a comic strip and her performance art piece as ways of explaining to herself and others what it means to be disabled.

Los Angeles, with its size, impersonal nature and high cost of living, is a far cry from the small-town feel of Boulder, but right now it's giving her what she needs — a rich and stimulating environment, a world class art school and accessibility second to none.

Part of what got Gretchen to L.A. was feeling that she needed more schooling in technique and process. Since enrolling in the Art Center College of Design in Pasadena, her schoolwork now consumes her life— four to five hours of classes, nearly as much time in homework, as well as some independent work. Her course work includes a creative writing course in which she's toyed with some loosely autobiographical fiction of early post-injury experiences.

"It might be therapeutic," she says, "and it's been long enough since my accident that I like writing about it and want to remember it."

What little spare time she has is filled with museum hopping, walking her dogs and taking care of herself with yoga, standing, exercise and eating well. She says her vegan diet contributes to her good health and high level of energy by eliminating meat, dairy and eggs.

Her studio, down a ramp in the back of her house, is a large, high-ceilinged room windowed on three walls and filled with works in progress and a number of self-portraits done both recently and soon after injury.

Back From Hell

Gretchen was 16 and a high school sophomore when the Jeep she was riding in outside of Boulder went down a 100-foot embankment and left her with broken bones, collapsed lungs and a ruptured aorta. There were doubts about her survival.

Once she was stabilized, her doctor bluntly delivered the not so pleasant news: "You've been in an accident. For some reason you survived but we don't know why. You'll never walk again."

She was still a mess when she got to Craig Hospital. Severe blood loss to her spinal cord had caused an L1 injury; she had jaundice, was still very banged up, and steroids had taken most of her hair. At 5'10" then, and barely 97 pounds, she was a rail.

The change of scenery at Craig helped. "It was so nurturing there," she recalls with a smile. "We went rafting and out to different places. There was no school and I made some good friends. The hardest part was leaving." Powerful experience was how she describes rehab.

"Raw" is how she describes getting back into life that first year or so. Only a few weeks out of Craig, she returned to school for her junior year and for Gretchen it was a double whammy.

"It's a blur and it just sucked," she says. "High school is awful enough without a chair. My school was four stories of carpeted ramps and of course I wouldn't let anyone push me. I didn't have the bowel and bladder stuff figured out yet and I didn't have a car, so if I had an accident I was just stuck there.

"I was embarrassed and ashamed about my body. I had wanted to be a model and now I certainly didn't look like one. The body image thing is difficult and hard enough on the ego for all young women. The chair made it that much harder. I thought maybe I deserved this or that if I had worked harder in rehab I'd be better.

"I got depressed about being in a chair, but I got depressed about all the other teenage stuff too: You know, all the normal stuff like 'you're stupid, you're ugly, your life is worthless, you're a burden, you'd be better off dead.'" Oh yeah, that stuff.

When a minister friend suggested she give the "why me?" question about three years before demanding an answer she came unglued.

"I told him I didn't have three years and that this was hell and I needed to feel better now! Things eventually did get better, but not right away. For a couple of years I would occasionally ask myself, 'Why me?' Eventually the answer I got was that the accident was changing my life in good ways."

Good ways?

"I started changing for the better," she says. "I stopped letting my insecurity show. I became more assertive and stood up for myself more. When I did that, people stopped treating me badly. When I held my head high and felt I had value, people responded positively and I started feeling better about myself."

Needing something to do besides think about her situation, Gretchen began volunteering in after-school programs for young disadvantaged kids.

"It felt so good to help others and be able to give back," she recalls. "I liked that I could be the teacher."

She also spent time watching how other crips did things and saw that they had lives that went on after injury, that the television and movie images of disability ("That melodramatic 'Either you get cured or you die' crap") weren't reality.

Though she wasn't afraid to cry or let people know that she was angry or sad, eventually she decided she didn't have to be bitter or helpless and much of the anger went away. Slowly she found herself focusing less on what should have been and more on how things actually were and might be. None of it was very conscious.

"It just sort of happened, like someone asking 'Can you take this?' My answer was 'Hell yes, I can take it!'"

What hadn't changed was her friends, who transported her and joined her for the usual teenage fun. Two years out of rehab, Gretchen moved into her own apartment and began college. That was big, she says. "I'm grateful that my parents gave me a lot of leeway and support to do that. Some parents are so overprotective that kids stay really immature. As a young woman it was important for me to not let that happen and my spirit wouldn't allow it." That spirit explains most of Gretchen's post-injury life.

The Harley Connection

While in rehab, she'd met a wheeler who rode a Harley-Davidson equipped with a sidecar. After he took her for a ride, she was hooked and eventually bought his bike. "I'd never ridden one before, but somehow I always knew I'd be a biker chick. The speed, the independence, the wind in my hair; it was great. Riding in the mountains sort of made up for not hiking."

The bike gave her back some of that power and youthful sense of invulnerability, as if she'd paid her dues and was now bulletproof. Things were turning around.

Then the call came from an off-road wheelchair manufacturer. "We built this chair; want to race it?" Looking to build a racing team, they'd seen her picture and wanted to sponsor Gretchen as the sport's first woman racer. After training on dirt roads they headed for the mountain slopes of Colorado, Utah and California.

"The races were all on ski slopes and very steep, rocky and rugged," she says. "I got to travel for free, even to Japan, and at first I was pretty fearless. It was a lot of fun being outside and in the mountains again."

Eventually the pull of art outweighed the lure of physical adventure and she gave up racing after a bad off-road crash. Adventure lost again when she moved to Los Angeles and the traffic there made her say good-bye to the Harley. "It's too dangerous out here," she says. "Maybe I'll have another one in the future."

At times Gretchen seems in awe of life and its unexpected twists and turns, like the one that brought her partner Peter into her life five years ago. They met while she was visiting her parents in Boulder.

"I first saw her in a store," Peter recalls. "When I saw her again a year later, I talked to her and asked her out."

The connection was instant, they tell me, and within days they were living together in her parents' home. She returned to her house in California several months later. Peter went with her.

"Peter was a huge surprise," Gretchen says. "It's still a little hard to believe he doesn't care about the chair, that he could love me more than be afraid of my disability. I'm 6 feet, he's 5-foot-eight. I'm not sure we'd be together if I wasn't in a chair."

"I saw an artist and mountain biker and beautiful blonde," says Peter. "I thought about the chair a little when we first met, but there were too many other things to think about. I'm always aware of the chair because there are so many outdoor things I wish we could do together. But I'm not with someone in a chair, I'm with Gretchen. I just wish she could cook," he deadpans.

Through all this, Gretchen remains convinced that her injury is no accident, though she's still not sure about the why. "If I had to believe this was just a random act of chaos I'd go crazy," she says. "I'm open to the belief that the accident was something of a choice on my part, that I was helped through it spiritually. I know that nothing in my life would be what it is without my disability, so maybe I needed it to get where I am now.

"The motorcycle, the racing, doing well in school, they're all results of my accident. I'm grateful to be alive, for having a low injury, for living in California. This helps me as an artist. Those are all things that happened that I wouldn't undo." ∎

Juan Garibay

"Sometimes I think, 'Damn, my life could be a little movie!' Never in a million years did I think this could be so good."

Juan Garibay has a huge smile on his face, surprise and wonder in his voice, as he talks of his present life. He's happy being a working stiff, a responsible dad, part-time college student and disabled athlete. The way he sees it, his reality is about five times better than any film would be.

Ten years ago Juan was a 19-year-old unemployed father to be, struggling to pull away from his gang and the friends who were living that life. Then he got nailed in a drive-by. Wrong place, wrong time. The .22-caliber rifle shot damaged his liver and a kidney before lodging in his spine at T12.

Now it's about noon on a lazy July Sunday in Redondo Beach, Calif. After greeting me with a big smile, Juan leads the way past the gate and into his apartment complex. My eyes get pretty big when I watch him pop a wheelie up an 8-inch step, grab a rail and pull himself up. He smiles, motions for me to wait and quickly returns with Marilyn, his partner of nearly 10 years and, coincidentally, his rehab PT. She helps me up and we're greeted by the Stones on the big screen when the three of us enter their apartment. Juan and I settle at the dining room table to talk.

In a phone conversation about a month earlier, he'd told me how much he loves the struggle of being disabled. That's where we start.

"I do love the struggle, man. When things are hard and difficult, that's what keeps me going. This has been a long battle for me to make the change, to do right after being in a gang. If you had met me 10 years ago, you would have met the toughest 19-year-old banger possible, somebody with no future."

Would I have been afraid?

"Yeah, and with good reason. But being bad, dealing drugs, those things are all easy. And we all want to do what's easy. But I know the outcome of those old ways and I don't want that. Still, it's a struggle to not slip back into the old life."

If change were easy, everybody would do it?

"Exactly. I never thought this life—going to college, having a good job, being close to my daughter, meeting someone like Marilyn, knowing so many good people—I never thought any of that was possible. It's so good, but it's still a struggle."

Struggle aptly describes Juan's past 10 years; they've been neither straight nor smooth. Following a month in acute care recovering from the gunshot, fusion and exploratory surgery, he transferred to Rancho Los Amigos for two months of rehab. Having never envisioned a future other than jail or early death, he says he never got depressed.

"It was weird just laying there," he says. "I accepted the chair right away because I never expected much of life. I thought 'whatever' and figured I'd just go back to the gang."

Which is precisely what he did for about three years, returning to the old life of partying all night with the boys. But things weren't totally the same. His friends backed away from him, telling him there wasn't much there for him anymore. They said the chair made him an easy target.

Juan needed to support himself, so he went back to doing what he did best and dealt rock for a couple of years before getting busted for possession in 1996. Twenty-two months of minimum security in several facilities were ugly enough to get him thinking about some lifestyle changes.

"They messed with us a lot in there," he says. "Cold food, sometimes no hot water. The doctors didn't know anything about SCI and had to ask me about catheters. I saw guys who knew that life and seemed to like being there. No one in a chair was having a real bad time, but after talking to some of the old-timers I knew that life wasn't for me. Jail made me want to change."

The Fool No More

The changes began as soon as he was released and he says they're still going on. The best change was finding his partner

Marilyn. They've lived together since he got out of jail in late '97.

"She was a surprise," Juan says. "She's always trying to do the right thing, putting people she loves ahead of herself. She gives me unconditional love and is always keeping my spirits up and encouraging me. She's very smart and dedicated to what she believes and loves. I've never met anyone like her; probably never will again."

You're terminally fortunate?

"Yes I am. She sticks with me and understands me better than anyone else. She's my role model."

For the past several years, Juan has worked full time in Rancho's Research and Education Institute, where he's an assistant coordinator for an outreach program. He also answers phones, does data entry and other general clerking. That's the part of his job that motivates him to go to school. Another part of the job is research on improving leg braces.

"But the best part," he says, "is doing presentations on rehabilitation engineering to junior and senior high students. I talk about myself to the kids and try to help them stay straight. We introduce rehab engineering by talking about gang violence. I love talking to them and giving them advice. They're like I was: angry, confused, scared, neglected, picked on. I like helping them with life choices. It feels good to give back and be a service to my community."

Up each day before 7, Juan and Marilyn are out the door by 8 to fight commuter traffic, work at Rancho from nine to five, and get home to chores each night. He spends weekends sleeping in, visiting with his daughter and playing hoops.

He likes the new predictability of his life.

"It's worry-free and I'm not looking over my shoulder," he says. "I never worked before I got shot because I was too busy acting the fool, so I'm still learning as I go. This is OK for now but I need to make more money. I want to get my degree and do rehabilitation counseling or maybe work in a high school with at-risk kids."

Juan talks about responsibility a lot. What does the word mean to him?

"Being responsible means taking care of my daughter, caring for others, meeting my financial obligations, my emotional obligations. Being responsible means being concerned about something bigger than myself."

His responsibility to his daughter Sarah is something he considers bigger than himself. He's frequently on the phone with her, and two to four weekends a month he picks her up so she can stay with him.

"We go to the park or to movies. I need for her to know I care about her and want her to be part of my life."

If Juan's new life has been a learning process, then Rancho's wheelchair sports program — hockey, tennis, basketball, skiing — has been a large part of the curriculum.

What's he learned from sports?

"Setting goals, learning how to lose, taking things in stride," he says. "I get a rush from the competition. It's great stress relief. I've learned discipline and focus. I try to take those things into work with me."

Just before his arrest, when he was still dealing and living some of the old life, he decided to take classes and get a GED. He liked the positive environment of school—nothing gang-related there—but never tried to reconcile his old and new lives.

"Growing up in the inner city, all I saw was gangs, jail and early death," he says. "That's what I saw for all my friends and that's what I saw for myself."

Grim outlook.

"Yes, it is. I started college because I was bored and had too much time on my hands. California has fee waivers based on income, so it was free. I liked it and it sounded cool to say I went to college. I used it as a pick-up line."

Now he's going after a degree on the installment plan — two classes at a time with an occasional semester off. Presently out of the classroom, he's looking forward to getting back soon.

Strength, Help and Teddy Bears

Juan's been smiling almost non-stop for two hours. What's that about?

"When I was banging I had to be tough and hard-core," he says. "Now I can be me, without that image. We're all teddy bears; it's bad environments that make us gorillas."

Many people I talked with said that old friends and old habits got them through hard times. Juan had to turn his back on all that in order to have any chance of making a life on wheels. That's a much bigger order. By changing his focus from gangs, drugs and violence to family, sports and work, he also changed both his friendships and the direction of his life. He was able to do that, I think, because he sees it as a challenge and looks for the lessons he might learn. As he's already said, he loves his struggle, his second chance for a new life.

"This is a good life compared to what I had and it's possible if I keep my head up and stay focused. I ain't gonna bullshit you though, it's still hard."

Hard, but filled with possibilities, many because of, not in spite of, the chair.

"My life surprises me. It surprises Marilyn and my family. People go out of their way to help me. My boss took a chance and offered me a NIDRR [National Institute of Disability and Rehabilitation Research] scholarship and then hired me. I never thought I had much control of my life, but now I know I can be in charge of myself. I'm stronger than I thought because I've let others help me. "

And why all the support and help now?

"Because I've changed, things around me changed. I got so many positives now, Marilyn, my daughter, my family. I got love and sports and college. I'd turn down the cure if I had to go back to the old life.

"The chair can make you a better person," he says, "or cause you to fall apart."

What would he tell a newly injured gangbanger?

"I want for other bangers to know this life is possible. I'd like to tell them to learn from my mistakes. Life is about what you want it to be, whether you're in a chair or not." ■

Kevin Wolitzky

"I went to college, got a good job, met someone special, got married and now I have a family. My friends and most people I know like me. God loves me. Except for not being able to exercise, SCI hasn't stopped me from doing most all of the important things I've wanted to do, so my life is pretty much what I imagined it would be."

Kevin Wolitzky is 31, a C5 quad, and living that life outside of Parker, Colo., about an hour southeast of Denver. Kevin, his wife Leda and their daughter Ella just moved into their new home. It's big, open

and top of the line with its hardwood floors, big-screen television, roll-under cook top and a huge bathroom with roll-in shower. And if you have any doubts about finding in-home care in a rural area, this guy's proof it can be done. He lives 10 miles out from a small town, in a place some people would call close to nowhere.

His days begin between 6 and 7 a.m., when his attendant shows up to help him out of bed and get ready for the day. Out the door by 8, he's at work a half hour later and home at about 6. His wife Leda stays home as a full-time mom with one-year-old Ella. In the evening Kevin plays with the baby, watches a little television and, with some help from Leda, makes it to bed by 10.

The family spends weekends sleeping in, attending church and catching up with high school and college friends. Kevin's also a volunteer baseball coach for his old high school, plays fantasy baseball with several friends and spends time counseling newly injured people at the local rehab center.

His work with Raytheon Systems, a defense contractor, is classified, so he can't divulge details about his job. He is able to say that what he does provides information to troops all over the world. Since he can't serve in the military, he sees his work as a way of helping the country. With a physics degree in hand, he was hired three months out of college and has worked for the past seven years.

Does working for a defense contractor mean you make bombs?

"Not with these hands," he says with a smile. "I wanted to work for a cool company and what I do is pretty cool. I like the people I work with and the pay is very good. If I can't be a TV baseball announcer or bench coach, this'll do. The job gives me a purpose, lets me make my own way and prove myself to others and to myself. I see myself as being like everyone else—working, paying taxes, having a schedule, keeping my mind occupied. It feels good to do those things."

Good fringe benefits, too. When a wheeler friend who works in the same building as Kevin introduced him to Leda, a co-worker, she and Kevin quickly began dating, married within a couple of years and are now proud parents.

"I guess that being in a chair sort of led me to Leda," he says. "Marriage changed my life and gave me a lot of security. I still hire and train aides to help me most days, but I don't lose sleep worrying about attendant care any more. I don't want to wear Leda out by relying on her too much so I've learned ways to help her get me into bed without having to lift me. "

Taking Charge

An exceptional athlete in high school, Kevin received all-state honors in both track and baseball during the same spring season, a first in Colorado. Though track was his passion, it was baseball that earned him a partial scholarship to the University of Northern Colorado. On campus less than two months, he snapped his neck diving headfirst into a six-inch deep mud pit as part of a team initiation.

"The pit was a tradition for the freshmen on the team," he says. "When it was my turn I dove in like it was a swimming pool, at way too steep an angle. I lost sensation immediately and didn't feel any pain. I never even felt cold. I knew right away and when my friends pulled me out and rolled me over, I told them I was paralyzed."

Following two weeks spaced out on morphine at University Medical Center, he moved on to Craig Hospital for four and a half months of rehab. Kevin never held out much hope of walking and once there saw many people with conditions more disabling than his own.

"At first I wondered if I really wanted to live like this, and to tell the truth, I wasn't really sure. There just wasn't much to be optimistic about. I'd always been able to take advantage of opportunities and now I couldn't because I didn't see any. It took a little while to get motivated."

Then he hunkered down and hoped for the best. He had others hoping with him.

"When I heard my family and friends all expecting me to return to college and then find a job, I began to believe I could and I started thinking I could have a better life than I first thought was possible."

Did you think then that what you have now was possible?

"I wasn't really sure. I saw people who were working and had families, so I knew it was possible for them. As I improved and was able to do more things, I began to see and believe that more would be possible for me.

"One day a doc came in and asked me how I planned to manage my bladder, either an indwelling catheter or a suprapubic. When I asked her about the pros and cons, she looked at me and said, 'Well, with a suprapubic, your girlfriend can just hop on.' That sort of shocked me and I started thinking that if that was possible, if I could have a girl friend, then maybe someone wanting to marry me was possible too. From there, things just started snowballing."

Kevin calls those eight weeks in a halo probably the worst of his life. He felt light-headed and nauseous for at least a month. When he asked a doctor about medication for low blood pressure, drugs solved the problem. He learned from that experience.

"Even when you have world-class care, you still have to take charge and figure things out for yourself," he says. "Once I got home I had other things to figure out, like putting food in the oven *before* turning on the heat. We all end up finding our own ways of doing things. I made a grip for my hand controls that makes driving easier. I use my quad grabber and Velcro a lot. You find ways."

He found less tangible ways as well. Ten months post-injury and back in school, Kevin immediately built a network of people to help him with meals and getting around campus. He paid his roommate, a high school friend, for occasional assistance. The university honored his baseball scholarship, Medicaid paid for attendant care and health expenses, Student Services provided note-takers and SSI covered basic financial needs. Because he was living on campus and didn't need transportation, he was able to put off driving until Voc Rehab helped him with a van after graduation. First things first and all things in good time.

The People Connection

College was fun, he says. Besides going to class he made friends, dated, drank and learned about people in general and himself in particular. The more he did the more confident he became.

"I met people by being me, smiling a lot, showing an interest in them and what they liked to do," he says. "When I touch people's compassion, they want to help me. I was never really afraid of rejection and had always been fairly confident. I liked dating and it was pretty easy for me, maybe because I wasn't looking to get very serious. What I really liked was the challenge of getting someone to like me."

Connecting with people is a skill he's mastered. I saw him in action when I introduced him to my wife. He spent about five minutes sincerely complementing her on her gardens and interior decorating, all the while looking her straight in the eye and smiling. They quickly connected. Because he likes people and shows an interest in them, they reciprocate. It serves him well.

When curiosity led him to Bible study, Kevin quickly developed a deep and abiding faith in Jesus that gives him peace of mind, helps him cope with the "why me's" and provides the optimism and will to focus on the joys of life. His faith, along with his positive perspective on disability, helped him focus on all he has rather than on what he's lost.

"It's not always been this way," he says, "but that's how I feel now. I'm alive, I'm productive, I have family and friends. If all I did was sit around, I'd just worry about what might happen, so I stay busy, enjoy what I have and try not to make my problems bigger than they are. I'm an ordinary guy living an ordinary life; it's just not exactly how I pictured it. One of my goals after I got hurt was to not change and I don't think I have. That's been hard, but I've done it. I really love the life I have.

"I made things happen by adjusting my approach and attitude, and I haven't let my life be just about the chair. I need three hours of help a day and do fine on my own the other 21. To me that means I'm independent. I'm happy with it." ■

Greg Adcock

After we'd discussed the nature of his job for 15 minutes, I was still unsure just what Greg Adcock does for a living. I asked for the short explanation.

"I'm a Control Systems Engineer and utilize the latest in control and communication technology to control large industrial plants from one central control room. Also, I maintain the Information network, the LAN. Currently, our office is in the process of designing project execution methodology. It basically involves developing all the supportive software and databases, as a tool for all of our employees working out in the field to work consistently, efficiently and safely."

So now you understand.

We meet at a hotel where Greg has come for a friend's wedding. He's quick to smile and seems to fit easily into any setting from ranching to academia; he knows half the people who walk into the lobby.

"I need interaction and to feed off other people," he says. "Since I got hurt I listen more and can read people better. I try not to put up barriers or make the chair an issue, and I'm not afraid to express my feelings. I like the simple things, soft shirts, the sound of tall grass blowing, the warm sun in fall."

I tell him he sounds like a personals ad. He smiles and says he's comfortable with who he is. It shows.

At 32, he's a busy guy—up by 6 a.m., out the door of his Salt Lake City home by 7:15 and not home again till 6 p.m. to walk his dog and grab something to eat. On top of his 45-hour work week, he spends another 20 or 25 hours on grad school, which he began two years ago. Rarely crashing before midnight, he operates on about five hours of sleep a night. The pace doesn't slow down much on the weekends, when he mows his lawn, plays in the dirt of his garden, and tends a busy social and recreational life. Even with work and grad school, he finds the time to teach himself guitar and banjo.

"My life may not be very exciting," he says, "but it's what I have to do right now."

The Schools of Rehab, College, Life

Greg was rated second on the Colorado motocross circuit in 1989 when he was thrown over the handle bars of his bike while doing a jump. He landed on his back, and the bike landed on his chest. Vital statistics: T4 incomplete injury, surgery to stabilize his spine, a month of rehab in Fort Collins and two more at Craig Hospital.

For him, rehab was a blend of making strong friendships with other patients and doing whatever it took to have fun, including racing down a nearby six-level parking garage. While he very much appreciated the encouragement and compassion of the staff, he struggled with what he saw as a cookie-cutter approach— the same rehab for everyone.

"Rehab was like a giant support group for us and our families," he says. "The aides were the absolute best. In fact, it was an aide who taught me to credé. I broke the rules and expanded what I learned there, making an effort to learn from everything. I tried to

96

replace what I'd lost with new things, like the guitar, and slowly started to live my life again."

His new mantra: adapt, modify, improve.

Though clueless about what his major would be, Greg began classes at Colorado State University in Fort Collins within six months of injury. Switching from motocross to college seemed pretty logical to him.

"I'd been racing motorcycles and detailing cars and knew I needed an education if I wanted something better," he says. "I also knew I didn't want to be dependent on SSI and Medicaid. Because I couldn't base a love relationship on a common physical interest like hiking or climbing or skiing any more, I figured a bit more upscale lifestyle would help offset what I couldn't do and make attracting someone easier."

Despite his engineering focus, his description of higher education sounds more like a major in partying. He spent his first year in school getting used to the chair, learning to meet and to be around people and being pulled to bars by his dog.

"I didn't really care much about grades initially," he recalls, "but once I got into engineering I kicked ass."

And he continues kicking now that he's an engineer. For the past seven years he's worked as a consultant to the mining industry, first doing electrical drawings, then designing and engineering control systems. Now he's in charge of software and developing methods to get clients' plants on-line and turning a profit as quickly as possible.

Why the mining industry? "I like the environment," he says. "Flannel shirts, pot bellies, down-to-earth people. I'm one of the few disabled people working on mining sites, going where people in chairs don't normally go. I like that."

Greg's present life came only after a lot of change and acceptance.

"I had to get used to being disabled, then I had to be sure others were comfortable and accepting of me and that I accepted myself. Looking back, I think I had those last two backwards. I was so worried about how others saw me and if they accepted me that I wasn't sure if my perceptions were accurate. Instead, I needed to get comfortable with myself in order to reach some kind of resolution with this."

As he tried new things such as school, dating and recreational pursuits, he learned from his successes and failures and found ways to prevent future headaches. When he wanted to go to college, he got Voc Rehab to pay; when he wanted to get someplace he couldn't go, he found friends to help him; when he wanted to mow his lawn, he invented a way to do it; when he wanted to go off-road, he learned how to load his ATV onto a trailer without help; when he wanted to make a good impression in the work place, he used the social skills he'd learned in college. What first he did with difficulty, he soon did with dispatch.

Independent by Design

"It took me four or five years to figure this all out," he says. "I had to try new things and different ways and then learn from my mistakes. I'm a pretty smart dog, but I know I can't figure out everything and when I can't, I find someone who can help me. That's what I did to design the downhill racing chair, which got me back into the mountains and having fun. My truck became half my attitude and gave me the confidence that I could go anywhere I wanted. Independence is using whatever assistive technology, social programs, or physical help it takes to achieve or maintain function. I focus on small goals and build on them, rather than one big goal like walking in five years."

Sometimes he sounds as if he might prefer being in a chair. Not true, but he will admit to enjoying surprising people when he jumps a 10-inch curb. His goal is to have others see that he's comfortable with himself and that having a disability isn't a helpless experience. As something of a disability ambassador to the ablebodied world, he tries to cut ABs some slack rather than being rude. "I might be the only disabled person they ever meet," he notes.

Greg points to Christopher Reeve as a hero, praising him for using his celebrity and high profile to educate the public. Reeve, he says, has stepped up to push for greater societal awareness on multiple fronts including government, big business and religious organizations. He thinks the overall message is that all of us, disabled or nondisabled, are far more alike than different.

Unlike most people, who bottom out during rehab or the first few months after discharge, Greg waited about seven years. When a relationship broke up, he went into a tailspin of drug and alcohol abuse, which he compares to a death trip.

"Just after she left," he remembers, "the dog I had since injury died. Together, those two things were way worse than the chair. When you break my heart, you bust my spirit. I consciously tried to hit bottom then because I knew that once I was there, things could only get better."

Have the last 14 years taught him anything?

"To think outside the box," he says. "When people told me I couldn't do something, then it was on me to try harder, learn more, get people to help me or make more money to pay for a solution. I didn't want failure to be the result of not testing my limits or challenging myself. I had to be true to who I was and am."

Any grand design to all this? Sort of.

"Shit happens. We have to deal with it and control as much as we can. I could die in a car accident tomorrow. Is that fate? If it is, then I think fate sucks."

He says that one thing surprised him after injury.

"When the sports door closed, my mind, spirit and soul all opened up. Some of the best things in my life have happened since I've been injured. I try to temper optimism with realism and anticipate what could go wrong. If I dwell on all the bad things, it only drags me down, so I'd rather look for positives. Things can *always* be worse." ∎

Eric Gibson

"People who knew me back then knew where I was headed," says Eric Gibson of his pre-injury life. Right to prison or the morgue.

In a sense, he'd achieved a measure of success. At 25 he was a drug dealer and OG (Original Gangster), known, respected and feared in his world. He'd already been shot several times in gang-related incidents, so his career looked ripe for abbreviation.

"If you told me I could have the life I now have, I would have called you crazy."

If you saw Eric on television back in 1993, it was because the crew for the *Cops* show was in his neighborhood and followed the ambulance to the crime scene where he'd been shot. If you saw him on television today, he'd probably be on *Oprah* or *60 Minutes*, featured as someone who has turned his life around. This guy's an interesting mix of two very different lifestyles.

A rags to riches story?

"Yeah, but rather than money, my riches is peace of mind," he says.

Marina Del Rey seems an unlikely locale for a former gangbanger, but that's where I found Eric, in a quiet townhouse complex, complete with an on-grounds day care center, in the middle of the L.A. 'burbs. His place is middle class and comfortable, with a lived-in feel that's probably imparted by his 16-year-old daughter who lives here with him. After settling in at the kitchen table, next to the phone and the fax machine, he tells me his story.

The chair and his T12 injury are the most obvious indicators of his old life, along with the four kids he has with four different mothers. His oldest was born when he was 18, the youngest four years later.

Evidence of his new life are a computer, that fax machine and a phone that's constantly ringing with business calls related to his two jobs. His new realities are supporting his four kids, volunteer work with newly injured people and a busy social life with the ladies. His three younger children—two more daughters and a son—live with their mothers about an hour east of the city.

"Better environment. No gangs, less pressure." He says it with a big smile, in a deep, Barry White, "we're gettin' it together, baby" voice.

Career Change

Eric moved to L.A. from Mississippi when he was 12. Within a year he was prepping for the gang life.

"I was lovin' to go to school and hang out," he says. "There was graffiti everywhere and hot girls who were ready. I'd never seen anything like it. The gang stuff was a big rush and selling drugs was good money. But it came with a high price tag—being busted or being robbed. After a dozen years or so of that, I wanted something better."

The first real job Eric ever had came a couple of years post-injury, when he formed his own company selling medical supplies full time. After making an $800 investment, he sold on consignment. With little overhead and no inventory, he did well enough that six months later he jumped on an offer to sell the company for a healthy profit and take a position as an executive salesman with the company that bought him out. He began meeting with clients all over greater L.A., eight hours a day, five days a week. In time, he began working more and more by phone, fax and cell, and now he's down to about four hours a day, selling for two companies, mostly out of his home.

The transition from dealing drugs to selling medical supplies was fairly easy, a simple product-line switch from cocaine to equipment, with the bonus of better money and less danger.

"I already knew how to handle money and read people, so it wasn't hard. I met clients everywhere," he says, smiling. "If you're in a chair and I see you, we're gonna talk and you're gonna be my customer."

OK, but after banging, doesn't this middle class lifestyle get tedious?

"What I do now is right and legal and I help people," he says. "That excites me. I need to help people and I need challenges. I like the feeling I get from getting everything on my to-do lists done. I feel like an adult now."

Up by 7:30 and on the job by 9, he's checking e-mails and faxes, making phone calls and hawking his wares. He often spends a couple hours at Rancho Los Amigos with newbies before heading home to meet his daughter from school by 3. This dad stuff is serious business.

"This new life of mine, the grass is greener over here, thicker and nicer. This is where I want to be, where I should be. Now I talk to others about coming over here."

Turning Points

He was shot five times. A 13-year-old girl who was standing on the sidewalk with him died at the scene.

"It could have been that 13-year-old girl talking to you," Eric says. "The fact that I'm alive was a message to me that I needed to be doing something different."

Following 72 hours at an acute care hospital and nine weeks at Rancho Los Amigos in Downey, he left with a driver's license and the skills he needed to live independently. Rehab was much more depressing than elevating, filled with all the usual questions, uncertainties and doubts. He didn't see much future for himself, even after seeing some old-timers who were doing well. He figured life was pretty much over.

Once home, he smoked weed, watched television and looked backward. It took about eight months for that to get old, and when it did he began to go out, occasionally to Rancho. He saw others there, many much more severely injured than he.

"I saw guys in chairs who were working and guys who were deadbeats," he says. "I knew wheelers who were still in gangs. When I saw people who were in worse shape than me but doing better, I made up my mind to change and start movin' on."

Leaving the old life wasn't easy. Because he grew up surrounded by well paid dealers selling on every street corner, a life of crime still looked attractive.

"I had to give up a lot of friends if I wanted to stay clear of the old life," he says. It didn't happen all at once, and he still dabbled in drugs after injury. Yet he saw wheelers like himself with jobs and good-looking women, and that appealed to him. Getting busted and locked up for 24 hours gave him more motivation. He decided to at least try a different path.

"The first time I saw a successful black man, dressed well and with a good car, I thought 'He knows the things I need to know. I want that; I can do that!' I couldn't stop talking about him."

He got out more, and when he went to a local chapter of the National Spinal Cord Injury Association (NSCIA), he began surrounding himself with positive people, asking questions and learning more about his injury. Before long he was working. Three years later, he accepted an invitation to sit on the Board of Directors of national NSCIA. He'd turned the corner.

"My doctor pushed me to be on that board and I'm glad he did," he says. "It was a challenge to fit in because there were only three other people in chairs. Most of the others were doctors and lawyers. In the old days, whenever I'd been around a lawyer I was paying him to get me out of trouble; with doctors, they were pulling bullets out of me. By the second day of that first meeting I was comfortable and people were asking me what *I* thought. I was the first black man on that board in 40 years."

"The Chair Is My Culture Now"

NSCIA wanted to develop violence protection programs, so Eric helped put together the Project Peace programs in both Washington and Atlanta. Now he speaks about gangs, peer pressure and drugs in high schools, juvenile halls and detention centers for Teens on Target, an L.A. prevention program. All the speakers in that program are wheelers and he says he likes being around them.

"They're like me and they accepted me as I was. Being on wheels gives us a shared experience, a shared struggle, and I felt in my body, my mind and my soul that I was where I was supposed to be. We're a community. The chair is my culture now, more than race."

The idea of building community resonates with Eric. He's set up a support group in East L.A. so he can share his knowledge about equipment, employment and being out in the world. It meets once a week. Because initial rehab stays keep getting shorter, Eric tries to serve as a "life coach," teaching skills to newbies and encouraging them to find their own ways of coping. After all, he says, we're all in this race together.

And he got into sports. In 1996, he wrangled an invitation for a team he'd formed in L.A. to the '96 Atlanta Games. They did a trial demonstration of relay brace walking, an event featuring contestants on crutches and braces or using walkers. During the opening ceremonies he handed the torch to Mark Wellman, who then climbed the tower and lit the flame.

Has he learned anything in the past decade?

"To take my time, experiment and learn from my mistakes," he says. "It took me eight years and a lot of hard work to get here. I rolled an 11; lots of people roll craps. It's not easy for anyone. You have to get your act together, get out the house, be responsible and not expect a lot of sympathy. Nobody's entitled to a bad attitude. You gotta know how to take care of yourself. You can't make excuses."

Given all that's happened in the past 10 years, what do the next five look like?

"Nothing but positives," he smiles. "I'd like to buy a house and choose a wife. I want to own a company again, maybe have my kids working for me. And I'd like to start a non-profit and travel around meeting other people in chairs."

Life is good?

"Life is *very* good!"

Eric isn't the first person to tell me that he's glad this has happened to him. He says it gave him a second chance at life.

"I know that sounds like bullshit, but I also know I've got a much better life now. I've got my kids, my health, and I'm not looking over my shoulder. Life's better; I appreciate and enjoy it more. I wouldn't trade this lifestyle, these friends, the lessons I've learned for walking." ∎

Keith Davis

At 6 feet three inches, 170 pounds and with arms the size of legs, Keith Davis looks like a jock. His rating as the top wheelchair racer in the U.S. and one of the top five in the world for three straight years probably qualifies him as one. But once he begins speaking, he's more thinker and seeker than sweaty gym rat.

As we talk about life with SCI on this overcast summer morning, Keith, a T10 para and a former Paralympian, prefers discussing the meaning of life.

"I'm a spiritual being having a physical experience," he says. "The more physical experiences I have, the more spiritual I become. Being injured gave me the opportunity to define a more challenging and exciting life."

Pacific Palisades, Calif., just north of Santa Monica, is where Keith, at 29, is defining that life. We're sitting in his dining room, which holds a small table and a big piano. A sliding glass door looks out past his dogs and the sandy back yard to the ocean beyond. Though the neighborhood has a quiet, family feel, this home says a bachelor lives here.

Those physical and spiritual components Keith speaks of existed long before he was injured as a passenger in a rollover near Los Angeles in 1989, but it's clear that he's used his injury to explore their meaning in his life.

Prior to injury, he excelled at basketball, soccer, triathlons and surfing, and dreamed of the NBA. Afterward, sports on wheels was a natural. Eight months out of rehab he was playing basketball and on his way to the University of Illinois on athletic and academic scholarships to study music. U of I boasts an elite wheelchair sports program— the nation's first—with talented coaches, high expectations, strong competition and a five-hour-a-day training commitment. This is the big league, not weekend recreation, and Keith excelled. He played on a national championship team and in 1996 was offered an alternate spot on the Paralympic basketball team. After college came more competition, this time in track.

"Racing's the toughest sport and demands a very high level of spiritual, physical and emotional strength," says Keith. "It's all on you. That's the kind of athlete I wanted to be. My goal was to be the best within five years." He did it in three.

"I formed a racing team, Revolution X, as a way to stay motivated and draw sponsorship, because the prize money isn't enough to live on. We were all young and hip and tried to present an image that said 'I wish I could do that' with cool clothes and hot chairs."

Racing, for Keith, was self-exploration, each race an opportunity to develop discipline, commitment, perseverance and teamwork.

"You're totally in your head, asking, 'Can I do this? Do I have what it takes?' Excellence requires passion and motivation to move through the disappointment and pain and try again. Those are lessons I used in dealing with hard times. I can say, 'Yeah, this is tough, but not as tough as mile 20.' I got better by being blown away."

In 2000, he landed a spot on the Paralympic racing team by qualifying for six events, but there was a catch: over the course of several days he was competing in as many as three races daily.

"I didn't do as well as I had hoped because I may have peaked at the trials or maybe got too caught up in the excitement. So many things can keep you from winning; you get boxed in or make a mistake or get momentarily distracted. But not winning didn't erase the five years it took to get there."

One day, out on a training run less than a year after the 2000 Paralympics, he realized he was done with racing. "I was racing solely for myself anyway, and had gotten what I needed from it," he remembers. "I was a couple miles from home when I got it and understood I didn't have to race any more."

A Forrest Gump moment?

"Totally. I'd done what I wanted to do and can honestly say I don't miss it."

Hip Hop and Indies

For Keith, music provides a slightly different opportunity for self-exploration, requiring more thinking and creativity. When the performance track of his music major demanded the same five-hour-a-day commitment as athletics, he transferred to composition and used music to offset the physicality of sports. He continues to play piano, using a headset with a switch to operate the sustain pedal.

"In sports and racing you're basically imposing your will on someone else," he says. "Music demands interpretation and that's what makes it unique, even though you still must answer the same personal questions and the same passions as athletics."

Music has always served as an emotional outlet. Now he's made it a career and is presently producing a hip hop album. Already well-versed in music, he's spent the past year on a self-directed crash course in commercial production in all its varied technical aspects. Producing demands fluency in several different trade languages to communicate with artists, technicians, distributors and marketers. With hip hop, he hopes to use his training in theory, structure

and composition to polish an urban art form rooted in rhythm and blues, soul and jazz.

Keith's pre-production work begins in his home studio, where he can work on a whim with writing, keyboards, tracking and sequencing. Then he's off to the studio for edits, vocals, effects, overdubs and mixing. Getting an album to market successfully, he explains, is very complicated and time consuming. Even with the best material, musicians, mixing and marketing, if the timing's off the project will still miss. Keith sees music, as he sees all things, as a growth experience.

"Music is sort of a calling for me," he says. "It's a way to express myself, tap into my emotions and feel more."

And Keith, predictably, wants to do still more. He has recently tried his hand at film, serving as executive producer and music supervisor for an independent comedy called "Death to the Supermodel."

He'll tell you that he's lucky in one major way. An insurance settlement from the automobile accident makes work optional for him. Once given the opportunity to do what he loved, he decided that instead of living the life of the idle rich, he would pursue personal excellence in every way he could.

"I've always looked at the money as a benefit and opportunity to do something meaningful," he says. "I've invested and taken risks on people with it. Money can be very limiting. Some people who have it don't do anything with it because they're afraid of losing it. Mine could be gone tomorrow and it wouldn't matter because I know I can make a living and I know I'm loved."

Enjoying the Ride

When asked how much the chair interferes with his daily life, Keith brushes it off, telling me it's right up there with, oh say, a sunburn. He's serious when he says this.

"I'm just living my life without thinking that I'm doing it from a chair," he says. "When I need help is when it enters and that's a very small part of my life." Because his house accommodates his chair so well, he says his disability is a non-issue until he leaves home.

Injured a day before his 17th birthday, he describes himself then as a cocky golden boy, sarcastic, elitist and a bit too smart and funny for his own good, waiting around for someone to come and hand him a bag of money. Then he was in the car, suspended upside down with no feeling in his legs. An hour later he was in a helicopter on his way to a trauma center and surgery.

He'd asked for a challenge and now he had it. Because the accident was serious enough to have killed him, he saw being alive as a win and paralysis as an opportunity. While he was at Northridge Hospital his sister helped him shape his approach to life in a chair. She told him his accident was "unfortunate," and Keith read a lot into that one word.

"Calling it unfortunate meant that this was not the end of the world, that people die every day, that this wouldn't define who I was. It meant that I was still worthy of love and that there was something to gain and share from this."

He's not the first to tell me that SCI was a teenage midlife crisis. He put that pre-injury confidence and swagger to work and went on an eight-month "healing journey," learning all he could about meditation, nutrition, acupuncture and other holistic approaches and using all of them to learn his new body and prepare for the future. One year post-injury he signed on for the ultimate California experience—a Landmark Forum personal empowerment seminar— and used it to get past what he refers to as his sense of entitlement.

At times he sounds like a combination of Stuart Smalley ("I'm good enough, I'm smart enough and doggone it, people like me.") and personal empowerment guru Tony Robbins. He's on a quest to take life seriously while laughing at himself.

"The seminar is about getting over yourself, not being a victim and letting go of fear," he riffs. "It got me away from getting caught up in the little everyday dramas and more focused on the big picture. I can choose not to be a victim. I can choose to love myself and believe I'm worthy of love. I'm not ripped off because I can't walk. Letting go of entitlement with grace and humor is huge and can impact others. I can decide what being in a chair means."

Disability, he tells me, has become a big, funny test of being fearless and responsible and in control. It's the challenge of being the person with the grin, not the regrets; the person who doesn't worry about what others think; the person responsible for his own happiness. Life on wheels has allowed him to become a catalyst for change in others.

A *funny* test? Absolutely.

"I want to enjoy this experience of being disabled and I want to do it without having any expectations. Sometimes that means going dancing in China or climbing the Great Wall out of my chair with my legs spasming the entire time or following the bowling ball down the alley to make sure I get a strike. I won't be idle and I don't do things half-assed. I'm not going to be afraid of this.

"The best piece of advice I got was from my rehab nurse," he adds. "She told me, 'You're young, you heal fast, go do things.' What I heard was that it was okay to be like I was, that the chair wasn't a big deal, that I shouldn't worry about all the bad things that could happen." And that's still the heart of what he says he's learned.

"I can never be happy being afraid or being a victim," he says. "This is an opportunity for self-exploration, creativity and challenge. Life is like a match. You can choose for it to be a slow burn or something intense that you use to start a fire." ■

Angel Watson

Angel Watson is a study in contrasts. She's assertive and bold, yet she was a shrinking violet when it came to accepting her injury. She's a big talker who loves to laugh, yet isn't afraid to let the tears fall when recalling those early post-injury fears. She's all woman, fond of flashy clothes, but her military background comes alive every time her country goes to war.

"Just send me over there," she says. "Give me a chance to kick some butt."

Angel's story is about reinvention. Several reinventions. When she went from soldier to wheeler 16 years ago, she assumed a new identify and put the skills she learned in military life to new uses. When she became a single mom, she went through another transformation. And in a strange twist, although she lost much of her old life's context when she was injured, most of it has returned to her.

At present, she raises her daughter, works part-time, sings with her church, and is active with the Paralyzed Veterans of America (PVA). Tomorrow she might change again.

This woman is a dynamo. On the walls and shelves of her office, you'll see a "Spirit of the ADA" award, accessibility manuals and a host of ceramic and glass butterflies. As the ADA coordinator for the Caring and Sharing Center for Independent Living (CASCIL) in Largo, Fla., she has—naturally—many identities. She conducts continuing education credit coursework for architects and teaches businesses and people with disabilities about accessibility laws. She lobbies legislators and serves on numerous state boards and committees. She instructs all the Florida ADA coordinators on changes in the ADA and its accessibility guidelines. She wears all these hats, not only in the greater Clearwater/St. Pete area but throughout the state. In almost everything she does, she finds her wheelchair an advantage.

"The chair gets me to the front of the line and helps me meet people," she says.

"When I lobby, I can position myself next to people I need to talk to.

"I've found parallel areas for most of my pre-injury life," she adds. "I was a member of the military and now I belong to the Paralyzed Veterans of America. I was working in a technical field and now I work in a people field."

She's still a warrior as she advocates for clients and deals with problem landlords. As a soldier for access, her weapon is her knowledge.

"I do a lot of fighting with all the condo commandos and provide training on building codes for restaurants, hotels and other public buildings. I'm the reigning expert on restrooms with accessibility problems. I'm the Latrine Queen."

Charmaine G. Brown, *A Royal Flush*

I caught up with her just as she was finishing work on a Friday afternoon. Her daughter Gloria and I talked as Angel returned phone calls, then Gloria entertained herself while her mom and I talked of the past and present.

Rocky Beginnings

Angel's reinventions began in 1988, after she hit a patch of ice while skiing in Pennsylvania. She slid into a tree, spun into another, then fell off a 30-foot cliff into a rocky ravine where she struck her head on a boulder. Brain injury, T8 fracture, coma for two and half weeks. In ICU for months, a nightmare of broken ribs, bruised kidneys and liver, open heart surgery, UTIs, renal failure, lung infections, chest tubes, a morphine pump, a DNR order and several "say your good-bye" visits from relatives.

When she finally stabilized, she had the function of a quad and the use of only one arm. And things didn't improve much at first when she transferred to rehab at what is now Healthsouth Rehabilitation Center in York, Pa.

"I fought with the therapists and nurses," she says. "I was *not* getting out of bed until this bad dream went away. They were getting $500 a day, so I figured they could dress me. I wouldn't push my chair. They fixed everything else in ICU; I figured they'd fix my back, too."

The injury totally rocked Angel's world, and she fell into a deep angry funk. She feared that her life and future—kids, productivity, employment—were over. The picture she had of disability and paraplegia, she says, was of some little old lady sitting in a window and crocheting. "I couldn't imagine the chair would ever be OK."

Getting this 5-foot woman out of bed took an army of six, and her attitude didn't improve when an "out-of-her-mind, dragon-lady PT" instructed her to list the Top Ten Things about being in a wheelchair.

"I wrote a list of what I hated to do before injury and wouldn't have to do anymore," she says.

"Like waitressing. All I could see were negatives and barriers."

That changed when Doug Heir, a Paralympic medalist and motivational speaker, came to her rehab facility to speak. He was a wheeler and an athlete who was successful, funny, productive and had a life. The effect was profound.

"He talked about traveling, sports, working and being successful," she remembers. "I finally had an image of someone my age living a conventional life. It was maybe the first time I laughed." Laughter and hope helped turn things around.

Angel learned to use her anger as motivation to master the basics of wheelchair life. Return of muscle function helped too, and she was eventually able to stand and try walking with braces. Walking proved impractical, but she liked her new ability to get upright to cook, negotiate narrow doorways or mop hard-to-reach areas. And the more she did, the more she wanted to do.

When she needed cash she baked cakes and took in sewing and laundry. She started driving. She got help from Voc Rehab and Pell grants and returned to college. She got used to being around people by working at Dolly Parton's Dollywood theme park for two summers. She worked as a secretary for a psychologist and a law firm.

"You can sit at home and imagine all the bad things that might occur or go out and deal with them as they happen," she says. "Things were rarely as bad as I expected. I learned how people reacted to the chair and how to be with them. In retail, people didn't care that I was in a chair; they'd still tell me off about poor service and that helped me form some boundaries. The office work was good because of the high expectations. I had to be on time and do my job despite my problems. Eventually I just stopped caring what other people might think of the chair."

With the difficulties of chair life magnified by Pennsylvania's snow, wind, rain, hills and steps, Angel figured there had to be a better way for her, or at least a better place. After checking out Florida, Arizona and California a few years after injury, she settled on St. Petersburg. Then, two weeks before graduating from college, she was both surprised and pleased to discover she was pregnant. She didn't feel close to the father, nor was she interested in a long-term relationship, so she decided to go it alone and headed south. Moving to Florida, she says, was a bold move.

Smooth Landings

Six months after graduating from college and a month before her due date, Angel began a new adventure as a single mom. The first few years of raising Gloria were an exercise in invention as she learned how to care for an infant, then toddler and preschooler, from her chair. Now she's parenting a 10-year-old 4H Club member.

How does she manage? Quite well, thank you. The two of them are up at 6:30 each morning and out the door by 8:15. Once Gloria is off to school Angel works out or swims, spends an hour as a classroom mom and then works at CASCIL where she limits herself to part time to protect her SSDI and Medicare benefits. Then it's errands, homework and taking Gloria to activities before getting home for dinner and to bed by midnight. Gloria's unfazed by the chair,

probably because her mom has integrated it so well into both their lives.

During almost nine years of active and reserve military duty before her injury, Angel had traveled, modeled and rappelled her way around C5 cargo planes doing inspections. She had always been physically fit, active and strong.

She still travels, both on the job and now to Washington to lobby for the PVA. Her contributions to that organization have given her camaraderie, peer support and opportunities for hunting, trap shooting and archery. PVA's Spinal Cord Injury Outreach Network, disability advisory boards and dating clubs all compete for her time. She still models, and when she has time she works with stained glass and plays the guitar. She's still fit. But all that takes a back seat to Gloria.

"Being a mom is the best job around," she says. "Gloria is certainly what I'm most proud of."

Angel feels her adjustment is complete, but that everyone has to do it for themselves.

"You're the only one who can make a difference in how your life turns out. It takes work, but you can make your own destiny by educating yourself and then learning to do for yourself. You *can* do it. You have a right to be angry and depressed, so take some time to be angry and depressed and then get over it. Get yourself out of the *me* attitude. Do things you never had time to do. Smile even when you don't want to. Thank people for all they do for you, because they don't have to. Go ahead and laugh!

"When I was in rehab, it was all about me but when I got out I realized the world didn't stop because mine had. I had to lose the entitlement attitude. There's a big world out there and I found out it was OK for me to fit into it, as me, the way I am. I had to accept myself to do that." ∎

Amit Jha

Amit Jha's 35, his career is on track and his life is moving along pretty much as he'd always planned it. Married for several years, he and his wife are now thinking about starting a family. He's got a couple of good jobs, a house, a car and big student loans to repay.

As a physiatrist practicing academic medicine, he splits his time between a clinical practice at one of Denver's general hospitals, co-directing a university-based residency program and working in Craig Hospital's Research Department. More on that below.

Amit was 19 and home from college for Christmas vacation when the car he was riding in rolled down an embankment on a mountain road west of Denver. The roof collapsed and he broke his neck at C7. After four days in an ICU, he went to Craig for four months of rehab. He wore a halo for three of those months, then, after a fusion surgery, a cervical collar for another month before discharge to his parents' home.

"After about a month I started thinking about the implications of SCI and about the future," he says. "I started thinking about getting back to college and doing all the things I liked to do."

Rehabbing in the same city where he lived helped him maintain a social life, and once he was discharged, the same friends who had visited him in the hospital went out of their way to drag him out of the house to meet new people.

"I wasn't a hermit but I needed physical help to go places. Without my friends I may not have gone out at all. They were very helpful and 16 years later I still have contact with some of them."

Living at home also had its drawbacks. Amit's family had moved to Denver from India when he was four. They brought many cultural differences with them, including the common misconception that people with disabilities require constant care and shouldn't try to be independent. As a result, they became very protective of him

and wanted him to stay home, change majors and learn to walk.

Since his injury is incomplete, both he and his parents thought maybe walking with braces would be possible. It took long months of trying before he realized that it was impractical for him.

"Walking was so physically demanding," he says. Still, Amit felt more accepting of the chair than his parents did. "I never felt talked down to or disrespected, so being at eye level with people wasn't all that important to me.

"But being Asian, I felt a great deal of pressure to succeed and I think my expectations were much higher than those of my parents, though that may have been a defense mechanism. If they had done my care, that might have changed everything and what I've done may not have been possible. I still worry that maybe I'm not the same son."

Compulsive overachieving?

"Maybe."

Amit was back in Chicago at Northwestern University and majoring in biomedical engineering within nine months, and he had his eye on medical school, just like before his injury.

The Academician

Getting into medical school was no picnic. As a resident of Colorado, Amit wanted to go to the University of Colorado and avoid paying high out-of-state tuition. The school balked, insisting on a physical exam and a test to see if he could adequately perform CPR.

"I'd already been accepted at Pitt," he notes. "They were very accommodating but didn't offer me any financial aid. Part of me felt that all these requirements at Colorado made sense, but another part said they were pretty bogus, so I filed a complaint with the State of Colorado. The day before I was scheduled to move to Pittsburgh, I got a call telling me I was accepted at CU. I started classes two days later."

Med school went smoothly and the university provided all the necessary accommodations, even building ramps and platforms so he could work on cadavers in anatomy class. Then he was off to the University of Washington, where his needs were equally well met, for his residency and a research fellowship.

"Occasionally, people outside of rehab medicine were very impressed and tended to treat me like a superstar," he says. "Sometimes the chair helped, like in surgery, where I was the perfect height."

In 1996, after his second year of residency in Seattle, he met his wife, a nurse who worked at the same hospital. They dated for a couple of years, then lived together, then got married and moved to Denver in 2000. His wife works as a psychiatric nurse and administers pediatric immunizations.

Amit spends two and a half days a week at the Denver Health Medical Center, where he teaches residents while he runs an amputee outpatient clinic, does acute care consults for patients with SCI and brain injuries, and participates in EMG nerve-conduction studies. He spends the other two and a half days in Craig Hospital's Research Department, where he studies aging with

SCI, satisfaction with healthcare, and sleep disorders and fatigue after brain injury. He does clinical research work with the hospital's medical director, and is a co-investigator for part of Craig's macrophage clinical trials.

In addition, Amit is co-director of the University of Colorado Medical School's residency program in physical medicine and rehabilitation, and teaches at least a course a year on topics like prosthetics, orthotics and spinal cord injury as part of its lecture series.

"I wanted to go into academic medicine because I wanted more than just a medical practice," he says. "I enjoy the variety. I like doing the research and trying to figure out what all the data means. For me, forming hypotheses, running experiments, doing statistics, the reading, writing and math, that's all fun.

"Those are different skills from the diagnosis and treatment skills I use in my practice. I enjoy the patient care and especially like dealing with the families."

Many of the people he treats use wheelchairs. Does his using one himself make a difference?

"Some seem to feel I may have more empathy and understanding for their situation because of the chair, but for the most part I think it's pretty neutral," he says. "I'm their doctor. That's how they see me."

Accepting Change, Resisting Change

Has he applied any formula for dealing with a C7 injury over the past 16 years?

"I tried to keep as much as possible the same while minimizing the impact the chair has on my life," Amit says. "I try to accept the things I can't change."

As he sees it, the chair makes him a prisoner to schedules more than before, but he suspects that this self-imposed structure is as essential for success as it is an inevitable part of life with SCI.

Because he thought that fewer post-injury changes would make his injury less traumatizing, Amit held on to as much as possible. How successful was he?

"I stuck with my career in medicine. If I hadn't been hurt I may have gone into something a bit more physically demanding, like surgery. I probably dated less and I put off looking for a relationship until after my internship. If I hadn't been injured, I think I'd probably have a family by now.

"I gave up sports because I was afraid disability would become the dominant aspect of my persona," he says. "I wanted to downplay its impact rather than highlight it. I felt uneasy around other people with disabilities and thought that if I hung out with them the chair would become the biggest part of who I am. I might have felt I was different from others with disabilities, and some of that's still there. I don't want to have to deal with the stereotypes that come with disability."

While that attitude might not win him many friends in the disabled activist community, it's an extremely common one. With Amit, it has softened with time, and he concedes that the chair has crept into his identity.

"If I had written an autobiography five years ago," he says, "I may not have mentioned the chair. Now it's a significant part of who I am. As the years pile up, perhaps I'm more willing to accept its significance."

Despite the changes he has made to accommodate his disability, most aspects of his life—education, career ambitions, marriage—remain the same.

"I never thought about *not* going back to school, so education was more a question of where and for what," he says. "After I was injured, education became even more important and I became more serious. I was confident about how I'd do academically and throwing myself into it was a good distraction. I didn't think much about my career; I just focused on classes."

Once back in school, he was able to maintain a fairly active social life. Some of his old friends shied away from his disability, but his easy outgoing manner made making new ones easy.

Amit has seen life on wheels from both sides, as physician and consumer, and I'm wondering if he's got any advice.

"As a professional, I give people medical advice, but mostly tell them they're the experts on their bodies. I think everyone has to make some changes and accommodations. Not changing just invites disaster. A classic example is bowel management. You make adjustments because who needs accidents?

"More importantly though, rehab doesn't stop when you leave the hospital. In fact, without the backup of the hospital staff I had to be more creative and so I kept learning how to do things. I had to, necessity pushed me. Those are the real changes I made. Two years later, much more was possible." ∎

Joe Jeremias

Take healthy doses of humility and intelligence, combine them with a fierce and often dark sense of humor, mix in introspection, a sense of perspective and a dash of acceptance. Over the past 16 years, after letting all those things cook, Joe Jeremias has emerged as an English teacher, quad rugby player, homeowner, happily married guy and, according to his wife Chris, a real smart-ass.

Joe's World sits in West Hempstead, on Long Island about half an hour from New York City. A 32-year-old C6 quad, Joe's been in a chair for half his life, after being hit by a car while riding his bike at 16. Following three weeks in acute care at University Hospital in Newark, N.J., he went to Kessler Rehabilitation Institute in West Orange, N.J. for six months. He's one of the few people I've met who has fond memories of rehab, which he says was a bit like summer camp or the best year of high school.

He was the youngest guy in rehab and something of a celebrity, running with the twentysomethings and surrounded by good-looking female therapists who always had their hands on him. He eagerly volunteered for everything, being especially accommodating to female staff who needed to practice cathing the quads. "I'd just sit back and say, 'line 'em up and enjoy yourselves!'" He knew how to find the positives of a situation.

Joe made the best of his time at Kessler, constantly comparing himself to others and working to master skills as well as the paras he watched. He figured the more he knew and the more he was able to own his injury, the less scary life would be.

"Rehab was a great time," he says, "one of the richest experiences I've ever had. I learned so much and I want to remember it all, especially the people—the nurses and docs and therapists and the cleaning lady in ICU. It's selfish of me really, why would I want to forget?"

Happiness Happens

Joe saw education as his ticket back into life. Tutored throughout rehab, he returned to high school part time and graduated with his class. Then he went to Montclair State College and got a degree in English with Voc Rehab footing the bill. When he'd held down writing and graphic design jobs for several years and still hadn't found his niche, he returned to college for a master's in teaching, paying for it with a graphic design assistantship. A year and a half later he was instructing New Jersey high school seniors in British literature, a job he held for five years.

When he and Chris married a year ago and bought their home on Long Island, Joe switched schools and now teaches freshmen and sophomores in a nearby high school.

"I'm hooked on the material and want to

pass along my excitement about it," he says. "I have a love for this stuff."

He also has a love for the kids and a drive to make a difference. The feeling is obviously mutual: several former students from New Jersey crashed his wedding and two full pages of their wedding album are filled with photos of them. Seems he's found that niche.

Joe and Chris met on the quad rugby court. He had played for several years after college and had just rejoined the team after taking a few years off. Chris, who has been involved with wheelchair sports and rugby for years, had worked with Joe's EPVA (now known as United Spinal Association) team before he reupped.

"I'd been living on my own for about four years and had dated a good deal," he says. "I'd had a lot of good moments with women, but I wanted more than just moments. I'd just gone through a dark period and had sort of given up on relationships. One day at practice a friend said, 'Joe, that's Chris, she's a teacher, go talk to her.'" He did, and they got to know each other while sitting on the sidelines and grading papers.

Chris had dated several wheelers in the past, and she eventually asked him out. "I'd pretty much sworn off rugby players," she recalls, "but I liked being around him. We went out and had lots of fun. Things moved on from there. "

Things moved on well enough for them to be married within two years.

"When we started getting serious my family was concerned about what my life would be like married to someone in a chair. They don't even see it now."

Did he think this American Dream trifecta of good job, marriage and home was possible? "Possible? Well yeah, I was an Eagle Scout, so I believed most anything was possible. And I knew guys in chairs who had all those things. I just wasn't sure it was going to happen for me."

Just Your Average Joe

Joe gets by with humor, contact with other wheelers, staring down his demons and maintaining a sense of perspective.

He likes to laugh and uses self-deprecating humor—the darker the better—to connect with others. In rehab he and his friends would trade such nuggets as, "Look at us; we're quads, we're pathetic, we can't even pull the trigger. It's easier to stay alive."

He finds disability to be an endless source of material, especially in the company of nondisabled people. In his classroom he'll tease students with threats of tire tracks on their foreheads. "ABs want to laugh, but they're not sure they should."

He sees other wheelers as both a resource and a cure for isolation. "You learn from them," he says. "They let you know you're not alone and give you someone to laugh with. Put a bunch of SCIs in a room and eventually the conversation degenerates to bowel, bladder and sex. You have to laugh at this stuff."

It's not all been laughter. He spent a good part of college uneasy in social situations and unsure that others accepted him. Projecting something of the brooding English major persona, he became a magnet for unhappy, insecure people of the misery-loves-company sort.

"I slowly realized how much I was missing and started taking the initiative more," Joe says. "Making jokes about the chair gave me more to talk about; it's a hell of a topic for conversation. Later, I did the 'Think First' prevention program with high school kids. So many of their questions were much more about me than about the injury, and I began to believe that people could be interested in me rather than what being in a chair was like. Time and experience helped me accept disability for what it is and get past it."

Getting past it, he tells me, means choosing to move forward rather than wallowing in self-pity. He doesn't deny the ongoing frustration of living with severe spasms, bowel and bladder hassles and the time lost to living in a chair. Things like a creaking chair or not finding accessible parking when he needs it still annoy him. They just don't ruin his day.

"It sets me off that I can lift my body weight but can't use a paper clip, or that a half inch of snow slows me down as much as a flight of stairs," he says. "But there are lots of things in life that are worse, and I know people whose situations are much tougher than mine. I keep that in mind and it helps me deal with all the day-to-day stuff."

Dealing with those day-to-day tribulations is not what he sees as the stuff of inspiration. In fact, inspiration is a compliment he'd just as soon live without.

"I'm inspired by good writers, people who create things out of nothing. I get up; I go to work; I get through my days just like everyone else. My life isn't the kind that books are written about or movies are made of. My accomplishments are very average, maybe boring. I'm no Willy Loman. I know I'm average."

Boring is not the description that comes to mind, and it makes Chris roll her eyes. She reminds him that he's forever complaining about not having enough time to do everything he wants to do, that in the past year he's been to Vegas and Hawaii, and that eight months ago, in the span of two weeks, they got married, moved into their home and he began a new job.

"I can't argue with that," he says with a smile, "I love my life the way it is. It's all I've ever aspired to."

The Right Destinations

"We all have choices about the roads we take through life, and they don't all lead to desirable places," Joe says. "I'm pretty satisfied that I've found OK destinations. Being a quad is only a little piece of who I am. It's not my defining characteristic, but it's helped make me what I am and it colors everything I see."

Joe is confident that, on average, things work out for the best. He's got this wonder and excitement about all parts of his life— his marriage, teaching, life in general.

"You never know what the next moment will bring," he says. "One day I could turn a corner and see a unicorn. The possibilities amaze me."

With so much going on in life and mystery waiting around every corner, Joe is always looking. He doesn't want to miss anything.

"He finds inspiration and joy in everything," Chris says. "He's always reading something to me, sometimes just because he loves the way it sounds. He gets excited about simple things like clouds or sunsets."

But he's no Pollyanna. He sees the world without windowdressing and looks for what it has to offer.

"Living with this is such an individual thing," he says. "There are upsides of being in a chair for me. I got a college education, I met my wife, I got a small settlement that helps make ends meet. Being in a chair changed who I am. I think I'm less self-centered, less materially focused, more introspective.

"I take this for what it is and look for the positives. Some of the rotten things have helped me grow, and when things are good I let them be. Overall, this has been a good experience. Don't get me wrong, I'd kneecap someone in a minute for a place in the cure line, about number 10, so they'd have the kinks worked out. But if I waited around for the cure to happen, I'd miss out on too much. I live the life I have and don't pine away for what I don't have."

No regrets?

"I never envisioned all the possibilities at first and wallowed around for four or five years. I didn't begin doing all I wanted to do until the last 11 or so. I wish I had believed in myself sooner.

"It's hard to realize you can get out of bed in the beginning, hard to see very far into the future. You have to give yourself some time, so I can't say you just have to suck it up. But you can't just sit around and wait because all the rehab and money won't help if that's all you do. Everyone needs to mourn, but you can't get stuck. You have to do this yourself. If a schlep like me can do it, anyone can. It's a choice."

News Flash: This recent e-mail from Joe reading: "I would assume this qualifies as BIG news: Christine and I are expecting our first child." ∎

Karen Hwang

"When you get off the highway, take about three rights, then go a mile or so, I think, until you get to a light. Make a right there and go until you get to my street."

With those directions I figured on about four phone calls from places unknown before finding Karen Hwang, who lives in quiet, wooded Watchung, N.J., about 45 minutes west of Newark. Instead, I got there early. Like her directions, which only sound vague, Karen is very precise about who she is and what she thinks.

"My life with a disability is like an absurdist drama," she says. "The conditions

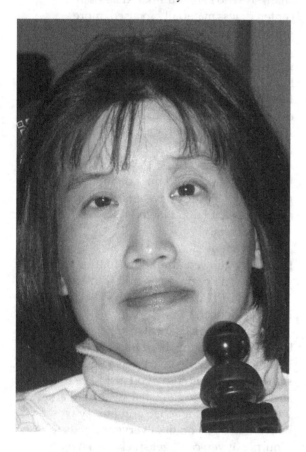

make absolutely no sense at all, but you can't stop to question it, you can just try to function within those parameters. I've never believed in God or karma or anything like that, so I'm not bothered by randomness or the fact that some things have no apparent meaning. Things are what they are and then you move on. I try not to ask why me?"

In 1988, when Karen was 21, she was injured in an automobile accident. C3-4. At 37, she still has no recollection of the accident or much that followed—a month in ICU, another month in acute care at Thomas Jefferson Hospital in Philadelphia and rehab at Magee Rehabilitation Hospital, also in Philadelphia. After discharge, she went home to live with her family.

Accustomed to the independence of living away from home for nearly four years before her injury, she struggled with her new living arrangement. With a bed set up in the family room, she had no privacy whatsoever and was in nearly constant disagreement with her overprotective parents over how best to handle her health and self-care issues. Despite needing personal care attendants 24 hours a day, she returned to school within six months to finish her degree.

Accessible housing is hard to find in New Jersey, so once she finished her undergraduate work Karen reached a mutual decision with her parents to build an addition to their house which gave her the privacy she needs and the ability to come and go as she pleases. Her wing of the house—a kitchen, living room and two bedrooms—seems almost compulsively neat and organized. Yet I quickly felt relaxed and comfortable there and music played the entire time we spoke.

Karen is quick to point out that her external circumstances—supportive parents, good insurance coverage, access to good medical care at nearby Kessler Institute and now separate living quarters—are more cushy than many others with SCI will ever have.

"There are plenty of people who are confined to institutions or nursing homes," she says. "I'm sure their lives are less fun than mine. I've been lucky."

She's also been skillful in securing help from several quarters. School provided scholarships, Voc Rehab helped with equipment and people at college went out of their way to meet her needs. Now that she's employed, the only benefit she receives is healthcare from New Jersey's no-fault auto insurance. Probably because of her education and involvement in Kessler's peer counseling program, her dealings with medical professionals have become more collegial than is typical in a doctor/patient relationship.

Informed, Rational

Call her a cynical realist or a person who speaks her mind without benefit of euphemisms or political correctness. She finds being a C3-4 quad difficult, often much more difficult than she cares to deal with. Don't expect her to tell you there's some meaning or explanation for her disability. She bristles when I ask her about reaching some point of acceptance of SCI.

"I really hate that term," she says. "In rehab they use the Kubler-Ross grief model—denial, anger, bargaining, depression and acceptance—but it's totally inappropriate for SCI. Many people just never get there. You don't have to like or accept being in a chair. You just have to deal with it."

For her, dealing with it means to focus on the day-to-day details of life and to steer clear of big-picture thinking. Instead of trying to imagine what life might be like five or 10 years down the road, she attends to what's here today. When she found her Ed.D. dissertation overwhelming, she focused on individual sections to make it more manageable. She does the same with her life.

"So many things are out of my control," she says. "I figure if this day, or hour, or sometimes even this moment is under control, then that's good enough."

In fact, Karen expressed some skepticism about being part of this project, suggesting that many others were doing far better than she. She also pointed out that she probably would have chosen to die, had she been given that choice 15 years ago.

She's obviously given this issue a good deal of thought since then, and feels that physician assisted death should be an option for people in her situation. For her, it's not about depression or fear of a nursing home but about her quality of life. She doesn't like being told she's not competent to judge her own circumstances.

"I'm educated, employed and have good healthcare and personal attendant coverage," she notes. "I think I'm perfectly qualified to make an informed, rational decision about the quality of my life." Feeling her situation is probably as good as it's ever going to get, Karen sees moving on as her only option. "I think it's OK to be *not* OK with this. You don't have to beat yourself up over not being happy. You're entitled to your emotions and if you try to fake or deny them, eventually they'll boil over like a pot of spaghetti with a lid on it."

Suicidal thoughts and SCI are no strangers. Several people profiled here either contemplated it or even made an attempt. The issue is as much a reality as is the dependency Karen lives with each day.

When we first spoke, she laughingly passed along a question from her boyfriend: "He told me to ask you if you realized I'm suicidal. He's probably the reason I'm still here. I'm in love with him and would never do anything to hurt him. But apart from the occasional quip about my being around only because Dr. Kevorkian rejected me, I usually don't think much about it."

A Low Boredom Threshold

This is a woman who gets through her days by staying very busy, and she does busy very well. She's included here on the strength of the recommendations of several people I respect who told me of what she's done and how she's dealt with her circumstances. If you have doubts, check out this résumé.

Since her injury, Karen has maintained a mutually supportive relationship with her family, created a relaxed and functional living environment, found reliable personal care assistants, is nearing completion of her Ed.D., written numerous articles for professional journals and consumer magazines, done peer counseling, sustained a pre-injury relationship with her boyfriend for 16 years and, in general, stayed productive. None of these things happened by accident or in a vacuum. They required skill, commitment and ongoing attention.

"I have a very low boredom threshold," she says. "I always have to be doing something. I can't just lie in bed; I get too fidgety."

She says graduate school was a good way to consume 10 years of her life without having to plan anything. She always knew what was coming next. When she receives her Ed.D. she'll gain both a skill and a credential and with any luck, she should gain a full-time job as well. These days she's up by 7 each morning, out the door by 9:30 and at her internship by 10, where she puts in about five hours a day at a center for people with developmental disabilities. It keeps her busy with clients, attending meetings or consulting with staff and others. Now free of classes and assignments, she submits professional papers for publication.

"I might be the only person who writes journal articles for fun," she says. "I write for myself, to get things out of my system." She also writes intelligent, balanced and well considered articles for *New Mobility* magazine, expressing her opinions on topics such as family, cure, religion and quality of life. In them she consistently addresses the need for inclusion, personal autonomy and choice.

There are unexpected sides of Karen Hwang. Several years ago, at a friend's insistence, she entered the Miss Wheelchair New Jersey Pageant, not once but twice, just for the hoot of it. In answer to a question asking how disability "added" to her quality of life, she predictably and straight-forwardly suggested that the pageant shouldn't be about quality of life.

"I was second runner-up both times," she says. "That's actually pageant-speak for 3rd place. Shows you what they know."

She feels some responsibility to those who are newly injured, and as a volunteer in Kessler's peer support program shares her experiences of school, equipment and the social aspects of disability. When things get to be too much for her, she calls on a friend, a disability advocate, for personal support.

Weekends are for Ali, her boyfriend of 16 years, who she says provides immediate stress relief by simply walking through the door. When they're together on weekends, they hang out at her place or go out for dinner, sleep in, get up late and spend time working on the play list for his late night bi-weekly radio show, often tossing Coltrane, Bach and Talking Heads into the same sets.

"He makes me happy," she says. "He gives me unconditional love. I'm surrounded by hardware on three sides and it's not easy for people to get physically close to me, but he does. Non-clinical touch is very important to me; Ali gives me that."

People have many different ways to cope with life after injury. Karen's done it by being flexible, realistic and productive. Above all, she's done it by staying very busy. While she speaks of what she sees as the absurdity, randomness and meaninglessness of life, she's chosen to live hers by pursuing an education and profession that seeks to provide explanations for that life. In doing so she offers both the ideal and the example of a life rationally and productively lived. ∎

Curtis Lovejoy

When Curtis Lovejoy was in rehab at Shepherd Center in 1986 with an incomplete C5-7 injury, he was 29 and so terrified of being in water, even with a life jacket, that it took him four or five sessions in the pool just to calm down. Sixteen years later he holds numerous world records, more than 300 medals in swimming—over 245 of them gold—and 25 more for fencing.

"When I was 12, people told me my smile would take me around the world," says Curtis. It has. It's taken him to Europe, South America, the Pacific Rim and Australia. In fact, the smile is the first thing you notice about him because he's always wearing one.

He stayed with that pool therapy after discharge and learned to swim 18 months later, though he took another year and half to lose the life jacket. Ten years ago, before Curtis found a coach at the YMCA and got serious, he took three hours to swim a mile;

now he does it in 35 minutes. He began competing in 1993. Within three years he set a world record in the breast stroke and picked up all the gold a quad could win in other international competitions but missed the 1996 Paralympics.

That's when he hired a professional coach to help him to relax and maintain a better rhythm in the water. He improved dramatically again. "It's all about rhythm and beat," Curtis says. "I sing and talk to myself while I swim."

In the Sydney 2000 Paralympic Games, despite having the flu, Curtis shattered the 100 meter freestyle world record by 32 seconds, and went on to set a total of five world records in two days.

"I was on top of the water," he says. And since? "I haven't come close to the old record, let alone the one I set."

At 45, how much longer can he compete? "It depends on how my body holds up, on how I feel," he says. "I'm good for 2004, maybe 2008. I love it, so I have to keep doing it."

Curtis is hardly a passive bystander in these achievements. Living the life of a world-class athlete, he's up at 5 a.m. and in the pool by 6 for two hours of training, then two more each afternoon. He's serious about nutrition and drinks well over a gallon of water a day to keep his 6-foot frame at about 165 pounds.

After his first gold in swimming, he tried fencing. Liking the idea of whacking people with a pointed instrument, he decided that the sport would be a good balance to swimming.

"Swimming gives me peace of mind," he says. "Fencing's fun."

He modified fencing moves to fit his function and invented his "whirlybird" move, in which he leans back, rotates the foil above his head and strikes.

"I holler when I see a point coming, and that scares my opponents. I can't stop the momentum when I lean forward and strike, so they feel the pain when I strike them. I'm always smiling during competitions; that's what they see. If I'm not smiling I know something's wrong. It's part of me."

Showdown with God

Back in rehab, when things were still grim, smiling wasn't part of Curtis's program. Admitted to Shepherd Center the day of his auto accident with an incomplete C6-7 injury, he was soon in a power chair, could barely lift his arms, and used a universal cuff to eat. That didn't stop him from working from his hospital bed—as a regional manager for Church's Chicken in Atlanta. Still, he hated how he looked, hated how others looked at him, and worried his wife would split and he'd be alone forever. He seriously contemplated suicide.

"That's when I had it out with God," says Curtis. "I told Him what I thought of Him and gave Him three days to heal me. He didn't answer. When I told my mom about that conversation, she told me I needed to repent—fast. I wept with shame and embarrassment listening to a nurse read me the Book of Job. God never left me; I'd left Him. Once I realized everything we do is a choice, things began to get better."

Things getting better included some remarkable return of function. He began to stand on his own, his arm function returned, as did abdominal and back muscles. Within two months he switched to a manual chair, and now uses one with a low 12-inch back. Limited hand function is his only remaining claim to quad-dom.

Some would call his dramatic return of function incredibly good luck; others might call it the residue of hard work. Curtis calls it a miracle, the result of his having been chosen to give hope to others through his unremitting faith in God. He doesn't care what you call it because he's a true believer.

"I didn't have much to do with it and can't claim any of the success personally," he says. "It's all God. If something didn't happen, like making the Olympic team in '96, it meant He didn't want it to happen."

In rehab, Curtis took control of his treatment, eliminating people who wouldn't listen to him or didn't believe he could improve. When his doctor told him doing sit-ups with a rope tied to the foot of the bed was a waste of time, Curtis fired him, feeling that if he was unsuccessful, the professionals were unsuccessful as well. He steered clear of those who confused sympathy with empathy.

He worked hard to keep physically fit and experimented with alternative treatments such as meditation, chiropractic and, of course, hydrotherapy. Using biofeedback, he found out he still had some muscle activity in his legs, and then figured out a way to use visualization to help him with bladder control. When his injury got him down, he used meditation and hypnosis to help him deal with the stress. Both helped, and also kept him relaxed while swimming. While he never thought he could fix his injury, he was convinced he could control and avoid problems like scoliosis and lower back pain through visualization, as well as enhance other functions like bladder control.

Even with all the progress he made in rehab, Curtis left Shepherd feeling angry, rejected, self-conscious and antisocial. After his wife left him three months later, he got a clue that his anger was one of the reasons for the divorce. He hated the chair and wanted to get rid of it, so he became obsessed with working out—to the point that his life consisted of eating, sleeping and exercising.

"I wasn't mature enough to accept my appearance or lack of function," he says. "Almost everything was out of my control and I was afraid that people only saw the ugly or disabled Curtis. I was afraid to share these feelings because I didn't want people to think I was weak."

He got unstuck by pumping himself up with pep talks while brushing his teeth. He took risks by talking about his fears and made sure people understood his feelings. He started to believe hard work really would pay off. From desperation to patience and learning.

For Curtis, injury became a second chance at life. First he set very high personal expectations, then committed himself to helping others, changing their attitudes about disability and being a role model to others. He wanted to use his swimming as a way of giving hope to all those he had met all over the world.

Change in Focus

"Before I got hurt," he says, "life was all about me and money. I figured 'I got mine, you get yours.' Not anymore; now it's about helping people. I want to show that people with disabilities have feelings, that we cry, that we're responsible, that we work and earn a living. I take things one day at a time, and I'm in the moment more. No matter how much I give, I always get more back."

Chronic pain, especially in cold weather, limits Curtis to part-time work. Early on he dispatched for the AAA and did public speaking for the "Arrive Alive" driving safety program. Now he works mornings in Shepherd's Health Information department and coaches swimming a couple of times a week. And he's parlayed his athletic achievements into regular speaking gigs with the Worldwide Sports Speaking Bureau, an organization that also books world class athletes like Lance Armstrong.

Appearing at churches, schools, colleges and corporations, he talks about faith, the Paralympics, coping with adversity and following dreams. Spending so much time at Shepherd has allowed him to use his degree in therapeutic recreation to conduct workshops on physiology, nutrition and fitness, and to act as a personal trainer for a number of staff members there.

"This has been an amazing experience," Curtis says. "I've learned how to get back up, back into life and how to be a warrior. Now I think I know how to help others and how to be me. Before I got hurt I asked God for opportunities, but I never imagined that they'd come in this kind of package. It's all been worth it though, because my accident opened up so many doors. It's taught me way too many lessons to take any of it back now. It's been worth it—all of it, every bit of it." ∎

CHAPTER FOUR
Finding What Works

People usually use broad terms to define their obstacles—inaccessibility, discrimination, low expectations, overall adjustment. But what about the day-to-day stuff, those things that gnaw and wear at you? If you had to put your finger on one thing that drives you up the wall or sets you off, what is it? What stands out? When the question turned more personal, so did the answers coming from this group.

Q: What are the most difficult things you've had to deal with since injury?

- Physical/medical specifics: bowel, bladder, skin
- Attitudes of others, acceptance
- Relationships
- Dependence
- Finances
- Loss of activities

When this group talked about their biggest obstacles, they started with the physical ones.

Eric Gibson says learning his new body, especially bowel and bladder care, was the hardest. Benj Anderson still occasionally struggles with his morning routine and begrudges the time it takes. Bowel, bladder and skin problems may seem mundane to some, but are ever-present considerations for most.

Michael Slaughter has bad memories of enforced bed rest to heal a skin sore. Don Dawkins, too, regrets the three years he spent in hospitals recovering from sores.

For Angel Watson, it's household chores: "Taking out the trash, doing laundry, vacuuming, those are the most difficult."

Eventually, everyone got their self-care and body management issues under control, at least to the point of finding tolerable routines. Pain was a different story, and for some remains an ongoing trial.

"Back pain is so difficult," says Susan Douglas. "That and the attitude of others. Some people just don't have a clue."

After body challenges, people named many others ranging from relationships to lack of accessibility to loss of independence to money problems. As before, most of these external problems had to do with fitting in, feeling accepted and dealing with other people's attitudes.

Richard Famiglietti struggles with how people perceive him now: "It's the pity factor that's hard to deal with." For Charlotte Heppner it was one good friend who couldn't cope with her chair: "It took him a couple of years to come around." Keith Davis talks about accessibility issues but also expresses appreciation for living in the U.S. and in California, where access is relatively good.

Most of the problems people brought up—acceptance by others, relationships, accessibility, body function, finances or loss of a much-loved activity—are very specific in nature and limited to one or a few aspects of life. Most people say they've found ways to deal with these problems so that now they are solved, they come up only occasionally, or have become manageable or tolerable. Even so, few dismiss these problems as inconsequential, and say that maintaining a perspective on how far they've come since those early days after injury reassures them that they can manage whatever's thrown their way.

Some challenges come with rewards. Anne Herman says that pregnancy and raising a newborn were the most difficult things she dealt with since her injury, but that she'd do it again in a heartbeat. Her son Donald, she says, is simply "the best."

Others, like Robert Statam or Juan Garibay, say their toughest lifestyle changes, such as moving away from drugs, alcohol or gang life, were epic struggles they are very pleased they waged.

As noted before, people managed to get past most major obstacles within a year or two. Does that mean all hassles go away? What about the long term? Does anything *stay* difficult?

Q: What's the worst thing about having a spinal cord injury and using a chair?

- Health issues: bowel and bladder, pain, pressure sores and fatigue
- Other people and their attitudes
- Personal Issues: self-image, frustration, depression, loss of confidence
- Inaccessibility
- Nothing major comes to mind
- Loss of spontaneity

While there are no real surprises here, this list does suggest that whatever was difficult at first often stays that way. Who would argue with the one-third of the group who say their lives would be easier without the worry and time restraints of bowel and bladder management, skin sores and fatigue? Yet few of that one-third see even these "worst" things as constant concerns, and instead call them occasional ones. No one said any of their problems were insurmountable.

Interestingly, about 15 percent—the hard-core optimists, presumably—answer this question (What's the worst thing?) with comments like "I just don't see it that way" or "It's foolish to speculate" or "This just isn't that horrible." These are the people who expect good things to happen and find positives in almost everything.

The fact that the answers to this question are all over the charts indicates how individually and personally SCI affects us all. Many in this group seem much more bothered by the secondary limitations of paralysis—the loss of time, spontaneity, travel or roughhousing with their kids—

than they are with not being able to walk. They also say that looking at the "worst" things in such specific ways helps them keep losses in perspective and remember how much they can still do and how much of life is still intact.

When the question moved away from "worst thing" and into the area of specific losses, the answers changed again.

Q: What would you say was your biggest loss due to injury?

- Physical activities and the loss of social interaction
- Career interruption or change
- Appearance
- Relationships, divorce, parenting issues
- No big losses: It's been all gains or the gains outweigh the losses

Loss of physical activities again tops the list, but just as often people quickly qualify their answers by putting those activities into a context: "I miss wrestling and roughhousing with my kids," "I miss dancing with my wife," "I miss the interaction that comes with shooting hoops or playing catch," or "I miss the adrenaline rush of running the quarter-mile."

Qualifying losses in this way seems to decrease the loss and help them replace activities or do them differently. People still dance, but in their chairs. They still interact with friends, but in less physical pursuits. Parents still roughhouse with their kids but maybe not on the floor. Limiting the context limits the loss.

Some people lost their marriages, had their existing careers slowed down or lost potential careers in athletics, modeling, the arts, the military or law enforcement. Most lost dreams and favorite activities. Everyone lost something. But they saw even the most painful losses as affecting only one or a few aspects of their lives rather than affecting all aspect of life. By viewing even the worst consequences of SCI as specific and limited seems to be an important factor in coping so well with their injuries.

That hard-core 15 percent of eternal optimists shows up here, too. They say that overall, SCI has given them more positives than negatives, that they've gained much more than they've lost. And while their average of more than 17 years on wheels no doubt has helped this group adjust, mature and come to terms with SCI's challenges, some of the most optimistic in this bunch are the twenty-somethings most recently injured. Apparently hopes of youth do spring eternal.

A state of optimism is not where most of these people started. Instead, many of them struggled during those first weeks and months after injury to imagine anything worse than being paralyzed. Some admitted wishing they had died, wanting to die or thinking that maybe paralysis really was a fate worse than death.

While in rehab, Kevin Wolitzky asked himself if he really wanted to live "this way." Many others asked similar questions. But over time, those attitudes, as well as many of the questions about living "this way" disappeared, lost intensity or at least changed substantially. As people acquired experience and learned of possibilities, they gained a more balanced perspective.

But still, SCI can be seen as terrible, so I asked people if they saw it as the ultimate worst-case scenario.

Is SCI the worst thing that ever happened to you?

- No, this is not the worst thing to ever happen to me
- Yes, this is the worst thing to happen to me
- No, this isn't the worst; in fact, it's been positive
- No, I can think of worse things

Initially, almost everyone thought SCI was the worst thing that had happened or could happen to them. A few years later—a few decades later for some—nearly half felt this was certainly *not* the worst thing that had happened to them, while others came to feel it wasn't even the worst that could

happen to them. For perspective, one-third still feel SCI is the worst thing they have ever experienced.

What's worse than spinal cord injury and a life on wheels? The death of a parent or child, a divorce or the breakup of a relationship, a family suicide, severe depression, drug and alcohol dependency, and gangbanging all qualified.

Matthew Seals' son died in the tornado that injured him. Don Dawkins watched his mother suffer for months before she died, as did Donald Collier with both his parents. When her ex-husband unexpectedly left the state with her kids, Marina Conner spent years after her accident not knowing where they were.

George Taborsky lost his father, grandmother, a close uncle and his dog of 17 years, was plagued by severe back pain and blood clots, caught pneumonia every summer and broke up with his live-in girl friend, all in the first three years after his injury. He calls that stretch much worse than his paralysis. "The bottom sort of fell out and it took me some time before I was able to move on."

Ryan McLean speaks for many: "This isn't the worst. I used to feel it was but there are lots worse things that could happen."

Some say SCI has been a positive experience. What, you ask, could possibly be positive about SCI? People speak of the perspective and insight they have gained and say their personal growth or needed lifestyle changes are worth the costs of paralysis. Others point out the opportunities that came their way after SCI such as athletics, travel, funding for school and the motivation to get an education.

"I think I've gained rather than lost from this," Jason Graber says. "It gave me direction and some focus, sort of a nice kick in the ass. I have to find some meaning to it and make the best of it."

Robert Statam calls SCI his second chance at life: "I spent years abusing alcohol and drugs and never thought I could get off that roller coaster. This gave me an opportunity to start out fresh and find out what I wanted out of life. Most people don't get that chance. The wheelchair may have saved my life."

Angel Watson sometimes saw it as not having much else to lose: "What are they going to do, take away my birthday?"

Nobody was happy about being paralyzed. No one told me their accident was the best thing that ever happened to them. Most struggled for some time to make sense of their injuries. But they still found positives and they still maintained perspective.

Many people soften the impact of misfortune by comparing themselves to others who are less fortunate or by imagining how much worse their situation could be. That doesn't mean they relish other people's misfortune, but rather that they place their own in a broader perspective.

Doing so helped many in this group see SCI in relative terms. Considering *what might have happened*, they say, things turned out pretty well. Patty Rivas says SCI is the worst thing that's happened to her, but quickly adds: "In some ways that's probably a reflection on how good my life has been." Jason Regier tries to stay aware of all the positives: great rehab, a super support system, a van, state-of-the-art chair and living in the USA as opposed to, say, Bosnia. "If I was living in a foreign country this would be so much harder," agrees Anne Marie Hochhalter. "If I complain and say 'oh poor me,' nothing will ever be enough."

Q: Tell me something about your problem-solving skills

- Analyze
- Seek help when needed
- Trial and error
- Creativity
- Persistence

Don Dawkins has developed an almost perverse sense of confidence in himself. "Because of the obstacles I've faced along the way," he says with certitude, "I *know* I can ride the whitewater."

The whitewater Don's talking about is all those assorted problems and obstacles that come with SCI. Riding it means solving them as they come along. Most people on these pages say that knowing how to solve problems is what living with SCI is all about and that SCI problems, because they are so unusual, often require unusually creative solutions. Most say knowing how to solve problems was essential to coping and doing well. You might think they'd all been talking to each other, because their philosophies are remarkably similar.

These are analytical people who face problems head-on. More than half their responses contained the word "analyze," and many others included the phrases "thoroughly examine," "logic," "step by step," "assess and evaluate," and "weigh all the facts." These people face problems quickly and directly, and they're not afraid of asking others for help. They know how to get creative to find solutions. They do whatever's necessary. Yet their styles vary widely.

Keith Davis uses a formula, "assess, evaluate, take action." Susan Douglas analyzes "to a fault." Ryan McLean writes about problems in her journal, sometimes listing them so she can see them all. Jamie Peterson tries anything he can think of until he finds a solution. As an engineer, Aric Fine examines problems from as many perspectives as possible and doesn't hesitate to ask others for help.

"I look for the easiest way and try not to make more problems," says Glenford Hibbert. "I think ahead."

It's no surprise that the engineers, businesspeople, independent living advocates, those who repair or repaired mechanical devices, as well as doctors and counselors would favor an analytical approach to problem solving, but even those who don't solve problems for a living also analyze their way to better lives. They all have one style in common: they define the problem, collect as much information as possible, define a potential solution and, after a trial run, evaluate ways to improve it.

They keep in mind that many SCI problems defy conventional solutions, so they rely on experimentation and trial and error. In fact, admits Juan Garibay, it's all trial and error. Wardell Kyles falls back on his motto of improvise, adapt and overcome. Brian Johnston built a business around his problem-solving skills when he began marketing adaptive tools for wheelers. Most spend time comparing notes with other wheelers who are likely to have answers.

Vincent Dureau thinks ahead as much as possible, mostly to make sure he can live with his solutions over the long run. He avoids gadgets—"they break"—and leans toward simplicity.

Several emphasize the need to include people when solving people problems. Realtor Mark Bussinger solves his attendant-care problems by solving his attendants' housing problems. In the process, they both win. Wally Dutcher's style in solving people problems is to involve them in the solution. Solving non-people problems, he says, is usually just a matter of learning the pertinent details. When he's in doubt about either type of problem, he falls back on his SWAG principle—that's a Sophisticated Wild Ass Guess.

Everyone speaks of the need for persistence, patience and confidence when solving problems. They say what they lack in patience they make up for with confidence gained over time. People with spinal cord injury, they say, solve more problems in the course of a day than most ablebodied people solve in a week or more. If, as this group claims, solving problems is an acquired skill, one learned over time and through experience, you can count on becoming an expert at this problem-solving business.

"We know shit most of the world will never know," Kevin Williams opines. "Because we have to put up with so much, we can cope with most anything. We're the most resourceful people in the world."

Angel Watson agrees: "There's not much else to lose. If you can learn to adapt to a wheelchair, you can learn to adapt to anything."

The resourcefulness these wheelers have developed over the years has given them confidence that there's always a solution and they'll always be able to find it.

Q: What do you do when you get stressed out?

SCI is stressful business. That spilled cup of coffee, the shoe that seems to be leaking, the unexpected surprise in your pants, even the full parking lot that makes you late— these nasty little bummers can ruin your day if you let them. Waiting for disaster and wondering what else can go wrong can get old. Here's how this group says to roll with the punches:

- Exercise and sports
- Relaxation: deep breathing, visualization, yoga, music, meditation
- Faith and prayer
- Distraction: TV, movies, video games, other people
- Marijuana and/or alcohol
- Analyze stressors
- Go for a drive

Exercise is a popular option with this group, perhaps because at least half of them are under 35 and more than 80 percent are under 45. But age doesn't deter some who are well into middle age and still work out regularly. Many swim, and those who do manage to find accessible pools nearby. Anne Herman may be in her mid-50's but she's willing to trade an hour of changing clothes in the locker room for the stress relief of 45 minutes of laps in the pool. Coaching and competition helped Ryan McLean turn her personal corner and now she stays in shape and on an even keel by hitting both the pool and gym regularly. Many belong to basketball, football or rugby teams, and a few continue to race. Others lift weights, play tennis or take a handcycle out for a spin.

Some find relief in meditation, yoga, visualization or deep breathing. Most who do have taught themselves, practice at least a couple times a week, and say they like the results. Paralympic athletes Keith Davis and

Curtis Lovejoy have used several of these methods for years, both to keep their racing edge and to manage stress. Fred Fay uses meditation, biofeedback and self-hypnosis to stay relaxed and maintain his go-with-the-flow attitude. Deep breathing keeps Marina Connor balanced both at work and at home.

Don't discount the power of prayer for stress relief, solace and guidance. "Any time I'm down and out, prayer gets me through," says Cathy Green. "It gives me peace and assurance." After his injury, Matthew Seals' faith deepened and strengthened, helping him enormously. "Thank goodness for it," he says. "I can't imagine not having hope in something." Prayer, many say, connects them with something bigger than themselves, giving them comfort and the feeling of support and guidance.

Distraction works too: live music at local pubs for Kevin Williams, theater and films for Susan Douglas, NASCAR with his friends on the big screen for Joel Lorentz. Joe Jeremias gets lost in "some mindlessly violent video game … or a power nap." Glenford Hibbert heads for the beach.

People aren't particular and use whatever works, be it reading, playing with pets, ignoring problems or running away from stress as fast as they can. Some eat, others take warm baths or get facials. A few occasionally rely on the time-honored methods of alcohol and minor illegal substances.

And a few let their problem-solving styles carry over into stress relief, analyzing even their stress levels. Amit Jha reads self-help books and tries to get knowledgeable about the source of his stress. "I always think I can find out what I need from books or on the Internet," he says. "I intellectualize everything."

Recognizing the high costs of stress—frazzled emotions and health problems, for example—this group consciously and actively avoids stress as much as possible and feels that having a plan to deal with it is mandatory. Managing stress, they're convinced, keeps them on an even keel, feeling better physically, more even-tempered and pleasant to be around, less anxious about disability and more open to life's possibilities. ∎

The School of Luck

Feeling down on your luck? Not surprising, given the radical change of spinal cord injury. It's hard to feel lucky while lying in a hospital bed or trying to understand a new body and an expensive piece of hardware. Lady Luck sometimes seems to have taken a powder.

We've all heard stories about unusually lucky people, like the woman in New Jersey who won the lottery twice in four months or people who can't seem to make a wrong move. The result of smiling gods? Some psychic gift? Cosmic coincidence? Who knows? Whatever the reason, many in this book think of themselves as lucky. Many others call themselves blessed.

Richard Wiseman, an English psychologist and researcher, claims luck is a skill people can learn. He says you can actually learn how to be lucky.

Wiseman ran experiments and interviews with over 400 people to find out why some people are frequently lucky while others seem to constantly attract misfortune. He came up with Four Principles of Luck:

- Creating Opportunities
- Thinking Lucky
- Feeling Lucky
- Turning Bad Luck into Good

Wiseman's principles bear a striking resemblance to the steps many in this group have used to rebuild their lives. He just might be on to something. It's clear that they are.

Charmaine G. Brown, *A Royal Flush*

You can't win the lottery without entering. You won't get the job if you don't apply. You'll never find your true love if you don't make yourself available. Wiseman found that most lucky people are active, open and willing to try new things. They meet and get to know a lot of people and then they stay in contact. This helps them create a wide net of potential opportunities and raises the odds that good things will come their way. When those good things happen, they call it luck. Wiseman calls it *creating opportunities*. Sometimes, 90 percent of luck is just showing up.

Because they have a relaxed attitude toward life in general and tend to be flexible in their expectations of how things are supposed to be, they're able to recognize and take advantage when chance opportunities pop into their lives. Lucky people seem to invite unexpected opportunities. It's a matter of numbers. The more people you know, the more things you do, the more places you go, the more activities you try, the more good things can come your way. When Ryan McLean struck up a conversation with a stranger at the gym, it led to a job. When Aric Fine accepted an invitation to try water skiing, it led to a berth on the U.S. Disabled Ski Team and several world records. When Mark Bussinger opened up to Internet dating, it led to a partner.

Ever heard someone say "Well, I just had a hunch and sure enough …"? Ever had a bad feeling about something and backed away at the last minute? Ever not backed away and wished you had? Lucky people, says Wiseman, *think lucky* by listening to their intuition and going with their hunches. They're especially likely to do so with personal relationships and career decisions.

James Lilly and Anne Herman both listened to their intuition, and found life partners. They met them at parties, listened to that inner voice, and followed through. Both couples remain together today. Wiseman adds that you can hone your intuition. He found that many people who call themselves lucky increase their intuition with meditation, concentration and whatever else works to get them in touch with themselves and their inner voices.

Thinking lucky also means expecting good things to happen. Wiseman, echoing Seligman, says that when lucky people have setbacks, they assume their bad luck is temporary and that they'll quickly get past it. In this group, many felt sure they'd learn new skills such as transfers, cathing, driving and bowel management, and then go on to better things. Brian Johnston expected good opportunities to come his way and they usually did. Michael Slaughter expected his skill as an auto mechanic would carry over to computers and it did. Positive expectations gave them the confidence to take risks and pursue bigger goals of college, work or dating, even when the odds seemed steep.

Wiseman's principles hold up well in human interactions. Because lucky people expect that the people they meet will be fun, interesting and exciting, they tend to act more interested and engaged, drawing people to them in the process. Their expectations then become self-fulfilling prophecies. Wiseman calls this *feeling lucky*.

Lucky people maintain positive attitudes and expectations and this gives them an uncanny ability to *turn bad luck into good*. People in this group often say such things as "I've met some great people, including my wife, because of my accident." Others tend to feel their luck could have been much worse, offering statements like "I could live in Africa," "my injury could be much worse," or "I could have had a brain injury and become a different person." Anne Marie Hochhalter had an endless string of negatives in her life. When she grew tired of feeling down on her luck, she stopped dwelling on all that was wrong and addressed problems one by one until her circumstances improved. "Focusing on the positives is what gets me through now," she says. It's the same for Don Dawkins. He gave up constantly focusing on the negatives because, as he puts it, "I didn't survive so I could be miserable."

When Wiseman taught his principles to a group of self-described unlucky subjects, they reported a significant turn of events and an increase in luck. You can't deny the good fortune of those born into riches and supportive families or the ill fortune of those born into poverty and negligent families. But once the race begins, Wiseman says, it's up to you to make your own luck.

Wally Dutcher, a man of many professions, agrees, saying that preparation creates opportunities. He says first you do the research, become knowledgeable and then go for it when the time is right. "You never know when the spaghetti will stick to the wall," he says. ∎

The School of Luck Curriculum

Create Opportunities: Be active, persistent, keep an open mind and show up.

Think Lucky: Find that inner voice and listen to it.

Feel Lucky: Expect good things to happen, expect bad things to improve and remember that Opportunity + Preparation = Luck.

Turn Bad Luck Into Good: Problem-solve bad luck to your advantage, focus on present positives, let go of past negatives.

PROFILES IV

Clockwise from top: Jamie Petersen, Aric Fine, Glenford Hibbert, Vincent Dureau, Charlotte Heppner, Kevin Williams, James Turner, Mark Bussinger, James Lilly, Richard Famiglietti; Middle: Kathy Green, Susan Douglas.

Richard Famiglietti

Richard Famiglietti is cocky, bold, self-assured and quick to smile. He's equally comfortable playing pool at the pub or chess at a bookstore. He's also angry, and he uses his anger well. It's hard to argue with a friend of his who refers to him as a teddy bear inside a gorilla.

Some people might call him a guy with an attitude. Others might see him as relentless, the kind of person who doesn't stop until the job is done and done right. Or as a loyal friend.

How would he describe himself?

"You always know where I'm coming from," he says. "I get very driven and intense when I'm going after what I want."

Richard lives within a stone's throw of I-95 in New Haven, Conn. He's invited me there for dinner, and we both arrive at the same time. After he unloads his chair from the Cartopper of his Taurus, we wheel up his ramp to be greeted by Kaiser, his big German Shepherd. His front door opens into the living room, which houses little more than a pool table and a stairway with a platform lift to get him to the second floor.

Richard reminds me of the blue collar guys I grew up with and worked beside in steel mills and hard rock mines. He says what he thinks and means what he says. He is a bright and passionate man.

We spend most of our time at the dining room table, first with his friend Diana eating the chicken he has grilled, and then talking about the past 17 years.

In 1985 Richard was 20, a tool and die maker. He was on his way home from the gym—feeling like Superman, he says—when he laid his motorcycle down, scraped a guardrail and went airborne. He broke his neck at C5-6 and came out of surgery on a vent and wanting to pull the plug. Instead, he struggled through rehab at Gaylord Hospital in Wallingford, Conn.

"I hated OT because they always wanted me to stack stuff like a freakin' two-year-old," he says. "I couldn't do any of my self-care and didn't think I'd ever do anything. I wore sweats for two years."

Fifteen years later he went to work part time at the New Haven Independent Living Center, and now he's the center's full-time transition coordinator. Much of his job is springing people from nursing homes into the community, and his chief tool for doing that is *Olmstead v L.C.*, a 1999 Supreme Court decision affirming that healthcare must be provided "in the least restrictive environment appropriate to the needs of qualified individuals with disabilities." He works with consumers and helps them lobby legislators at the state capital in Hartford.

All the professional lingo is there as Richard describes how he identifies and educates nursing home residents who want to live in the community and would benefit most from such a move. He often must argue with uncooperative social workers and nursing home administrators, and speaks of these encounters as if he's resolved them all his life rather than only during the past nine months. He is, after all, well motivated.

"I know that with some bad luck I could end up in a nursing home," he says, "and I'm not going to let that happen."

He also builds partnerships with a variety of state agencies and works to catalyze change through legislation. Because of the way his job is funded he can't lobby state representatives directly, so he coaches consumers on how best to advocate for themselves. He speaks with passion and frustration about a state government that eagerly spends tax dollars on a stadium to attract the New England Patriots while it cuts funds for social programs.

"The real change happens in Hartford," he says. "I'd really like to do more legislative stuff and set some precedents. I like to help people and if that means a confrontation or causing trouble, that's OK. There's plenty of that in the nursing homes and at the statehouse. I could get 150 people out of nursing homes this year, but there's not enough affordable housing or accessible transportation. The legislature could change that."

Despite his frustrations, he likes both the job and his work conditions.

"I like that my job acknowledges my disability and accommodates the hassles of all the quad stuff. They give me some leeway and flextime if I need to be late now and then."

As with many working quads, his days are long. He's up by 5:30 every other morning to get his self-care out of the way so he can be out the door for work by 8:45. In the course of a week he also swims once, goes to the gym two or three times and to rugby practice every Saturday.

Bumpy Roads

Richard's present life follows a number of not-so-rosy years filled with potholes, hairpin turns and roadblocks. The potholes were predictable: self-pity, anxiety about the future and over-protective parents.

"For me, being a man means working, being married, having a family and being responsible," he says. "After I got hurt, I didn't see myself doing any of that. Instead, I drank, drugged and chased women I never would have considered when I was walking."

Living with his parents didn't help. His father preached caution to avoid further injury, while his mom, though less protective, liked to keep her house just so.

"It took me two years to get her to put the milk on a shelf I could reach."

Then he hit that hairpin turn.

"I got pretty down on myself and couldn't see things ever getting any better," he remembers. "I said screw it, took a bunch of valium and called some friends to come sit with me."

What he got was a good buzz and 30 days in a psych ward because his friends, instead of holding his hand, called an ambulance. That hospitalization, and the people he saw there, taught him that things could be a lot worse. When he received almost no assistance in managing his disability, he had to do the self-care he hadn't learned in rehab. He left a stronger and more independent person.

"I never want to go back there," he says. "Some of those people were really nuts."

Instead of going back he moved forward, beginning with sports. He raced, helped form a quad rugby team and found a sponsor to support it. Sports got him into good physical condition, gave him focus and put him in contact with other wheelers. He could be as competitive as he needed to be and, more important, he could excel. Schooling seemed like a logical next step.

Voc Rehab paid for tuition and helped with van modifications, and school got him out of the house with something to look forward to every day. As he studied for an associate degree in mechanical engineering, full-time work looked like a realistic goal for the first time since his injury. His aim was never to be a scholar, but he did well enough to assure himself that he was a smart, capable guy.

Those friends who saved Richard's life never left him. Instead, they often dragged him out, and dressed and cathed him if necessary. That reassured him, but he still struggled with being disabled. "I wanted ABs to accept me in a chair, yet I couldn't accept all the guys I played rugby with who all had disabilities. See a problem here? Over time, racing and rugby helped me grow out of that. It took me too long to figure out that I could learn things from them. They always had lots of different ideas about how to do things. Besides, they're the same height as me."

He had another friend, his dog. "He went to school, to practice, everywhere with me. Knowing I had to take care of him was a good responsibility for me."

Making a Difference

He hit the roadblock a dozen years post-injury when he was all dressed up for work but had nowhere to go. That's when his career in participatory democracy began.

"I had all this stuff in place," he says. "The degree, a van, a lift in the house, and then I figure out I can't work without losing Medicaid, and there was no way I could do without it. Today's incentives didn't exist then. When I found out that the Connecticut Women with Disabilities was sponsoring legislation for a Medicaid buy-in that would let me work, I joined their task force and threw myself into it. Eventually it got me my job."

Richard gets very animated when he talks about the legislative work he did and how he went from political novice to skilled activist. He sent e-mails to every legislator in the state, worked tirelessly for the buy-in bill and eventually gained a say in its contents. When his state representative and the governor both signed onto the bill, its passage was assured.

"I lived this for months," he says. "The more I got into it the more I realized I could make a difference."

Why the excitement, the commitment, the dedication?

"I wanted to work! Getting that bill passed was huge, bigger than getting my van. It got me my job."

In the first year the bill was law, 1,000 people with disabilities got jobs in Connecticut. Richard was one of them.

Richard's life has improved in a big way, but he doesn't buy the notion that there might be meaning or purpose in disability or that the chair makes him a better person.

"I'd knock people down to get in the cure line," he says. "This isn't who I am and I don't want to be in this chair, which is maybe why I'm so independent. If someone's angry enough they can use that anger to get by with as little help as possible. Look, I have to accept these circumstances, but I don't have to like them. Work, self-care, shopping, my dog—that's what I have time for. I don't even have time to tie my shoes. I've got Velcro."

He has used the creativity, resourcefulness and problem solving he learned from his machinist days to make the system work for him. "When I saw things like the van happen, I used my anger to stay on Voc Rehab for tuition and other things. People can turn their anger into stubbornness and willfulness so they can get what they need. Sometimes you just do what you have to do and not get caught."

What gets him out of bed every day? He's quick with yet another blue collar answer, telling me it's all about the satisfaction of being productive.

"Work makes me think and keeps me sharp. It builds character. Working every day can be stressful, but I think stress is a necessary part of life. It makes you tough, makes you think, helps you know yourself."

He knows himself and knows who helped him get where he is today. He plans on remembering those people.

"Good people were always around to help me. I don't forget about that. I remember people who give me a hand. I don't forget about my friends." ∎

Jamie Peterson

"At some point you accept the parameters of living with SCI and work them into your life. There are limitations you learn to live with, but this isn't as limiting as you think. The disability's there; you learn to deal with it. Still, I don't settle for much."

So says Jamie Peterson, a 40-year-old Colorado quad who's had an SCI for 18 years. When I tell him that might sound simplistic and rosy to some newbie sitting in rehab, he just shrugs his shoulders.

"Hey, I don't minimize the physical aspects of this, because a lot of it can be really hard. Obviously there are a lot of physical losses, but I don't think I've given up that much. I still get frustrated, but I've learned to pick and choose what I get upset about."

We're at the dining room table of Jamie's mom's home in Colorado Springs, where he lives and works. His office, adjacent to the dining room, is organized chaos. The sofa to the right is piled high with blueprints, sketches, a jar of trail mix and … stuff. The worktable to the left holds his computer and some floor plans he's working on.

Jamie's an architectural draftsman who turns hand-drawn sketches—hardly more than napkin drawings, really—of someone's dream home into finished blueprints that building inspectors approve and contractors build. His is the first step of turning dream into reality. All his work is done on a computer-assisted design program.

"I like doing what I do," he says. "My work involves a lot of creativity and responsibility. It's a challenge to figure all these things out and it's tricky sometimes making everything work and fit into where it's supposed to be. The structural aspects, such as the floor and roof and framing systems, are the most challenging."

Many of these homes are starter castles and mansions—3,000 to 4,000 square-foot semi-custom homes in the $500,000 to $700,000 price range. Some of his plans have

been for homes selling in the low seven figures.

There's irony in his work. He rarely sees, much less tours, what he designs.

"I can't get into 99 percent of them."

Jamie gets most of his work done while you and I are sleeping, usually getting down to business by 8 at night and burning the oil until 4 or 5 in the morning. Then he sacks out until his aide shows up at 8:30 a.m.

"I'm in my office during the day but sometimes I don't get much done," he says. "I usually nap for a couple hours in the late afternoon, eat and then get back down to business. It works for me."

Self-employment allows him both to work at home and maintain this eccentric schedule. Most of his jobs come from one local architectural designer who farms out work to a number of independent draftsmen. The majority of Jamie's work is done at home, but he does attend regular planning meetings and courses upgrading his skills. While he never saw himself in this profession when he was young, his livelihood is not a total surprise.

"I was always involved with construction," he says. "My dad was a bricklayer and I worked with him. Then I did framing and roofing. I always thought I'd be involved in construction somehow but I never thought it would be like this."

Intimations of the Good Life

That carpentry career came to an end in 1985 when Jamie was 21 and breaking in a new motorcycle. He was no stranger to bikes, having raced them for nearly a decade by then, and the fall, one he says he'd taken many times before, was nothing special. Broken neck at C6-7. Several people witnessed the accident and called for help, which got him to a local hospital in less than an hour. The two weeks of care he got there were another matter.

"They didn't seem to be set up to deal with SCI," he says. "I was so drugged up that my stomach stopped working, I was hallucinating and had no idea what was going on. Then the donor-bone site on my hip got infected and burst open. I'm not sure they knew what they were doing and I wasn't very stable when they transferred me to Craig, but at least when I got there I felt like they knew what to do."

The loose, laid-back atmosphere of rehab made a big difference.

"There was laughter and aides walking around in cutoffs and sandals and still a lot of partying going on, not like now. [Craig ended its party-hardy days during the 1980s.] Some guys I met had a nothing's-going-to-stop-me attitude and I started hanging with them. We did what we wanted and didn't care what other people thought. Maybe the biggest influence was meeting and talking to guys coming back for checkups. Some of them were doing alright and looked like they were having good lives. That really opened my eyes and let me see what was possible. I figured I could do that too, and it got me thinking about the future."

And there were the ones who weren't doing so well. "When some of them had a bad day—and everybody does—they'd lose it. That made an impression on me and I thought 'I can't be like that.' I can remember a few bad days in rehab, some of that 'why me?' But you get to where it *is* you and you just have to roll on. This is all about attitude."

When his mind was on motorcycles and carpentry, Jamie never thought he was the college type. Yet a couple of years post-injury and needing to do something, he decided to give it a try and paid for it with a Pell grant, a means-tested federal program for college funding.

"I had never thought about college before and enjoyed it more than I expected," he says. "Most of the classes I had to take were in areas I was familiar with and liked. I did better than I ever did in high school. Actually, the biggest thing college did for me was get me back out into the world and around people. It forced me to get organized and manage my time better. I had to have a schedule and I had to make a commitment to do the work, and that really helped."

He had an associate degree in architectural design and construction technology within four years and, because Colorado does not require draftsmen to have an architectural license to draw building plans, he found a job quickly. More importantly, he discovered a way to make money and not lose his Medicaid and home healthcare funding. That solution came with a little-known Medicaid provision called 1619B, which allows people to work and stay eligible for SSI.

"Before I started working, I called up a counselor at the rehab hospital and asked her how I could keep the attendant care. She told me about 1619B. It lets me work and keep SSI, which means Medicaid. I need attendant care every day, so I can't lose Medicaid. As I understand it, you have to stay under a certain income level, different in every state, to stay eligible. There's a grace period when you first start working that lets you make as much as you can. Then after a while, the income limits kick in. Not too many people know about it. As long as I stay under that limit, I keep Medicaid. "

Doing It His Way

While in rehab, Jamie wanted to learn to get by without daily assistance. Though he wasn't able to reach that level of independence, he's learned that needing and receiving help is not a major issue for him.

"It's just part of life now," he says. "I'm very independent. I'm still calling the shots, in charge of what these folks do and how they do it. I understand that it's a learning process for the aides too, and it all comes together over time. The only time it's an issue for me is if they're late, like yesterday when I had to do a presentation and my aide was late. I had to remind her that my day doesn't begin until she gets here.

"The hardest part is breaking in a new person. I'm still pretty loose and easygoing, but I'm clearer now about my needs and a bit more professional. Because I work and have a schedule, my life is more structured than before. I don't think you can understand all this in rehab; you have to experience it on your own."

He's not sure how this sense of independence came about, and will tell you it evolved over time in small steps that let him build confidence and get comfortable with new situations. After rehab, he was just relieved to be home, and his cautious, think-things-through style kept him from venturing out much. Relying on others to take him places, he took his time adjusting, finding and training personal care attendants and plotting his future. That changed when his parents bought him a van and his insurance paid for the modifications. He was mobile and enrolled in college soon after.

"I understood pretty early that this is all about solving problems," he says, "and I'm a problem solver. There wasn't much I couldn't figure out and find a way to do."

That can-do mentality gets him what he wants, including back into the woods to hunt with his friends. He sits on a small flatbed trailer and uses a chair-mounted table with a rail around it as a gun rest. He's often gone for a couple of days at a time, camping out and hunting deer, coyotes and turkey.

"The gun rest sort of evolved over a few years, by trial and error," he says. "I try to keep things as simple as possible. We're fairly comfortable and don't rough it or anything. It's just great to get away from everything."

I remark that Jamie sometimes makes SCI sound more like an inconvenience than a life-changing injury.

"In some ways that's right," he says. "I've lived with it long enough that it's just part of my life, part of who I am, and it doesn't cross my mind unless there's a problem or a health issue or I decide I want to do something I've never done before.

"I wouldn't pretend to know the best way for everyone, but I know what works for me. I think the most important thing is to stick with it and keep chugging along. You find out what works for you and then do it. I don't know anyone who's living hard and fast by the rules they learned in rehab.

"Sooner or later you have to move forward. Things change and you have to change too. I'm doing so much more than I did early on. I'm working and paying taxes and contributing. I drive up to Denver eight or 10 times a year for Avalanche [NHL] hockey games. I visit family and friends. I work out a bit during the warmer months and I travel occasionally. This isn't as limiting as people think." ∎

Cathy Green

"My husband and I have a pretty normal life. We spend most of our time with each other or with family and friends. We go to church, watch videos and occasionally go out to dinner. Mostly we go through the grind of making a living—just like everyone else."

When Cathy Green says she's like everybody else, she means everybody, not just wheelers. From what I saw, her description is very accurate. When we first spoke on the phone she didn't have much to say in response to questions about SCI and her everyday life. I thought maybe she was quiet, shy or possibly just not very interesting. After spending several hours with her I realized that she gave short shrift to disability-related questions simply because the chair is such a small part of her life. Most of the time she doesn't give it much thought.

We're in Birmingham, Ala. on a bright sunny Sunday in the middle of winter. When I called for directions, Cathy told me I'd never find the place and sent her husband Dale to come get me. She and Dale were married several years after her automobile accident and live in a modest home they recently purchased. Their neighborhood is hilly and wooded. Though only 15 minutes from the city, it's got a quiet, country feel that fits Kathy just fine.

Seventeen years ago, when Cathy was 21 and a junior at Jacksonville State, she drove off an embankment while rushing to work. Luckily someone saw the accident, and called for help. Medical care arrived on the scene quickly. She woke with a T12 injury in a hospital in Gadsden, Ala., where she had surgery and stayed a month. She went to Spain Rehabilitation Center in Birmingham, about 60 miles away, for another month. Spain was a positive experience, and she left having mastered most of what she needed to know to live independently.

Her first few months out of the hospital were difficult. Before injury, though she'd been quiet and somewhat shy, she'd been

active in cheerleading, dance team and several other high school and college activities. Losing that level of physical activity was hard, but support and help from her mom, siblings, friends, neighbors and church congregation helped her get past those early hard times and move forward.

"They were there for me in every way I needed," she remembers. "With all that support, I started thinking about going back to school right away."

When Cathy left Spain her mom took charge of securing all the necessary benefits: Voc Rehab for hand controls and making the family home accessible, Pell grants for school, SSI and Medicaid for support until she began working full time. Cathy found the system was helpful and fairly easy to access, and made it work for her without abusing it. She picked up a few more weeks of rehab at a different facility, got some driving lessons, and was mobile once again.

"Driving was pretty scary, but it was a big step," she says. "I felt independent again. Before that I was pretty isolated."

Where the Jobs Are

Life changed quickly. Injured in March, she was back in the classroom by August. After commuting the 30 minutes from home to campus for a semester, Cathy moved to Jacksonville State and found her own place. Though she says going back to school was initially difficult, the campus was accessible, and getting out with people again helped her gain confidence and confirm that she was still capable. She graduated with a degree in sociology.

"Maybe I was naïve," she says, "but I always thought I'd work, have my own place, get married and have a normal life. I just assumed I'd be OK. That first six months or so out of the hospital were hard; I didn't want people to see me dependent and in a chair. But then I decided wallowing wouldn't accomplish anything. After a while I just stopped caring about being in the chair and got on with my life."

Faith in God has been integral to Cathy's life, her ace in the hole for the day-to-day challenges of paralysis. Though peripherally involved with her church since childhood, she became a committed Christian after her injury. Daily prayer, Sunday services and a midweek prayer meeting are constants in her life.

"Without God, I'm not sure where I'd be today," she says. "I have a one-on-one relationship with Him that tells me I'll be alright. I still get angry or down sometimes and miss how active I used to be, but my faith helps me feel that things will be okay. Prayer gives me peace and reassurance and the strength I need to get through things."

And she had some things to get through. Unable to find work immediately after graduation, she returned to her mom's in Gadsden. Wanting to fill the time people normally devote to work, she volunteered at the local unemployment office.

"That was a good experience," she says. "It was pretty much like a job and gave me a schedule, a routine and some structure. It also got me out and I began meeting people." Why the unemployment office? "It's where the jobs are," she says with a smile. "I knew I would be able to see what was available and get to pick first. That's how I got my job with Alabama Gas. They worked with Voc Rehab and things worked out for me."

She's been with Alabama Gas for 13 years. For the past nine she's worked in customer service, taking 125 to 150 calls a day from people complaining about high bills, poor service and misread meters.

"The colder it gets, the more people call to ask why their bill is so high," she says. "They tell me they didn't use any gas. They compare their bill to their neighbor's and wonder why theirs is so much higher. I have to be very patient; I know they're not angry with me, but it's still very stressful."

The time she spent not working—between college and her first post-injury job—got her down. Working gives her a sense of normalcy, a feeling of fitting in and being just like everyone else. She enjoys her co-workers and likes helping people. Employment, she says, isn't just about staying busy or making money. It does wonders for how she feels about herself.

So does volunteering. In addition to her daily life and work, Cathy and a friend occasionally work with an attorney addressing accessibility in public buildings. She participates in the early inspection and filing work, as well as the affidavit process. And as a mentor at Spain, she offers newly injured people a vision of life after injury and tells them that independence is both possible and mostly between the ears. She tells them what has worked for her—continuing to strive for the things she always wanted in life.

A Good Life

Cathy found more than a job when she volunteered at the unemployment office. She also found her husband Dale. They had attended Jacksonville State at the same time, but had never been formally introduced. When they were, Dale didn't find the chair at all intimidating.

"She's an attractive woman," he says. "I liked her and I never really saw the chair. People thought I was a nice guy for dating her, but I never thought of her as disabled."

Though Cathy doesn't see herself as unusually busy, Dale will tell you she underestimates just how on-the-go she is. Up at 4:30 every morning, she's out the door by 6:15 and on the job by 7. She cooks dinner each night.

"She's more active than most ablebodied people I know," he says. "She works full time, she volunteers at church, she's out a lot and she's very sociable and outgoing. She's very independent. When people say I'm taking care of her, they don't realize how much she takes care of me. I don't think of myself as being married to a woman in a chair. I'm married to my wife."

So who wears the pants in the family?

"We both do," he laughs. "I certainly don't try to boss her around. I feel protective of her sometimes, I'm sure she'd say I'm overprotective. I wanted to put some grab bars in the bathroom but she says she doesn't need them and doesn't like how they look."

Cathy enjoys being married, and values both the companionship and the feeling of being part of a family. She says there are no secrets to mixing marriage and SCI. Just be positive and understanding.

These are friendly, quiet, unassuming people, and they have their quiet satisfactions.

"My life is pretty good," Cathy says. "I really believe I can do whatever I put my mind to, and that attitude has helped me. No one owes us anything; we have to work for what we want. I've always felt that a fulfilling life after injury was very possible and now I have one." ∎

Charmaine G. Brown   *A Royal Flush*

Susan Douglas

Susan Douglas loves her job because her job is helping people. A neurologist at the UCLA Medical Center in Los Angeles for the past 10 years, she's a T8 para who completed medical school, internship and residency on wheels.

Best thing about being a doctor?

"I know this sounds corny," she says, "but having other people trust you really is a privilege. Everyone needs to be needed, and my job gives me that. Helping people is the best part."

Cruising down Wilshire Boulevard in Westwood is pure culture shock. This is a tony corner of the world, filled with limos and high-rises, where almost everything seems new. This fantasyland lets me think I am somebody because people in uniforms are paid to park my car and open my doors. We're not in Kansas anymore.

After passing muster with the guy in the lobby, I make my way to Susan's fifth-floor digs, where she instantly puts me at ease with a welcoming smile. Her apartment, graced with a piano, has an elegant and formal feel, suggesting a professional lives here. That piano isn't just interior decorating; she began lessons when she was four and still plays every day. "I love music, love, love, love it!" she says, her entire face aglow. "It gives me some peace and tranquility. It's nice to have it in my life." Oh yes, she's now taking up the violin.

We camp out at the dining room table for a couple of hours and talk about what her 18 years of SCI have been like. We start with her normal day.

"I don't really have a typical day, except that most of them are pretty non-stop," Susan tells me.

Usually she's out of bed by 7, at work three miles away by 8, and not home again until sometime after 6. Some evenings find her going to movies, dinner, theater and out with friends. Normally in bed by 11, she reads for an hour or so each night.

Susan's medical practice splits her time fairly evenly between clinical work and research. Wearing her clinical hat, she sees patients, most with SCI, in the ER, in their rooms and in her office. The work is physically demanding because it's spread throughout the campus.

Does using a chair make a difference with patients? "Absolutely," she says. "They relate to me differently and assume I've been where they are and understand. That happens immediately. They also know they can't BS me."

Any conflicts with being both an SCI doc and consumer?

"I think we've all had the experience of knowing more about our injuries than our doctors. Like most people, I hate not being listened to."

Susan's academic hat has her doing research in the lab and teaching medical students on their neurological rotations. The lab work requires a commitment to the rigors of science that she finds totally engrossing. Her face lights up as she tells me that the technology, science and brain power necessary to find the cure are all coming together, *now*.

"I love sitting in the lab for two days straight, even if it yields nothing," she says. "My work is more than just looking for positives. I want to figure out how to be done with this," she says, motioning to the chair, "and I think I'll see other people with SCI walk. Neuroscience is very exciting right now."

What she was taught in med school about central nervous system injuries—that the damage is permanent and nerve growth stops—is much different from what she knows today. Her lab work confirms that nerves can regenerate and the spinal cord is plastic, changing over time.

Racism, Ableism, Sexism

Susan was 22 when, after her car skidded off a Washington, D.C. road and down an embankment, she spent 10 hours alone before being found. As a physician's daughter, she immediately understood what had happened. In addition to her broken back, injuries to her spleen, lungs and ribs left her in intense pain. She wasn't sure she would survive.

She spent a month in acute care having rods installed and internal organs repaired. After transferring to a rehab facility in Waterville, Iowa to be closer to her family, she got conflicting messages from therapists and doctors about what her future held. While some told her that returning to medical school was out of the question, others assured her she'd be totally independent. Finding the attitude of 'our way is the only way' far too rigid and discouraging, she left within a month and rehabbed on her own.

She was back in Washington at Georgetown University medical school within 10 months. She was hardly welcomed with open arms, but instead quickly met disability prejudice, racism and—as one of few women in a male-dominated, conservative Jesuit institution—sexism. Dealing with those headaches, she says, took as much energy as her classes.

The daughter of an African-American father and a white mother, Susan was familiar with Midwestern, small-town racism but was totally unprepared for the big-city version. Discrimination plus accessibility and housing issues made for a stressful re-entry.

Despite the hassles, she says getting lost in learning was a welcome distraction from the early uncertainties of disability. Knowing where she was going to be and what she was going to do for the next several years was comforting. As many people in this book have found, structure can be helpful.

"Having lots of day-to-day decisions made for me was useful," she says. "School extends childhood for years, and I had an automatic social group. I love to learn and I didn't need to use anything but my mind. It was great."

Regaining a social life was pretty easy; she began dating within months of returning to school and never gave fitting in all that much thought. Any secret?

"I plaster that smile on my face like we all do and try to make people comfortable."

What about getting around all the hospital equipment and keeping up with the fast pace of training rotations? Wheels plus the normal stress of medical training sounded tough to me.

"My first rotation was neurology," Susan says. "The department head was supportive and it was easy for me to bond with the patients, so that was a good start. Then in surgery the injury was sort of gone because the nurses pushed me around the operating table in my standing chair. I always assumed that medical school and becoming a doctor would happen," she adds. "I just didn't anticipate how difficult it would be."

Susan was a trailblazer for others at Georgetown University: the year she left, the school admitted a para as a first-year medical student. She left feeling that both she and the school had learned and grown.

A Clear Choice

She moved on to Los Angeles to do her residency at UCLA, and once there, filled an obligation she felt to other wheelers by starting a support group. People came out of the woodwork. Though helping others as a doctor was what she had in mind, she says the group helped her as well.

"As wheelers, we all share the same daily struggles and victories, regardless of our occupation or apparent level of success. Having them validated by people who are in the same boat, fighting the same fight helps. Just because I've had some success doesn't mean I don't get sad or forget about what I've lost. Being in a chair is hard. I didn't need this to be a better person and it's OK for me to say that I don't like being paralyzed. "

For a long time, she tells me, she was uncomfortable with the inspiration label that followed her around like a panting dog wherever she went. "It's like you're a hero for getting on with your life," she says. Now she appreciates the opportunity to give back through example and to answer questions from newbies about how she got from there to here. To her, the chair presents a clear choice: "Be pissed off or grow." She thinks that SCI helped her become more compassionate, modest and persevering, but she adds some qualifications.

"I mean it when I say I *hate* this. But I know I won't get far with a frown and a scowl, so I have to find the positives in order to make life more powerful." That viewpoint, she says, has given her personal and professional victories much more depth and meaning. "I've met some pretty amazing people and I've grown in unanticipated ways."

One of those ways has been a stronger belief in herself. The strength that comes from coping with SCI, she says, has helped her in other areas of her life, including her biggest struggle.

Which is? Her answer offers perspective.

"Being biracial."

Susan's one of those people who always needs more action. She serves on the board of directors of the National Spinal Cord Injury Association and reviews research grant applications for PVA's Spinal Cord Research Foundation. Then there are all those *de rigueur* work and professional functions to attend and it's still not enough. With little left to achieve in her first profession, she's now adding law school.

After spending years watching wheelers struggle with such arcane provisions as the Medicare Homebound Rule and other regulations that serve only as barriers to independence, she now wants to shake up insurance companies and the federal government. In fact, she wants to fight barriers wherever she finds them.

"I'm crazy," she says. "I can't believe I'm doing this. I want to learn insurance law and change some things. Part of the problem I see is that unless people have totally devastating injuries, play the game and be helpless victims, they don't get the equipment, care and help they need. Facing all that, I can't blame anyone who wants to just blend into the woodwork."

Advice? Regrets?

Listen to your body and what it's telling you. Learn the signs when something's wrong. And speaking for herself as well as others, she suggests that independence may be overrated.

"I may have overcompensated early by trying to prove I could do so much. Now I'm paying for it with pain and some overuse issues. I'm much more willing to accept help now.

"And remember to let people in. You can't get support if you don't let people in.

■

Glenford Hibbert

Glenford Hibbert's hard not to like. A big man with a booming laugh, a seductive Jamaican accent and a nonstop smile, he radiates a childlike, wide-eyed sense of wonder and surprise at just how good life can be. He's proud of his successful business and grateful for the free time, income and comfortable lifestyle it provides. He's proud of his kids, his apartment loaded with high-end electronics, his shiny new SUV, and his numerous female "associates" who accompany him to dinner and clubs.

"I will tell you the truth," he says. "I didn't think I was capable of any of this when I got hurt but I found out I could be. I didn't think people in wheelchairs could be happy but I'm very happy."

His story—one of those "against all odds" epics—is the kind local news channels love to feature. Sixteen years ago, Glendford was a 21 year old visiting America for the first time and attending a reggae concert in south central L.A. when he was hit by a ricochet from a nearby gunshot. The T9 injury ended his budding career as a chef, and left him broke and unemployed.

Though married to a U.S. citizen, he was an illegal. As such, he was unable to work and ineligible for any government benefits. His third world image of disability—helplessness, isolation and embarrassment—left him depressed and hopeless.

Not any more. Now he works out of his Marina Del Rey townhome making house calls to repair big-screen TVs. That might seem an unlikely career for a wheeler, but for the past seven years Glenford's been out there doing just that.

"Big screens—45 inches and up—that's where the money is at," he says. "This is a good living; I've always liked technical work and there's not much overhead doing housecalls. I'm out in the field most every day with one of my employees, going into people's houses and apartments and doing our work. People are always surprised and very polite when I get out of my chair and down on the floor to start working. They don't expect it."

Business is good enough that he has four people working for him. Up at about 8 each morning to shower, he's making and taking phone calls by 9. Then he's off making house calls with one of his employees. Because as often as not he's done with work by 1 p.m., he'll then head for the beach for some quality time. On weekends he's either checking out yard sales, where he buys things to turn over at his own sales, or he's out to clubs, concerts and dinner, living the proverbial life of wine, women and song.

A Quest for Who He Was

"Once a man, twice a child," Glenford says with a laugh. "I had to learn to crawl all over again." But he also remembers that it wasn't very funny to him at the time. Following a month of acute care and a fusion surgery, he rehabbed for six weeks in Glendale, Calif. Once discharged, he hid from the world.

"I was always having bowel accidents and when they happened I would take out my anger and frustration on my wife," he recalls. "Even though she was working I expected her to cook and take care of me and wait on me. I expected her to do everything. We fought a lot; she was a very large woman and sometimes we would get physical.

"I was mean to people and stayed at home a lot, afraid to go out. I didn't want to tell people I'd been shot because I was afraid they'd think I was a bad guy. I couldn't find work because of being here illegally. It was all very hard and took time to get over. In Jamaica there is much more judgment and embarrassment about being disabled."

Things slowly began to come together for Glenford and after six or eight months out of the hospital, he filed for and gained legal status, which helped him secure assistance from Voc Rehab.

"I was motivated, well dressed and made a good impression. They wanted to help me. Besides, I was a minority."

His road back began with an eight-month course in electronics at trade school, followed by a couple of years assembling printed circuit boards. Separated from his wife by now, he found a subsidized housing apartment and eventually went to college.

"When I first went to school and then to work," he says, "I was around people much more, which was good for me. Later, the people I worked with became my family. The job helped because I was good at it and doing a good job made me feel good. I was part of society and felt like I was going forward and getting on with my life. But still, it was so very scary when my wife left because there is no medication for a broken heart. Time was the magic that helped me heal."

And time also helped him regain some of his own magic, especially once he began feeling more comfortable with people, especially women.

"I kept getting out and meeting people," he says. "I started playing basketball and ping-pong. When I went to Santa Monica College I became president of the table tennis club there. All the exercise of the sports and going out was good for my health. When I started having fun I was able to gain some confidence and feel better. Now I know who I am.

"After I got my associate's degree in electronics and got promoted, I was able to move from Inglewood to the Marina. Things got much better then, because it was safer and I didn't have to watch my back so much. Then, when I became a citizen, the doors really opened up for me."

One door was gaining the financial ability to bring his son Adric and daughter Tanisha to this country and help them become citizens. Doing so, he says, is the best thing he's done since being injured. His son, now 21, lives with him and his 19-year-old daughter is about to be married.

"Getting them to this country was very hard and complicated. It's very difficult for many ablebodied people from Jamaica to do this, so I'm very proud that I did it. My kids motivated me and gave me a purpose. I needed to set an example for them. I'm proud that they look up to me and that I'm still able to help them."

Another door was television repair. When he began his business and it quickly

took off, he was able to help his kids financially. He was also able to buy the toys most men want.

About the same time he gained citizenship, Glenford discovered yet another door in the form of independent living movement. Spending time with a group of people, all of whom were disabled in different ways, had a huge impact on him and changed the way he saw certain things.

"Lots of people in the movement were very successful," he says. "Some of them were doctors and lawyers. They were all disabled. When I saw their accomplishments and how capable they all were, I thought, 'If they can do this, so can I.' We were very active in fighting for in-home health services and got thrown in jail a few times for protesting. I helped form independent living centers in Compton and Watts and was on the board of directors of them."

The Big Things in Life

From illegal immigrant to citizen, entrepreneur and political activist is quite a jump. From deep depression to happiness and optimism is, perhaps, an even bigger one. How did he do it?

"I will tell you the truth," he says, now getting quite serious. "It's not easy dealing with all the barriers and having people stare at you everywhere. It's not easy to make yourself go out and meet other people. But those are the things I had to do. First I had to meet and get to know others in chairs. Then I had to learn from them."

That formula—forcing yourself to go out to meet people and getting to know other wheelers—is a popular and effective one for many others in this book.

After a couple of hours with Glenford, I find it hard to imagine him without that smile or being unhappy or not wanting to be around people.

"I am the mentor now," he says, "and people learn from me and from my mistakes. I tell them how relying on my wife destroyed my marriage. I tell them that I could have been independent much sooner. I tell them a good life is not easy but very possible.

"So much of independence is in your head. You get it by going out, doing things, having a good attitude. Everyone needs some help, but it's bad to become too dependent on others and ask for help when you don't need it."

Divorce, education, working and dating, while certainly more challenging on wheels, are things all people, disabled and non-disabled alike, deal with. Glenford's talking about the stuff of life. When I share my observation with him, he smiles widely.

"I never thought of it like that, but that's the world I live in. Most people I deal with are walking and I want the same things they want. I want a house. I want more money and more success. I always want the best. The things that I want, the big things in my life, are not about the chair."

In retrospect, does he think his success was inevitable?

"Maybe this is easier for people who have always had difficult lives," he says. "Things have never been easy for me, but don't get me wrong, I still whine sometimes. Yet I know it's much easier here than in other parts of the world. It's easy for us to get spoiled in this country."

Note: Shortly before publication Glenford passed away in his sleep of an apparent heart attack. He had been in good health and his death was unrelated to SCI. ∎

Kevin Williams

When an occupational therapist told Kevin Williams that law school didn't seem very practical, he gave her a typical Kevin Williams response.

"Well, then you shouldn't go."

Don't tell him no. Don't cross him, either. He might nail you the way he nailed the mayor of Denver. When hizzoner commandeered an entire accessible parking lot at a music festival for "security purposes," Williams quickly had a consent decree enforced that ordered the city to pay a $500-a-space fine. It totaled $37,000, and he did it as fast as you can say ADA. When this dog bites, he doesn't let go.

Kevin, at 37, has made his mark on the disability law scene. He is the legal program director of the Colorado Cross Disability Coalition (CCDC), a grassroots non-profit disability rights organization that has grown in clout with Kevin's help. He has filed suits to enforce the ADA and other civil rights laws for people with disabilities ever since his student days at the University of Denver Law School, where his suit against the university resulted in many access improvements on that campus.

Acting for CCDC, he has sued Taco Bell, Wendy's, Toys R Us, a national movie theater chain, the Rapid Transit System, a shopping mall and two professional sports venues, all for better access. His practice includes air transport, education, housing and Voc Rehab issues, and has made Denver an easier place for people with disabilities to live.

"I'm surprised by how gratifying my job is," he says, "especially given all the cons of the profession—sleazy defense lawyers, hacks, long hours, the demand and necessity for precision, the bad reputation of the profession. I like being a lawyer. We change things. We're successful. It's more than just a job for me."

Kevin's schedule suggests the same. He puts in 55- to 60-hour work weeks, and carries a large caseload. The long hours may be at his suburban condo or at CCDC's office in Denver, and they're a result of both that satisfaction he speaks of and the need to generate enough money to fund CCDC's legal program. His aide shows up 5 a.m., and two hours later he's buried in research, intakes, motions, administrative work and phone calls until 6 or 7 in the evening. He crashes at about 10. During a recent trial, he worked 11-hour days for three weeks straight. For him, the workload is anything but a recipe for medical disaster.

"Actually, I've had fewer health problems since I began working than I ever had before," he says. "My biggest challenge is finding balance and making time for fun. It can't be all about work."

He finds that balance relaxing with friends in bars or at home, or satisfying his eclectic taste in music, theater and cultural events. Today he's at home taking a few hours out of what would normally be a working weekend to talk to me. After years of subsidized housing, he got ahead enough to buy this place, a modest one-bedroom with a large bathroom.

His desk is loaded with work and his computer beeps with an incoming e-mail every few minutes. Law- and disability-related books such as *No Pity, Make Them Go Away* and the civil rights compilation *Eyes on the Prize* line the bookshelves. A poster of Thurgood Marshall hangs on the wall, as does a gift from his father, a sign reading "Ask Me About My Bowel Movements."

Forty-Seven Steps

In 1986 Kevin broke his neck. He was 19 and a sophomore at the University of South Carolina when he dove off a floating dock and woke up in a hospital with a C5-6 injury. He was moved to a generic rehab facility about 100 miles away, in Greenville where his dad and stepmother lived, but he spent as much time in a general hospital fighting infections, fevers and blood clots as he did in the rehab facility hanging out with stroke patients and listening to elevator music. Once he was medically stable, he transferred to Craig Hospital. Life improved, but slowly.

"I had a pretty limited view of what was possible and was pretty pissed and depressed about being a quad, but I don't think I spent five minutes thinking about walking," he says. "That was several lifetimes ago and it's hard to remember all that. I was very sick at first and my main concern in rehab was where I was going to live after I was discharged."

Where he lived was Greenville. The only people he knew were his dad and step-mother, and the only time he got out of their house was to go to the rehab center.

"That first year was hard because nothing was in my control," he recalls. "I was living in someone else's house in Greenville and didn't know a soul there. I'd grown up in Ohio and I'd only lived in South Carolina a couple of months before I got hurt, so I had no long-term friends at school either. I was very alone, had no plans and my concerns were very basic, like how to turn a page or get a glass of water. I'd get up in the morning and then nothing would happen all day. I lived like that for well over a year. My dad and stepmother were great, but I needed a life.

"I was terribly depressed and I don't really know what got me moving. All I remember is being afraid that life was going to be meaningless forever. Finally I got to the point that I had to do something so my plan became going back to school. There was no single moment or turning point. Getting from my dad's house to living on my own was about 47 different steps."

Some of those steps: Getting Voc Rehab and academic scholarships to cover tuition. Qualifying for SSI and Medicaid to cover basic living expenses and healthcare. Finding an accessible room on campus. Those were huge steps, he says, and taught him he didn't need someone around 24/7. Good things began to happen and he lived on his own for a year until he ran into skin problems and needed surgery.

"I went back to Denver for surgery. I knew the medical care was better there, and with lots of time on my hands, I looked around at colleges and apartments," Kevin says. "When I saw that the accessibility and the home healthcare services were better too, I decided to move out there. That might have been a little gutsy, but I saw it as making my life easier and it wasn't like I was leaving anything all that great in South Carolina."

More Steps

It took a year and another 47 steps—the same ones he'd taken in South Carolina plus a few new ones—to move to Denver and find a roommate. Three years later, he had a BA and was in law school. He began volunteering at CCDC, then founded the legal program and became its director when he passed the bar in 1997.

"My education just sort of happened," he says. "I never planned it. I knew I needed a degree, so I kept going to classes until I had one. I knew I needed a job that would be flexible and pay well, so I went to law school, but never thought much about what I'd do when I was finished. If I'd known all that was involved in becoming a lawyer, I'm not sure I would have done it."

Has spending half his life with a disability made Kevin see the world differently? Dumb question.

"Look, we know shit most of the world will never know, and because of that we can cope with most anything," he says. "People assume we're needy, but we're actually the most resourceful people in the world. If you can get reliable home healthcare or make the system work for you, you can do anything."

Making the system work, he says, starts out as a full-time job for many. First people have to figure out what they want and need, then identify and understand the programs that can get them there, and then do the self-advocacy and maintenance work necessary to get the benefits and keep them.

"The world isn't set up for people with disabilities," he says. "Without Medicaid, people are going to die. Without SSI and other government programs, we simply won't survive. Most of us may require that type of assistance, but only a few of us are freeloaders. The fact is, I pick and choose what I use, and I'm using less than I need."

The primary program Kevin continues to use is SSI's 1619B provision, which allows him to make decent money and keep his Medicaid health insurance coverage. The program is little publicized by SSI, and therefore little known. It's complicated, yet essential to people who require expensive in-home care and want to work.

"Without this program, I'd have to make about $200,000 a year to cover my healthcare needs. The program pays for home health, meds, equipment and supplies. Most insurance won't cover all that.

"Problem solving has helped," he adds. "I had to figure out everything I needed and wanted, no different than if I was ablebodied. People with disabilities have to be assertive, have to make the phone calls, use the Internet, ask the questions and cover their butts. One way to learn to do that is by connecting with the disability community."

Attitude, he says, also helped him.

"A sense of humor and perspective. You have to be able to laugh, and you have to laugh at yourself. You have to be able to step back from disability, because it's so easy to let it be the center of your life, even though it doesn't have to be. When I'm at a concert it's me being there with a disability, not a disabled person there. At work I'm a lawyer first, then someone with a disability. I can't let my life be about disability, and I'm not about to let the world prohibit me or others from living fully because of disability."

What about independence?

"Independence is about making the decisions, it's about control. My attendant Anna comes every day to help me, but I'm in charge."

Advice?

"Anything I say will sound lofty and no one will buy it, but I think this is all about making choices. It's easier to be happy than sad, and there are things we can do, factors in our control, so we can avoid sadness. Life is worth living and so many things are still possible. The platitudes are true.

"The biggest thing I've learned in 18 years as a quad is that life with disability isn't abnormal or unusual. You do what you always did." ■

James Lilly

James Lilly is a family man. Each morning he gets his seven-year-old son Jimmy up and started on breakfast, then wakes up and dresses two-year-old Christian. The three of them head out together to walk Jimmy to his suburban Chicago school. James then heads back home to feed Christian. At about 2:30 p.m. he picks Jimmy up, supervises homework and playtime and cooks dinner. Evenings are for family time with his partner Nora and the boys.

"Being a dad is very important," he says. "It's number one."

After meeting me at the gate of the fence he built to enclose his yard, James takes me around to the back door and into the family room, avoiding the steps leading into his two-story house. A pair of incredibly light, handbuilt racing chairs sit in the corner, both bare metal with little attention paid to appearance. Trophies and plaques are everywhere—the mantle, the shelves, the walls. Most of the living area of the house is upstairs. No Stair Glide, no elevator. He humps up and down the stairs on his butt. "I like my privacy," he says, smiling.

Welcome to the life of James Lilly, public speaker and wheelchair racer.

He might be a private guy, but James doesn't mind a bit of the public eye that comes with racing and speaking. He does five to ten marathons each year, all over the country, and occasionally takes the family along for a vacation. Several years ago, when a friend asked him to share his story of going from gang life to racing, he began a part-time speaking career and now does several presentations a week to students in schools throughout the Chicago area. At his busiest, toward the end of the school year, he's doing two school assemblies a day.

While James makes a good living, coordinating care for the boys is a constant challenge and balancing act. With Nora working full time—"triple time" James calls it—they take advantage of before and after school programs for Jimmy and rely on Nora's mother to watch Christian. It's a dilemma they share with millions of other families.

This is a far cry from 20 years ago. Back in 1984 he was 15, brainwashed and living what he thought was an exciting life when he became an incomplete L2 para in a gang-related shooting. When his friends glamorized his injury as a martyrdom, he did what it took not to lose them and continued to bang. Following the example of others in his neighborhood who'd been shot and paralyzed, he relied on fellow gang members to take care of him. His parents couldn't get through to him and eventually his dad kicked him out. He lived from house to house for a couple of years, until he went through what he calls "a sobering Monday."

"I'd gone to a lot of funerals and as we were sitting reminiscing about our dead friends I realized just how many of them were gone," he says. "I knew that if I kept banging I'd either be hiding, locked up or dead." He didn't want that, but letting go was hard. "I'd been with the gang so long and knew so much, I had to take a pretty good beating before I was able to get out."

Classroom in the Bus

James's "mature life" began when he realized how much trouble, pain and heartache he'd caused his mom, how many tears she'd shed over those first five years. Now he wanted to make her proud. But with no high school diploma, little experience and still looking like a gang member, he couldn't find a job.

"No one would hire me," he says. "I had the feeling I was doing job interviews just so I could be told no." He supported himself by selling roses on Michigan Avenue in downtown Chicago, often crawling up and down the stairs to the train to get there. His road back started with a GED, earned while he was still on the streets.

"Then I bumped into a guy I knew who was visiting here from Texas and I decided on the spur of the moment to go back there with him. I went out for a haircut and ended up living in Dallas for a summer."

While in Texas, he got interested in wheelchair sports, gave junior college a try, and paid for it with help from Voc Rehab, SSI and a job at the school maintaining physical fitness equipment. When Todd Hattfield, a coach from Southern Illinois University, invited him to take a look at his program, James went to Carbondale for a semester and then on to junior college. Eventually he played basketball and raced for the University of Illinois in Champagne, looking to qualify for the Barcelona Games in 1992. Though he didn't make that team, he did make it to the '93 International Games. His days of marathoning had begun and continue to be a primary focus. While traveling the racing circuit in college, his classroom for SCI was the back of the bus.

"I think everyone should have to go on a bus trip with 20 guys in chairs before getting discharged from rehab," James says. "That was my education. Most of what I learned came from those guys, you name it—sex, driving, cathing, jobs, public transport-tation—all from the bus. I learned from these other guys what they did, how they did it, how they succeeded. That's where I got serious about school, where I learned about Voc Rehab. Some of them had been drug dealers or gang members. I figured that if they could do it, so could I."

It was about this time, at a college party in Champagne, that James met his partner Nora. They've been together ever since.

"I was getting ready to leave, but when I saw her I knew I had to stay," he recalls. "Now she's more a part of my life than I am. She's the backbone of our family. If I didn't have Nora and the boys, I'm not sure where I'd be."

Several years ago, when James found the 26.2 miles of a marathon an insufficient challenge, he entered the world's longest wheelchair road race, 367 miles from Fairbanks to Anchorage. After finishing third once and second three times, he won it all in 2002. He trains several hours each day, either on the road or on rollers in his family room while watching his boys, complementing the roadwork with weight training.

"I want them to see what I have to do to earn those trophies," he says. "Now Jimmy's

running races. He watches me, then I watch him. He just won a 5K. I told him I wasn't sure he could finish and he goes and wins. That was better for me than winning Alaska. We motivate each other."

Just Do It

In his school presentations James shares his story of both gang life and sports, and uses his early years of banging as an example of what not to do. He tells them that the loss of his youth is the terrible price he paid. He speaks of what it took for him to accomplish his goals in college and racing. Public speaking, he says, is a good news/bad news deal. The upside is having the necessary time to train and be with his boys; the downside is meeting the challenge of saying the same thing day after day without getting bored.

"If I can touch a handful of kids at each assembly who begin to think 'I don't ever want to go through all that,' then I'm doing good. I get letters from kids telling me that what I said changed and helped them, and sometimes they make me cry. Those letters remind me of why I need to keep doing what I'm doing." And the money helps, he says. "Public speaking is a good living."

He works with two local injury prevention programs, as well as with the National Spinal Cord Injury Association giving school presentations about brain and spinal cord injuries.

A recent rough spot, during which his mother-in-law nearly died, gave James major cause for reflection.

"We had to cancel everything and put our lives on hold for a couple weeks," he says. "Sitting in the ICU gave me a lot of time to think about all the people who've been good to me. I thought about my boys. I thought about how I wanted my mom to be proud of me, how I wanted to make her smile and not be sad about what I'd done. I thought about how much I owe the people at Eagle who stood by me and gave me chairs even though I never won a major marathon."

That sense of perspective and gratitude is central to his approach to life with a disability. It's something like a Nike commercial: "This is the way things are," he says, motioning to the chair. "You just gotta move on. I've got two boys and bills to pay. It's life and it's got to be done."

Don't mistake this just-do-it attitude for a lack of sophistication. This is a pragmatic man who seeks out logical solutions to life's problems, whatever they might be. Priding himself on his handyman skills and remodeling jobs, he tells me how he's painted and drywalled a room or two, building ramps and scaffolding so he could work clear up to the ceiling. He's particularly proud of that fence he installed himself. While some of the pride comes from his competitive nature and a need to prove things to himself, a lot is just common sense to him.

He's not afraid to ask for help when he needs it, he says, but he finds doing so illogical if the price is wearing out the goodwill of family and friends. "Why would I pay someone to tie my shoes if I can tie them myself? The fence and the remodeling aren't any different. If I keep asking for help with things I can do myself, I'll chase people away. That's not stubbornness, that's life. And it's something that I feel and that I've learned."

All the talk and hope for a cure troubles him because he feels it leads to too much false hope and encourages people to sit around waiting to walk rather than getting out and living life.

"We should be teaching people the skills necessary for independence, showing them what opportunities exist. We should be teaching acceptance, quality of life," he preaches, "not telling them to wait for the cure. The same night I got shot, a friend of mine died in a shooting. I haven't heard from him yet and until I do and he tells me everything is cool, I'll wait."

James admits to still having what he calls his "pity moments." And he'll tell you that being a crip and dealing with UTIs and involuntaries are still hassles. He'll also tell you that the life he has created is worth those hassles.

"I'm not in any rush to check out. I've experienced and enjoyed and laughed so much in these past 20 years. You've got to smile and relax because life is about looking forward.

"People tell me 'If I couldn't have sex, I'd kill myself; if I couldn't feel, well, that would be it.' There's so much more to life than just that. I still get down and the chair gets old. But my family, the boys, my mom, they all motivate me and keep me going. When I think about all of them, well then the other stuff isn't so important." ∎

Aric Fine

By anyone's measure, Aric Fine is a successful guy. At 33 he's got a good paying job that he likes as a systems engineer for Bell South. He's married with two good-looking children. He lives in an upscale home, complete with a swimming pool, in a quiet neighborhood of Marietta, Ga., and he's got a cabin on a nearby lake. He holds world records in water skiing. This is a lot for anyone, but Aric disclaims any extraordinary accomplishment.

"Hey, I'm your common schmoe," he says. "I live a pretty good life and the chair occasionally enters into it. Am I an overachiever? Well, I pick and choose areas where I might overachieve. Am I exceptional? By no means."

In the summer of 1983, when Aric was 14, he was swimming in a river with friends. He dove in and felt his arms touch the bottom, but didn't think much of it. The next time he dove he hit bottom and broke his back. Care arrived quickly and surgery in Tuscaloosa, Ala., followed the same day. And talk of bummers: Although his injury was at T4-5, the fusion surgery was done at C4-5. The mistake wasn't discovered until he got to Spain Rehabilitation Center in Birmingham. He went to the Baylor College of Medicine in Houston for the proper surgery and rods, then back to Spain for rehab.

"I think being hurt at 14 worked in my favor," Aric says. "I grew up in a chair and did all the normal teenage stuff. I went back to school immediately and was with the football team, only now on the sidelines. I really didn't know what I was missing then and I still don't feel very limited now."

If the past 20 years or so are any indication, he's not limited at all. After graduating on time with his high school class he went to the University of Alabama, where he earned his degree in four years.

Aric enjoyed college. The campus was very accessible and, when necessary, classes were moved to accommodate his needs. The only accessible rooms on campus were in a freshmen women's dorm, insuring that his friends would visit often. His dorm had a workout room and many of his fellow disabled classmates would use an abandoned second-floor cafeteria to play football. "All of us had some kind of disability," he says. "Both teams shared a quarterback, a legally blind guy with only peripheral vision. We had a good time."

Perhaps because his injury precluded playing varsity sports, Aric stayed focused on his schoolwork. He felt he was in college to learn and liked going to class. It was a good experience from start to finish.

Firings and Hirings

As we talk it becomes apparent that the chair isn't a large part of Aric's life. It's just how he gets around. At work, he uses a conventional office chair as much as his Quickie. When he goes out to lunch with co-workers, they toss his chair in the back of his SUV. About once a month they all pile out and head into a restaurant, forgetting the chair and leaving him behind.

"They're back two minutes later, all apologetic and embarrassed," he says. "I think it's the ultimate compliment that they forget about the chair. We all want to be known for ourselves."

What I sensed in phone conversations crystallized when I met him. People see Aric and not the chair. Because he's so engaging, enthusiastic and friendly, people gravitate to him.

While in college he worked at the campus television station as a director and cameraman, doing productions for the long distance learning program. Then he went to a local cable company and interned at a commercial television station. After college he landed a job as a talent coordinator for a Cosby/Warner game show but it tanked within six months and the résumés went out again. He was heavily recruited by an Atlanta television station to produce and direct a local program.

"I essentially got hired over the phone," he recalls. "When I went in to meet the guy and when he saw I was in a chair, he told me the producer/director position had been filled and offered me a different position with less responsibility. I didn't realize until later that I didn't get the job because I was in a chair and I got quite angry. That was the first time the chair was ever an issue, and I realized then that I wouldn't be able to change people's attitudes without showing them the real me."

He worked as the media coordinator for a year at the Shepherd Center, in Atlanta, doing in-house productions and closed circuit programming. From there it was on to an internship with the Atlanta Paralympics, first doing press releases for the athletes and, eventually, for all the Paralympics telecommunications systems.

Aric's boss at the Paralympics was an on-loan Bell South executive, who later helped him get his present job as a network sales engineer with the company. Aric works with Internet service providers, designing their networks of phone and Internet communications, and travels with the sales team about once a month. He likes the job and, no, the chair has never got in the way. After the sales team does the pitch, Aric explains to the clients how everything will work.

"I'm the tech guy," he says, "and I basically say the same thing as the sales execs. The only difference is that the clients believe me because I say it all in technical terms. I'm the geek. I just don't wear a pocket protector."

When I point out the absence of big, thick glasses, he smiles: "Lasik surgery."

The Best Offer of All

While Aric worked at the Paralympics, a fellow employee offered to take him water skiing. He'd never heard of disabled water skiing and thought that perhaps he'd get pulled around the lake on a door.

"The first time out I had perma-grin," he says. "I literally could not stop smiling. I loved it and immediately did some clinics at Shepherd. I took the ski home so I could practice getting it on and off. My instructor was a quad."

Two years later he bought a boat. By 1997, he was an alternate to the U.S. disabled water skiing team, and when one of the 14 team members went down, Aric stepped up and won silver. Two years later he set a world jump record in England, flying 72 feet and exceeding the old record by 10 feet.

In the 2001 Worlds he won gold in jump, silver in trick skiing and silver overall. A year later at the Nationals, he took gold in jump and trick, silver in slalom and gold overall.

When I call him a stud he laughs. "My goal is to win all four. When I do that you can call me a stud."

Aric wears that perma-grin as he talks about skiing. He thought about giving up competing after his son was born in 1999, but got the family into skiing instead. He's taught his wife Kim and this summer will teach his son Braxton, 3, and daughter Aleah, 6. They belong to a local ski club and are on the lake every weekend. In the summer he skis three or four times a week.

"It's a relaxing, family outlet," he says. "We do lots of social stuff with the club. Skiing is fun and something to excel at, but my life is my wife and kids, not skiing."

Aric and Kim have known each other since high school, where they began hanging out together and eventually moved on to dating. In order to work on her RN degree, Kim enrolled in a community college in Tuscaloosa, where the University of Alabama is located, so she and Aric could continue to date. They've been married for 12 years.

When he and his family went to his family reunion last spring, he visited with many of his relatives who hadn't seen him in the 19 years since he was injured. They gushed over him having a wife and family, a very good job and even over simply being out and about. This puzzles him.

"I thought, 'Should I not be doing well?' I feel fine, I just have a spinal cord injury. People often seem amazed with my life, but it's really not much different than theirs. We all make choices; at 14 mine was to not sit around at home but to be productive and wear out my tires instead of my shoes."

So what's productive?

"It means doing something good, volunteering, working toward a goal. We get our self-worth from being productive. It doesn't have to mean employment. Being productive is how we grow to love and accept ourselves."

And how can a newbie do that?

"All the platitudes are true. Life does go on. There is something out there for you. The chair is simply a mode of transportation. There's so much pride in accomplishment, and usually we don't realize what we can accomplish until we try. You have to try new things and show yourself what you can accomplish. You need to try having *fun*. Everyone has so much to offer, not only to others, but to themselves. You need to offer *yourself* opportunities."

Update: We can't call him a stud. In the latest world competitions in Orlando, Aric hit the trifecta of gold, silver and bronze, along with a team gold.

"I'm not ready to retire. I feel I've still got some in me and I'm looking forward to the games in Europe in two years. The family still enjoys coming out to watch, so we'll pack them all up and go. And we got the kids both on knee boards this past summer, so they'll be skiing soon. It's all good." ∎

Charlotte Heppner

If she didn't have an answering machine, I'm not sure anyone would be able to reach Charlotte Heppner. Ever.

The first time I called she was out water skiing. A week later she was parasailing. We rescheduled again because she was riding the roller coaster at Cedar Point, then the Cleveland Browns got in the way. When I called for an update, just prior to publication, she was dancing in New York City. This is a busy woman who, at 51, does twice as much as most people half her age. Spend just a little time with her and you'll see that the chair doesn't interfere much with her life. The negatives, she'll tell you, simply consume too much energy.

"This is just a different way of living," she says. "I'm the same as before, just sitting down. I think you're successful when you're able to change your lifestyle to accommodate wheels."

When she was 32, Charlotte was diagnosed with a tumor on her spine. Surgery removed the tumor, which was benign, and she walked out of the hospital. But she had a great deal of pain and over time, as more and more scar tissue formed, the pain just kept getting worse. Repeated surgeries to remove scar tissue took their toll, eventually leaving her with the equivalent of an incomplete T12 injury.

"I knew going into each surgery what might happen, so this wasn't really a surprise," she says. "When I came out of surgery I was grateful to be alive. I'm really thankful to my surgeon, because he's always been so honest and supportive. He's never talked down to me. He's even come to watch me race."

Though she was able to walk some with braces and crutches, she lost most other function including bowel and bladder control. After a few years, when crutches became too much of a hassle, she began using the chair full time. She says life on wheels is much easier, more convenient and in many ways quite liberating compared to the struggle of walking with all the hardware.

While she found the transition to disability pretty easy, those around her struggled. Her fiancé left. A close friend broke down and went away until Charlotte drew him back.

"But my family was great and carted me around a lot until I began driving. They really helped the first year," she says. Volunteering and sports also helped. "I was never really depressed. I'm having a great time now."

Doing It All

Charlotte and her partner John, who's also a wheeler, have been together for 12 years now. He sells durable medical equipment and they met when she went shopping for her first wheelchair.

"They have a code they would use on the public address system at the store," she says. "'Code One walking in' meant someone good-looking enough to check out, which John did. When I ran into him at a couple of races about a year later, I finally asked him out. He tells people that I came over one day and never left. It was John who got me into a lot of the sports stuff. I was never all that athletic before."

But she has always been adventurous. Years ago she lived in a commune and later ran a head shop. Prior to injury she helped to spring vets from the VA hospital. A big lover of speed, she raced cars. That go-for-it attitude remained intact and along with John's enthusiasm, drove her to sports.

She did her first 10K on crutches before beginning to compete in the chair and then graduating to marathons. In addition to being fun, racing occasionally rewards her financially.

"Not that many women enter races like the Revco Marathon," she says, "so I usually do pretty well. Men might beat me, but I win the money."

Besides racing, she likes water and snow skiing. The first time she saw someone parasailing, she knew she had to try that too. When the founder of *Dancing Wheels,* a professional dance troupe of disabled and ablebodied performers in Cleveland, spotted her at a race, he asked her to join the company. "I never thought I could feel graceful, but after dancing for a while I found that I could. It's done wonders for my body. I love performing and traveling with the company. Dancing at the Atlanta Paralympics was amazing." In the coming year, she'll accompany the troupe in its travels from Nevada to South Carolina.

Charlotte volunteers at Cleveland's MetroHealth rehab facility, where she speaks with SCI newbies, sharing knowledge and answering questions. Lately, she's taken to bringing Wild Wiener, one of her dogs, along as a way of connecting with patients. About once a week she's with Youth Challenge, a program serving kids with disabilities, either swimming or playing tennis in the summer, or skiing in the winter. She likes working one on one with the kids and teaching them independence. I suspect she's so good at it because she's still a kid herself. She even makes wheelchairs look fun. When we met in October the spokes of her chair were laced with ghosts and goblins for

Halloween; at Christmas time she says it's lights and Santas.

"I enjoy being a role model," she says "It feels really good when I hear one of the kids say 'I want to be like Charlotte.'"

When repeated surgeries prevented her from going back to her job as a lot foreman for Budget Rent-a-Car, Charlotte began collecting SSDI and doing the volunteer work. Then, in the early '90s, she jumped at her local vet's offer of a part-time job. An animal lover, she found the clinic a perfect fit and is now there three days a week.

"Doc's been great to me," she says. "He pays me a salary that keeps me under the Social Security ceiling and sometimes helps out in other ways. Once he paid for my glasses, another time for car repairs. Those things really help because $850 a month and Social Security is pretty meager."

How can she afford world class amusement parks, parasailing and season tickets to Browns games on $850 a month and SSDI?

"I prioritize. The parasailing was a gift. Most of the skiing is with various programs. I set aside $20 or $30 a month for football. If these things are important, there are always ways to do them."

Trial and Error
Over the years Charlotte's chronic pain has increased. She speaks of doing transfers with tears in her eyes, not from sadness but from burning pain throughout her torso and legs, a pain which also interrupts her sleep. Yet she continues to plow through the pain with simple distraction or sheer force of will, refusing to let it interfere because life is too much fun. A couple of years ago, she went to a morphine pump. While it helps a lot, its placement in her body makes racing next to impossible.

As we talk about health and pain, I ask about her experiences with the medical profession. She's learned to deal with them, she says, but still finds them a chore at times.

"I've had some bad experiences with doctors," she says. "There's a lot of condescension and they seem to talk over your head a lot. Not many of them know much about pain and few understand or appreciate the experience. When I see them for pain, sometimes I feel like they think I'm looking for drugs. One guy, when I tried to ask him some specific questions, told me to not interrupt him."

Charlotte and John live on the first floor of a two-story house; her mom lives upstairs. This house has what may be the world's steepest ramp, climbing well over three feet in less than twenty. She cruises up, grasps the handrails and pulls herself up. I get about halfway before needing some help from her brother, who lives across the street. The front porch at the top of the ramp is littered with equipment—a racing chair, a snow ski, a water ski and more—and looks like a used sports shop for gimps.

Inside, her place has the feel of an old hippie haven. Like the front porch, it's crowded and cluttered with, well, stuff. Halloween decorations are up here too, and I suspect there are decorations adorning the place year-round. We're greeted by three big barking dogs and a few cats. Most of the pets were abused orphans adopted from the animal clinic where she works. She just can't say no. Next to the kitchen is an alcove housing a desk and computer, and a wall filled with photos of Charlotte with friends, family or John. Lots of smiling faces reflecting lots of good times.

Even after 20 years, Charlotte says she's still learning new things every day and still finding that each day has new challenges. Simple solutions like bungee cords or coat hangers help the most, she says. Her bathroom and shower are doorless to make getting in and out easier. She walks the dogs two at a time by fastening their leashes to her footrests.

"This is all about trial and error and being willing to try new things," she says. "I analyze problems; I'm not afraid to ask for help. You learn how to be optimistic and look forward to the future. If I was still working 40 hours a week I couldn't do the sports or the dancing. When people say 'But I'm afraid.' I have to ask them, 'What else can happen?' This may open doors; you might find other possibilities. You may *not* fail." ∎

Dancing Wheels; Photo by Al Fuchs

Vincent Dureau

"Disability is now part of who I am, woven into the fabric of my life. I've had to integrate it into my life without denying it and except for the occasional reminder, like falling out of my chair, I don't think about it."

How long has that taken?

"No more than 22 years."

Vincent Dureau, 44, is a C6 quad, the result of a diving accident in his native France. As the chief technology officer for Open TV, a digital interactive pay television service, he travels worldwide to meet customers and consult with engineers. His company provides Internet access, as well as digital video recording capacity through a set-top box. If you subscribe to Dish Network, you've got his technology.

His job is to tell engineers what to build, deal with the FCC, oversee the company's patent strategy and sell his products. That keeps him on the road 50 percent of the time, but even after accumulating more than a million frequent flier miles during the past decade, he still enjoys the traveling and confesses an addiction to flying.

Most crips I know would find that much travel an exhausting invitation to loneliness and health problems. Vincent finds it relaxing.

"I don't cook the food or fly the plane," he says very matter-of-factly. "I just read a book or do work. Traveling alone is a great opportunity to meet people."

His schedule suggests something a bit more demanding than the usual pleasures of travel. His recent and pending itinerary:

"Two weeks ago I was on the East Coast, then off to France, Germany and Switzerland. After a week at home and in the office [in Palo Alto, Calif.], I came here to Denver for a few days of back-to-back meetings. I fly to Paris for the weekend and then to Brussels to speak to the European Parliament. That," he says with a smile, "will be fun." Working in his Silicon Valley office, he tells me, is far more stressful than traveling the world.

Vincent does have free time occasionally, and spends it reading, visiting museums, training in his racing chair, seeing friends or with his family in France. And there's his home and garden.

"I especially love my garden," he says with a wistful smile. "There are redwoods, maples and birches and paths running through them. There's also a very large pool for goldfish. I created and designed it so that I could be outside and enjoy it during the rainy season, which is half the year in the Bay Area."

The Enduring Force of Gravity

Twenty-two years ago, rehabbing in France, Vincent's life and expectations were different.

"I assumed SCI would completely change everything, including the laws of gravity and relativity," he says. "The first time I purchased something after injury I was surprised when my money still had the same value."

Just as gravity stuck around, so did other pleasures of life. He figured out how to hold a pen, for example, and again began drawing what he calls snapshots of his life.

"When things happen to me, I draw about them. I don't explain them. I just put them on the walls for others, like Post-Its." And he puts faith in being methodical. "I took on being a quad as a project, a series of skills to be learned. Eventually the skills became integrated into my life."

Once clear of rehab and in an apartment, he resumed swimming, replaced long distance running with wheeling from one end of Paris to the other and competed in races around Europe. He returned to school, and that was a turning point for him.

"I was mostly done with my M.S. degree in agronomy when I had my accident," he says. "I wrote the thesis in the rehab center and then decided I needed to move to an industry that would offer more opportunities to someone with SCI. College helped me reconnect with who I was before. It was a very positive environment."

Needing work he could do from a chair, he studied computers then took a job designing them for a Paris firm. In 1986, when he had to choose between accepting a transfer or looking for a new job, he made a major move. Culture shock came in the form of Iowa.

"I spent the first six months in a Sheraton Hotel in Des Moines, devoting nearly all my time to working. I had little opportunity to meet people, I didn't know what a mall was and I was very lonely."

From the City of Light to farm country and from farm country to the City of Angels. After seven years in L.A., he moved to the Bay Area and helped launch Open TV.

Phantom Hurdles

Even after a couple of hours on the phone and five hours of conversation with Vincent, I'm still asking myself, "Who is this guy?" Always thinking, always examining, always evaluating, he seems to take nothing lightly and everything at least somewhat seriously. His mind seems to be always working. In a science fiction film, he might be one of those aliens with a disproportionately large head to accommodate a brain on steroids. He's a smart, successful, athletic guy who made the transition from walking to wheelchair look easy.

He's got it all, right? Didn't he once have the nagging fears we all had and some still have? You bet.

"I worried that the chair would become the center of my life, a black hole that would swallow everything," he says. "Discovering that I could still give to others saved me. Being able to give meant that I wasn't entitled to be the center of the universe and that SCI didn't have to be a tragedy anymore."

Fear of that black hole is the engine that drove Vincent early on and gave him the resolve to get out of bed each day rather than waste away and give up. It's a battle he wages still.

"I'm very attached to my routines," he admits. "I don't think or make decisions about them because if I did, I'm afraid I might bargain with myself and not get up. Staying in bed all day would not be a good choice for me."

When he speaks of himself, it's usually in a critical tone, telling me how his company could be bigger, or how he could have done things faster and sooner, or that he could and should be doing better now.

"I wasted a lot of time jumping hurdles that did not exist. I regret taking so long to wear jeans and laced shoes or go to a movie or a store or travel alone. I wish I had been more open to learning how to do the practical self-care chores or outdoor things. I didn't know where to focus my energy. I may have liked the drama of rehab and injury too much."

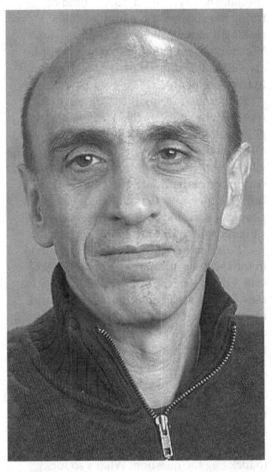

His fear of being defined by a wheelchair stuck with him until recently. He avoided the disability community because he didn't want to be part of a "disability ghetto." He regrets that he put off joining the peer support program at Santa Clara Valley Medical Center until about five years ago. Once there he found many people who had learned as much as he, but done it much faster.

As Vincent sees it, disability presents us with the dilemma of wanting to fit into the mainstream but yet being different. Communicating to others that we're just like them, only on wheels, allows us to connect with them, but the rub, the paradox, comes when people see us as special because we're living normal lives. In living those normal yet special lives, we risk isolation.

"Talking about living with disability is admitting that there's something to talk about, and that makes being disabled special," he says. "It's a double bind of trying to capture the banality of life or making a movie where nothing happens. Yet the chair may matter to others. People are vulnerable and we need to take care not to frighten them."

Rather than seeing the chair as a repellent, he suggests that it offers him the potential for a different kind of social interaction. When he puts out the right vibes, people come to him because they're curious or perhaps intrigued and wish to help. He then uses that knowledge to put people at ease and control whatever social situations he finds himself in.

"I used to be terrified of traveling alone in the third world," he says, "but it's all so safe. I'm no longer afraid of people because most people are good rather than evil and more disposed to show us their good side. I don't know why I worried so much about getting on a bus or finding a place to stay. I'm no longer afraid to go anywhere in the world."

Pure Luck

Vincent speaks a lot about his good fortune. Eventually his repeated references to luck beg the question: What's so lucky about a broken neck?

"Nothing," he says. "SCI really sucks. But my career was luck, a case of being in the right place at the right time. My injury was luck, in that it's low enough for me to be independent. I was very fit and healthy when I was injured and went to the best rehab center in France. I'm living in the U.S. That's all luck."

Is founding a 450-employee global company luck as well? No, but he credits that more to being a talker than a doer.

"I'm good at knowing where my company should go, but less so at actually getting it there. Other people do most of the work. I'm very lucky because I only have to do the things I love to do."

And what has he learned over the last 22 years?

"I think we all have a fairly universal sense of panic in the beginning. Most people have to move at their own pace and it's hard to speed things up in rehab and afterwards. Everyone needs to find their own path to reconstruction, in whatever form it takes, but at the least we should be able to point people in the right direction and suggest things they can do to get where they need to be.

"At the end of the day, life is a risk and shit happens. We're not invulnerable. Some things are inevitably stronger than we are and can defeat us. Right now I'm strong enough to deal with what I have but I don't see myself as a supercrip or doing anything exceptional. I'm not sure I could deal with a higher level of injury.

"Because we all feel very entitled to love, happiness and a walking life, we feel cheated if we don't get those things or if our only life is not a walking one. The challenge is to let go of feeling entitled to walking. That's not easy." He offers a wry analogy: "If we all felt entitled to immortality, then everyone would feel disabled." ∎

Mark Bussinger

When I asked Mark Bussinger the secret to his success, he just smiled.

"I've been active. I took charge of my life. I know a lot of people and I try to help them. I have a positive attitude and try not to let the whims of fate dictate what happens to me. It's not about disability."

So you're telling me that being a quad in a power chair doesn't matter much?

"If it does I've been in denial for 23 years."

Mark is not your average quad and certainly not your average real estate agent. He rarely goes into the houses he shows, but waits out front while his clients go in for a look-see. He's not lazy or crazy; he just can't get into most of the homes he shows.

How do you sell a house you can't get into?

"When I was starting out I had clients drag me into the houses," he says. "Now I have an assistant to take them through. My clients don't need me looking over their shoulders telling them what's right for them. I wait outside and only go into the homes they want to buy."

Why real estate?

"I always wanted to be an entrepreneur. It pays well and I can set my own hours. When the president of my real estate school said she thought I could only do either property management or commercial real estate and then when everyone else I talked to told me I couldn't do residential because 99 percent of it is inaccessible, I knew I had to try it. I had this naïve optimism, some call it denial. I've been able to use the obvious negatives to my advantage."

He has spent the past 15 years working primarily for himself as a buyer's representative, a sub-specialty of real estate he and several other agents pioneered together in Denver. He sees himself as a consultant who protects his clients in a business deal, and does whatever it takes to help them buy the house they want. If his customers believe he's competent and confident, he says, the chair doesn't matter.

"At first I'd lie awake at night anticipating that initial interview, trying to visualize everything that could happen and any questions that might come up. I know how uncomfortable people often are with my chair, so it's always on my mind. I've learned how they react in various social situations so I look for ways to defuse the tension by being attentive and taking the lead. Sometimes I'll tell a joke, other times I'll ask for help."

He's usually up by 6 each morning to greet his aide, who helps him out of bed and through his 30- to 90-minute self-care routine. After an hour or so of coffee on the deck next to his backyard pond and garden, he returns e-mails and does paperwork before leaving for the office. Home by 6, he usually makes his way to bed by 9.

Over the years, finding reliable attendant care has been his toughest challenge, and it's one that never ends. He responded by purchasing a home in his neighborhood, which he rents at a much reduced rate to his primary care attendant. That might seem an extreme measure, he says, but it's a surefire way to ensure loyalty.

Even so, he says, it's a still chore finding and keeping attendants. "I'm always looking and I always try to have a backup."

Off the job, he has his hobbies—theater, gardening, political activism and his remote-controlled sailboat. Occasionally he suffers through negotiating a deal over drinks at a local pub. And there's that 6,000 gallon backyard pond with its several dozen meal-sized fish. He doesn't have many idle hours.

Over the years he's volunteered with several community organizations including Denver Community Television (a local public access station of which he's currently the board chair), the United Way, the State Board of Social Worker Examiners and a city committee on economic development. The result of all this service is a huge network of influential friends.

"Sometimes I delude myself into thinking I can make a difference," he says. "Even in a city the size of Denver, only a few people run the whole joint and they all know each other. If you get to know them, you can create opportunities and good things will happen for you."

Mobility, Anticipation, Homework

In 1979, Mark broke his neck diving into a river in Michigan. C6 fracture, acute care and fusion surgery in Grand Rapids, 90 miles away. A couple of months of touch and go, struggling to stay alive. First he developed pneumonia, then a staph infection from the bone graft. When he went into convulsions and cardiac arrest, he snapped the fusion. Further complications put him on a vent and unable to speak for nearly four months. Then his jaw locked up from biting on a suction tube and he had to use a feeding tube. All the while his goals were simple—to stay alive and finagle an extra shot of demerol each day.

Dissatisfied with his care, his mom fought to get him released and transferred to better rehabilitation, even though he was medically unstable. He was admitted to Craig when he was still too sick for rehab and spent his first couple of weeks in Denver just gaining strength. Although he was injured in May, he didn't begin rehab until Thanksgiving. It was well into 1980

before he headed back to his mom and dad's home in Michigan. He was 20.

"Living at home again was hard," he remembers. "My mom was very protective. She knew I needed my independence, but my safety was her first concern. She was so worried at times that she didn't want to leave me alone in the house. She was being a mom. It was hard on her when I left, and we fought some before I moved out, but now we can laugh about it. I just couldn't live in that cocoon forever."

He got free by finding financial help to buy a modified van and getting strong enough to drive. Mobile again, he found a place of his own in nearby Saginaw and attended a community college. He majored in drinking too much and chasing women.

"I worried about how they would react to someone with a severe disability, but it wasn't the obstacle I thought it would be."

So the chair's a babe magnet?

"Well, I wouldn't recommend it as a way to pick up women. There's no substitute for getting laid but I'd prefer a different magnet."

Women might not have been a problem, but old friends were. He says he spent way too much time and energy detraumatizing buddies who knew him before his injury, so he decided it was time for a fresh start where people didn't know him.

"I'd rehabbed in Denver and liked the weather, the friendly people and the accessibility," he says. "I packed my bags and moved there."

As fresh starts go, it was shaky. He had Section 8 housing arranged, but the attendant care he'd lined up fell though just days before he planned on heading out. He moved anyway. Even though he didn't know anyone in Denver, he quickly found an attendant through an independent living center.

He pulled it off because he'd learned what to do: take the initiative, do his homework on government assistance programs, avoid all the built-in pit-falls, anticipate problems and find help doing what he couldn't do himself.

"You have to learn the system because it won't reach out to you," he says. "It may not let you hit the ground, but it has a way of capturing you and making you dependent and it's always looking to trip you up. The system makes disability an economic situation rather than a physical condition, so once I started working and making decent money, I was no longer considered disabled."

A few months after arriving in Denver Mark enrolled in a downtown college and got involved with civic organizations. He lived on SSDI and paid for school with low-income loans and Pell grants. After earning his B.A., he went after a master's, but halfway through the program decided to get into real estate. Once he was sure the business was going to work, in the spring of '88, he left school to sell houses.

Persistence Beats Fate

Mark rarely speaks of problems. For him they're "challenges." Is that just semantics?

"Not totally," he says. "Words reflect how we see the world. When I see problems as challenges it helps me stay more positive. When things go bad, whether it's SCI, relationships or business deals, you can't let circumstances dictate your attitude. You have to move on. We're disabled, but we're still people first. We still have to pay bills, we still need to work, we still want love and relationships. I like that W. Mitchell line, 'It's not what happens to you, it's what you do about it.'

"We can influence a lot of what happens in life. Instead of saying 'Fate will find me love,' I'd rather increase the odds by actively looking for women, and I look for them everywhere. I find them where they're at— school, work, hospitals, the Internet. I once got a date with the operator when I called information; you have to talk pretty fast to do that. I once met a woman, who I lived with for a time, in an elevator. I met my partner Jennifer on match.com and we're very happy. I've found love, but it wasn't fate. It was persistence."

Needing help every day to get out of bed and dressed has a way of keeping you sharp and focused, he tells me. He's learned to meet his challenges, get things done and to read people well. He's amazingly good at finding affordable people and teaching them to help him with *anything*.

Home maintenance and remodeling? Maintenance on his rental properties? The pond and gardens throughout his yard? He finds people to do them all, and he's always in charge. "I ask if they know how to do something, like dry walling, then I ask them if they want a job. If I have to, I'll teach them and train them to do what I need done."

Any wisdom for newbies?

"It's a mistake to think the future will be like things are now. You've got to give this a couple years. You can still have a good life."

Any purpose to all this?

"I'm still learning. Maybe I needed the challenge; maybe I needed to become more empathetic. Maybe I needed this to become a better person, but I don't think I need to be a saint."

What about regrets or missed opportunities?

"Did I refinance my house at the right time?" ∎

James Turner

"My life, everything I've done, is my greatest accomplishment. I played basketball in college, got an education, talked to kids about disability. I've been a leader and met people all over the country. I got married and I love my wife. I've got my relationships with people at church. I like my job. Every day is something new. It's all good, even the failures."

So says James Turner, 46, as we sit in the dining room of his suburban Denver home. When I first met James I found him smart, honest, funny and insightful, so when I began this project a few years later, I knew he should be part of it.

Injured in a 1979 car accident that left him with a C5-6 injury, he has lived in Denver since 1990 and worked for the U.S. Department of Agriculture almost as long. As a grants manager for USDA's Nutrition Services, James disburses and monitors more than $26 million worth of grants for school lunches, emergency food assistance, Meals on Wheels, and programs for women, infants and children in a 10-state region. He also assists in the oversight of billions in food stamps.

"I like the people I work with and I like the job," he says. "We're supplying food to the country, to the homeless, to those who need it. That's a good feeling."

That good feeling comes at the price of a long and demanding day which has him up at 4 a.m., out the door two hours later to catch a bus and at his desk by 7:15. After work, he works out at the office gym and is home by 7, in bed a few hours later. "I usually turn the TV off around midnight. When I'm tired, my body shuts down."

Twenty-five years ago, when James was attending Northwestern State University of Louisiana, he drifted off the road while driving, over-corrected, spun out into a ditch and broke his neck. He had two months of acute care and nearly six months at the Louisiana Rehabilitation Institute in New Orleans. He was 21.

"I had all kinds of support and encouragement from family and friends while I was in rehab," he says. "So much so that I started to believe it. I was scared, but I had the dream of a job, marriage, a house and independence and knew I could have them somehow. A guy I knew in a chair had done okay for himself and I figured if Cotton could do it, so could I. I knew I couldn't sit on the front porch with my grandfather or hang out with my friend Peanut for the rest of my life. And I didn't want to appear to be a quitter in the eyes of my younger brother Mark, who's been a big motivation to me."

Once discharged from rehab and back in Leesville, where he lived at the time of the accident and stayed while waiting to return to school, he became known as either Mister Do-It-For-Yourself or Mister Won't-Let-Nobody-Help-You, mostly he says, because he was just doing what it took to get independent. Within three months he'd regained enough strength to get through his days without assistance.

"To this day I don't like people pushing me or walking behind me," he says. "Eventually I got to letting people help some so they could feel good. I had to crack a lot of handicap jokes to get people to lighten up."

Professional Student

There were only a few accessible dorm rooms in small colleges back then, so James sat out 1980 at home with his mom, figuring things out. "I was making the adjustment and getting by," he says. "There wasn't a lot I wanted to do just then so I was just kind of waiting for school and enjoying the time off. I hit the bars, smoked a little weed, went to movies and hung out with my friend Peanut, Marvell Bowman."

When an accessible dorm room opened up at Louisiana Tech a year later, he transferred there. "School was harder than being at home," he says. "I didn't know what people thought of me and had to get used to them staring. I was still learning my body and having to pay attention to it. Working out and keeping all the handicap gadgets to a minimum helped me feel the same as before."

Things really began to come together when he took charge of reactivating the school's chapter of a social fraternity, Kappa Alpha Psi, which encourages community service, friendship and mutual support in the pursuit of personal excellence. Eager for a sense of purpose and to be needed, he wanted to serve as a responsible role model and example of a good Kappa man.

For a while the chair shook his confidence with women, and even though he'd gone to school on a basketball scholarship and been something of a lady's man, for a time he became more interested in friendships than romance. "But once I felt women were interested and accepting of me, I started trusting myself enough to want to have some intimacy and a girlfriend. I was afraid of rejection at first, but by the end of that second year I was willing to take the heartache to get some lovin'."

Life was good and James became a professional student, first earning a degree in psychology and then an M.A. in human relations before taking out some loans to pay for additional work in public administration at nearby Grambling State.

"I was on my own," he says. "I cooked, I cleaned, I did it all. I was back. I was all grown up and that's when I knew I'd be OK."

In 1990 he was awarded an internship in Denver with the National Conference of State Legislatures, an organization that does research for the country's state legislative offices. When USDA's offer came a year later, he took the job and stayed in Colorado.

People in small-town Louisiana had found his chair something of a novelty. Things were different in urban environs.

"I don't think people noticed me as much in the city and maybe they weren't as friendly," he says. "But there were curbcuts everywhere and I was rolling on sidewalks instead of the streets. I checked out bus routes and started asking people in my apartment complex where to go for fun. I got out and explored a lot. I began to network."

He connected with the local alumni chapter of his fraternity, and with his brothers began doing community service work by awarding scholarships, stipends and computers to students, and making food available to the needy at holiday times. "It's about camaraderie, networking and supporting each other in everything: jobs, family and personal life. We meet monthly."

While on his way to one of those meetings James met his wife Ramanda.

"I was wheeling down the sidewalk," he recalls. "She said I looked tired and offered me a ride. We talked, I gave her my number and a week or so later she came to visit me. We've been visiting ever since."

A Serious Clown

James and Ramanda have been married for eight years now and moved into their present home, a comfortable four-bedroom house with a big backyard for Bear the dog, a couple of years back.

Though James is a happy camper who clearly enjoys life, he still raised my eyebrows when he said he only spends about 15 minutes a year being depressed.

Charmaine G. Brown, *A Royal Flush*

"After 24 years in a chair I know disappointments aren't going to kill me and that I can get through anything. I don't like not being happy, so I let things roll off me. I've been blessed with my wife, a great church family, a nice home, good friends, an education and a job. I enjoy life and think I'm here to help others enjoy theirs," he says. "I like to make people smile. It lets me know I'm alright."

It's no accident that he uses the word "blessed." He's an associate minister in his Baptist church, the result of what he feels is a divine calling.

"God has helped me get through a lot of things since I was injured and I'm convinced He has a plan for me. The ministry is part of my personal relationship with Him. Still, it's been quite an adjustment from a life of partying and I'm still learning."

Connecting with people has always been easy for James. "I like people," he says. "I try to be a good friend and a good person. People have always been good to me and I'm not gonna fight 'em when they are. If people slap my hand when I extend it, I'll give them the benefit of the doubt and put it out again and try to learn what to look out for. If they don't respond, I figure they don't know what they're missing."

Getting to his current state of contentment has had its trials. Both his body and his grades took a beating from partying while trying to fit in at college. The difference with James is that he sees when he's headed the wrong direction, and when he is, he's smart enough to do something about it.

"I may not be the sharpest pencil in the box," he says, "but I'm *in* the box. When Voc Rehab told me to get my grades up, I recognized the problem and fixed it."

Ten years later some innocent experimentation led to a two-year love affair with crack cocaine. "It went from 'smoke a little weed,' to 'sprinkle some of this on,' to 'here, try the pipe.' After a while it wasn't about fun, just about getting high. I had so much to lose—marriage, job, house, people counting on me—and I did it anyway. It's insatiable. That part of my life wasn't good, not good at all, but getting through it was very uplifting."

Why share such a dark experience?

"I'm an optimist. I believe people are basically good and that life is good. How can someone knowing that damage me? If it will help someone else get past it, why not?"

That's the essence of this man. He seizes and enjoys life rather than being intimidated by it. While so many of us spend time worrying about what might go wrong, he searches for what goes right and then proceeds to celebrate it. He walks the talk of Christianity in both his thoughts and actions. It's a lesson and a gift.

And his optimism is strong enough to survive negative events. A few years ago, after he noticed a significant loss of strength, an MRI revealed a disc pressuring his cord.

Surgery relieved the pressure but he lost about a third of his muscle strength and some function. Yet, he doesn't see this loss as overwhelming, despite the high value he places on fitness, function and appearance.

"I'm just as mobile and independent as before, so there's no horror story there." As he says, it's all good, even the failures.

Has nearly 25 years on wheels taught him anything?

"Now you're asking for another hour," he laughs. "The chair was the start of a new life for me. When I was in rehab, I didn't know how I was going to get here, but I knew I could. I just kept pushing forward and always felt in charge. Life has been pretty normal and very rewarding, despite this so-called tragedy.

"I don't have any horror stories and I don't think I'm any worse for the wear. In fact, I enjoy the wear and the stress and the bad parts of life. I like pushing three blocks through the snow to the bus stop because when I'm there, then I'm going through the same stuff as everyone else. And because I'm a happy person, I like making people smile. If I'm not the class clown, I'm probably his assistant."

But behind this happy-go-lucky, sometimes pollyannish attitude is a very serious man.

"I'm serious about everything—work, church, my marriage, paying my bills—but what I'm most serious about is enjoying life and enjoying where I am right now. Helping others enjoy life lets me know I'm alright." ∎

Charmaine G. Brown *A Royal Flush*

CHAPTER FIVE
Salvations, Turning Points and More

Who doesn't want that pill or that surgery that will make all this go away, or that coping skill that will at least make things easier and get you back on track? Any magic bullets here? Judging from what this group says, probably not.

Q: Was there any one thing that was your "salvation" or key to your success?

- Support of family and friends
- Sports
- Faith in God
- College
- Belief in self
- Role models and peers
- Driving

The simple answer is that there is no simple answer. The wide range of responses to this question would suggest just the opposite. People struggled to put their fingers on any one thing that helped them put their lives back together. They couldn't point to any one way to do it. Salvations, if they exist at all, are as different as the people looking for them.

Support from family and friends is what worked most often and best for this group, often by providing encouragement, help in taking them places, lending assistance with securing benefits or finding attendant care, and often providing some of that personal care themselves.

Many in this group say anything that got them out of the house and interacting with other people helped. It didn't seem to matter whether it was sports, college, driving or meeting other wheelers or peers. What mattered was getting out and doing. Going to college or being part of a sports team lifted them emotionally and kept them active physically; for some, doing well in college was both gratifying and a surprise.

Many liked that they could control how involved they got in either sports or college. Some tested the water by taking a course at a local community college, some went full time to an out-of-town university, and others tried something in between. Sports gave many the options of dabbling or jumping right in in a big way. Being in charge of how involved they got was reassuring and they knew if it felt like too much, they could always back off.

A substantial number leaned on their strong faith in God and said it was the single biggest factor that helped them move forward and do well during rehab and after. Knowing God would help them get through hard times gave them trust and confidence in the future.

A few found that the best medicine was returning to whatever they did before, and doing so as quickly as possible. Amit Jha, Susan Douglas and Cathy Green wasted no time getting back to school. Steve Ferguson got back to leading his drum corps again as soon as he could get his power chair onto a football field. Joel Lorentz calls returning to work his salvation and a morale booster, helping him do a complete turnaround.

"Now I'm independent and away from the folks," he says. I own a home and am doing something worthwhile."

Because that first year or so is so hard, people use whatever's available, often something they can get totally absorbed in, to get them through. That not-so-magic bullet can be anything that puts a focus on competence, demonstrates accomplishment or pushes disability in the background for a time. Going back to work let Phillip Mann feel like he was one of the guys. Rugby gave George Taborsky an opportunity to excel and meet new people. Advocating for changes in legislation told Richard

Famiglietti he could make a difference. Activities such as these allowed people to realize they were still capable and whole, could still make contributions and do worthwhile things. Becoming active and involved helped them recognize that physical loss doesn't preclude skill and accomplishment. The magic bullet is everywhere. It's whatever works.

Q: Was there a turning point for you when you began to feel things were going to get better?

If there's no magic bullet, you say, is there at least a point where things start to feel better and the future begins to hold some promise? Well, probably not. Most people told me that turning the corner felt more like a series of baby steps around a huge bend. They said slow and steady wins the race. Here's what they said helped along the way.

- There was no single event but rather a series of events
- I was always confident and my progress was fairly straightforward
- Going to college
- Living on my own
- Sports
- Physical improvement
- Learning from successful peers
- Getting my first job
- A specific event: end of relationship, a conversation or decision.

People started feeling better about the future slowly and in a lot of different ways. They identified many small turning points, and gained confidence from each.

Getting from his dad's house to living on his own was "forty-seven different steps" for Kevin Williams, and those steps ranged from turning pages in a book or getting a drink of water to figuring out home healthcare and benefit programs. Things didn't happen overnight for Brian Johnston, either. "I began doing things—making a sandwich, cleaning up the apartment, doing transfers or learning how to do my self-care. As I gained confidence, I tried more." There

were times he slept in his chair or went to work without socks, but eventually he learned it all. Amit Jha began by getting back to college. "Then graduating, then going to med school. It was gradual."

Attending college, working, driving, sports or moving out on their own all put people in contact with the larger world and helped them gain confidence and experience. Taking action helped them feel in control.

Donald Collier had to let go his fears of being away from home during his early days of SCI. "The more time I spent away from home, out with a couple of other guys in chairs, the safer and better I felt," he says.

Marina Conner also saw the value of slow and steady steps. "The dating, the classes, working and singing all got me out and helped make me feel normal again," she says. "Those things were all part of my therapy. I began to realize I was the same person." Eric Gibson tells the same story. "When I started getting out more," he says, "things began to get better."

First Don Dawkins got a job and lived on his own for a year. Then he went to college. Eventually he found wheelchair sports. Along the way he joined a support group. Step by step he got over the hump. College showed Dan Wilkins some of the possibilities, and his first job taught him that he could affect other people's lives. Jamie Peterson went slowly, first learning to drive, then going to community college and eventually finding a profession he liked.

Rugby helped turn things around for George Taborsky. "I had a lot of sadness and loss in my life before I started playing," he says. "Rugby let me have fun and gave me something to excel at." He gained confidence, learned from teammates and went back to work, too.

Some people named specific events as their turning points. After hearing James Taylor's "Shower the People" over and over again, Bobbie Humphreys began putting the song's lyrics into action. She put out more positive energy to others, and in return they sent more back her way. Gretchen Schaper's pastor told her shortly after her injury to give herself three years to adjust. When that conversation crossed her mind three years later, she realized much of her pain and anger had subsided. A "sobering Monday" spent reflecting on how many gang-related funerals he had attended helped James Lilly turn his corner and start moving forward.

"I knew I'd be OK when I got a job," Felipe Antonio recalls. "Before that, my family was supporting me."

For others, independence from parents, learning to drive or moving away from the site of traumatic memories helped them lose some pain and feel better. A few spoke of seminal events like release from prison or the birth of a child as marking their personal corner.

If getting lost in activities and the necessities of day-to-day living was the rather mundane magic bullet for many in this group, turning the corner was more like rounding a long, long bend for many others. It took time.

One way or another, everyone made their way to the other side, to a place where they felt more comfortable and hopeful, a place where things felt more normal. What self-identified qualities or traits helped them get there?

Q: What personal factors, habits and beliefs have helped you the most?

- I'm strong-willed, motivated, confident
- I'm optimistic and have a positive attitude
- I have a lot of support from family and friends
- I have good problem-solving abilities
- I'm persistent and have a strong work ethic
- I have a strong faith in God

Most people who do well after SCI are convinced they have control over a great deal of what happens to them. They have confidence they can handle unexpected and uncontrollable events, including paralysis. Their answers reflect something most psychologists call *internal locus of control*. Fine you say, how do I get this thing called internal locus of control?

People in our group say they gained their sense of control by doing whatever it took to improve the conditions of their lives. They learned to do self-care and chores around the home (or how to supervise others who do it for them), they figured out government benefits, took college classes, learned to drive or use public transportation, and found successful SCI survivors to learn from. They took charge of their lives by using whatever pre-existing strengths they possessed, such as optimism, problem-solving skills, positive attitude, sense of humor, persistence, perspective or faith. They say they didn't think it was about specific traits, habits or beliefs as much as it was about putting whatever strengths they had to work in helping them feel in control. They took care of the drudgery of life by doing first things first, paying attention to details and assuming responsibility for their well-being. It may not sound glamorous, but doing so got them where they wanted to go.

"We can influence a lot of what happens in life," Mark Bussinger says. He uses government bureaucracy as an example. "You have to go find and learn the system because it won't reach out to you. Looking at problems as challenges helps me stay more positive."

Michael Slaughter's work ethic drove him to pull his own weight and be useful and productive around the house. In the process he gained confidence that he could handle more.

Glenford Hibbert regained his motivation by maintaining a good attitude and pushing himself to do things. "It's not easy dealing with all the barriers and having people stare at you everywhere," he says, "but that's what I had to do."

Some say they had no choice in the matter. "I could either accept the disability and go on with my life," Phillip Mann remembers, "or I could constantly complain and be a pain to be around. That's not much of a choice, really." It was the same for

Dennis Bossman: "I had to suck it up, move on and keep a sense of humor. I had no choice."

"I think what helped me was being optimistic and never looking too far into the future," says Ryan McLean. "I never felt I had to figure out how to do something right away."

Robert Statam gained control by keeping things into perspective. Looking back on all he's learned and how far he's come helps him say, "I'm real optimistic about the future. I got so many things going right for me now; I'm feeling about 80 percent whole and getting better."

Both Benj Anderson and Juan Garibay gained some control through the back door, by accepting help from others. With his parents in charge of securing his benefits, Benj was able to focus on school. "Otherwise," he says, "school would have taken me twice as long. I couldn't have done it without them."

Juan also let others help. "My boss took a chance, offered me a scholarship and then hired me," he says. Not wanting to disappoint his boss, Juan made the most of that chance. "I never thought I had much control of my life, but now I know different. I know I can be in charge of myself."

That kind of support has helped a lot of people. Those on the receiving end are rarely passive bystanders and usually do *something* in order to have it offered and know that people who extend support normally expect it to be put to good use.

Feeling in control may be especially important for woman, and several of them talk about an increased need to be assertive after injury.

"Women with SCI have some unique needs in areas like stigma, self-esteem and self-determination," says Anne Herman, who's a social worker. "They need to do things to empower themselves and find other women for support." Gretchen Schaper says she needed to be assertive so people wouldn't "walk all over me." Same thing for Marina Conner: "Occasionally I had to talk like a truck driver at work, but sometimes it was them or me." Ditto for Susan Douglas, who simultaneously had to deal with getting used to being disabled and the good old boys club of medical school.

What is it that sets this group apart? Differently phrased, what beliefs, habits and behaviors make them feel in control? Maybe a combination of things.

They say part of it is their beliefs: They're confident, motivated and optimistic. In fact, about half said their positive attitude and optimism were what helped them the most in taking on those early tasks and obstacles. They also credit their habits: They're persistent, good at solving problems, and many of them say they expect good things to happen instead of worrying about bad things that might happen. And they credit their behaviors: They do their best to learn from others and work to keep things in perspective. They get out and do things, take risks and build on successes, no matter how small. The combination has served them well.

They say they built on their existing strengths to enhance their sense of control and confidence. Now most are convinced they can do almost anything they set their minds to. What's more, they're convinced that if they can do it, others can too. ∎

Control and Happiness

Despite everything this group has said, you may still find it hard to imagine ever being happy again. You're down on your luck and it doesn't look as if it's likely to change any time soon. Yet most people with SCI eventually return to about the same level of happiness they had before they were injured.

How can that be? In theory, it seems we're born with a certain disposition which stays with us for most of our lives, and that goes a long way in explaining why some people wake up smiling every morning and others see only dark clouds. But there's lots of wiggle room in this theory and ways for those dark-clouds people to improve their moods and find some silver linings.

While studying learned helplessness and optimism (see Optimism 101, page 84), Martin Seligman developed a hypothesis suggesting that each of us is predisposed to a certain level of happiness, a *set point* similar to that of our weight. As we go through life we tend to hover around the same level of happiness. Every once in a while some significant event—marriage, death of a parent, a big promotion or a broken heart—moves us away from our set point into temporary highs and lows. But even after extreme disruptions we eventually return to whatever is normal for us. Studies of lottery winners found them to be about as happy a year or two after winning as they were before they won. The same usually holds true for negative events. We're a resilient species and adapt quickly. Grandma was right: Time heals all wounds. Time is our ace in the hole.

Seligman theorizes that our inherited level of happiness, our set point, accounts for about 50 percent of our happiness. Life circumstances—income, divorce, promotion or job loss, outstanding family support, loss of child or spouse, or spinal cord injury—account for about 10 percent of our happiness. That leaves nearly half our happiness level under our control. Seligman says we can work with that 40 percent by putting into action what he labels *intentional activities**—all the different thoughts and behaviors we can choose and control throughout each day.

Much of our happiness, and the intentional activities we use to increase it, revolve around control. Paralysis stole your control. You want it back. Sitting around in rehab or waiting at home for your PAS probably leaves you feeling totally out of control.

But if this group can tell you anything, they can tell you that getting back some control, lots of it really, is definitely possible. It may not look the same as it once did, but you can still have it.

The people in this book dedicated their intentional activities to regaining control by paying attention to first things first, mastering their self-care, finding reliable attendants, learning to navigate benefit rules, securing transportation and taking responsibility for their health. They remained hopeful by seeing problems as specific and temporary. They stayed busy and distracted from the negatives and focused on the positives. They reconnected to old passions and found new passions to replace some of their losses. They stayed in the present and looked forward to the future. All these intentional activities—putting first things first, seeing problems as specific and temporary, staying busy and looking forward—helped them build a strong sense of control and optimism and, in turn, a good shot at being happy.

By choosing to regain control, this group chose happiness.

*For more on intentional activities, see Seligman's Authentic Happiness, *listed in the resources section.*   ■

PROFILES V

Clockwise from top, Fred Fay, Wally Dutcher, Anne Herman, Brian Johnston, Don Dawkins, Phillip Mann, Dennis Bossman, Paul Herman, Bobbie Humphreys, Donald Collier; middle: Dan Wilkins, Marina Conner

Donald Collier

The first time I visited Donald Collier in Aurora, Colo., I couldn't get into his house. His aide had stepped out and he couldn't open the garage door to get me to his only ramp. We looked at each other through his picture window, laughed about our mutual predicament and rescheduled a time to get together.

Donald's C3 injury left him with no arm movement, and as I drove home I thought about how I'd deal with that level of dependence and disability. It looks pretty tough. Is it possible to be independent when you rely on others to feed you?

"I determine what I do each day. I'm able to come and go as I please," he says. "I may be limited in what I can do but I'm still independent because even if I need help I still do what I want. People don't have to feel sorry for me because I've got most everything I need. My life is very good."

Donald's life was also very good back in 1981. He was knocking on the door of musical success after years of dedicated effort. As a toddler he beat on pots and pans and was only seven when he began drumming in a local band. At 17, his band opened a concert for Earth Wind and Fire, just as that band was hitting the big time. He worked part time as a studio session drummer and had done gigs with B.B. King and Tower of Power. He was booked for a studio jazz album with Chuck Mangione when, three days before his scheduled flight to Detroit, he was mistakenly shot by an undercover cop.

"I was on my way to work as a computer operator," he recalls. "I was waiting in a Burger King parking lot when she came up to me dressed like a hooker. The next thing I know she shoots me. When I fell over and my foot hit the gas, the car jumped the curb and crashed into a convenience store across the street. I broke the steering wheel with my chin and got messed up bad."

He woke up several days later in a body cast and halo and on a vent, due to a collapsed lung and the C3 injury. The five weeks he spent in hospitals before getting to Craig are mostly a blur. What he does remember is the around-the-clock police guard outside his room and wondering if he wanted to live.

He decided fairly quickly into his six months of rehab that he wanted to live, but was hounded constantly by daily newspaper and television coverage, which was laced with sexual innuendo because the policewoman was working a solicitation sting.

"I was a stand-up guy," he says. "I had jobs from the time I was a kid. I was married and was a parent. I was always polite and respectful to women. Being accused of trying to buy sex was very hard."

He was eventually cleared, the shooting was ruled accidental and Donald, now 40 and divorced, received a settlement of $800 per month in compensation. The accusations still hurt twenty-three years later, but he has too many other things going on to let them consume him. First and foremost, he's a dad to two adult sons and a teenage daughter.

"When I was in the hospital and trying to decide if I wanted to live, I thought of my three-year-old boy Donnie. I stayed alive for him. My son Michael came shortly after I was shot. Raising them was scary at first," he says, "but I knew I could do it and I did."

Visitations began shortly after discharge and within months the boys were spending all day with Donald while their mother worked. His parents and sister helped out and the experience he gained raising the boys has come in handy with his adopted teenage daughter Portia, who he shares with her mother.

"It's been fun raising the kids," he says. "I think this might have happened to me so I could be a dad. Family's always been very important to me, and I'm proud of the job I've done with them."

All three still live with him, and now Donald and the boys share music through their music company, Mindblowing Productions. They do preliminary production from home, pre-recording on a computer in the kitchen, then refining on a mixer in the basement before the final mix and transfer to CD in a professional studio.

"Music has always been uplifting," he says. "It makes me happy—I can be creative, I meet a lot of people, I've been on TV." He also feeds his music jones by going out to clubs nearly every weekend or to City Park for free jazz concerts.

"I love watching people dance and listening to live music. My sons will drop me off at one club where I know the owner and it's on the house. Sometimes they'll stay with me, other times I'll take people with me to other clubs."

The Power of Mentors

Other wheelers steered Donald through those first few years. They gave him support, understood his hassles, and spent time with him so he wasn't so isolated.

"I met Barry at the rehab," he says. "He's been in a chair since he was seven and he became my mentor. He saw me crying every night in rehab and started talking to me, sharing his experiences. He helped me to get out and not be so afraid of being in a chair. A little while later Carl, another quad, started taking me out, driving me around, taking me to clubs and showing me that life goes on. We saw each other almost every day and he taught me the ropes."

Spending time with them was a strong reminder of the grass always being greener somewhere else. Each of them, at one time or another, felt some envy toward the other. "Carl wanted a power chair and I wanted to be able to push mine. Both of them were able to drive and I couldn't, but they were jealous of me because I had kids and they didn't."

Still fresh from rehab, he got help from the local independent living center and eventually joined its board of directors. Besides introducing him to people and sources of support, the ILC helped him secure a loan to buy a home.

Now Donald's on the giving end by meeting and advising inpatients and their families at the rehab center twice a month. That's what others did for him years ago and he wants to do the same.

"New injuries need support," he says. "They need to see what's possible. We've got to help each other out. I feel good when I feel like I helped somebody."

The independence Donald has achieved didn't happen by accident. He says he owes it to his rehab PT and his first home-health aide. "My PT Jackie kicked my butt and never let me miss therapy. She wouldn't let me out of rehab until I knew everything. Benitta was my first aide at home and she taught me all my self-care and how to teach it to other people. She also helped me when the boys were little. We're still friends after all these years."

Most people I've talked to say it's important to stay busy, and Donald's no exception.

"My mind's way too active," he says. "I gotta be part of things." In addition to music, parenting and mentoring, he recently started a lingerie business. Now he pours over wholesale and retail catalogs learning fabrics, figuring out the SSI work rules and, above all, seeking the answer to that eternal question, What do women want?

The answer?

"I don't know," he laughs, "but I'm asking all the time."

He's asking at lingerie stores, at trade shows, wherever he goes and sees an opportunity. He has staged fashion shows at a couple of clubs he frequents and recently bought a retail store. Eventually he would like to manufacture his own line of lingerie.

"This has been a lot of fun," he says. "I want to offer an alternative to boutiques and I'm trying to be all-inclusive by offering plus sizes and something for the gay population. I'm promoting all the time. I surprise people with the chair, but I make it work. They usually remember me because of it. If you're in a chair, you can't be bashful."

Hard Times, Good Times

Donald's had his share of bad times but feels he's gained from them. There was all the negative media coverage throughout his hospital stay, which he found hurtful, distracting and mean-spirited. He struggles with dating and finding a partner, but has learned the value of friendship.

"A couple of bad experiences with women have made me stronger," he says. "I know now I can't be torn down or treated badly. I've got enough going on that I never feel lonely and I know a woman can't hold sex over my head."

A small skin sore turned into a major problem for him when the three doctors treating him failed to talk to each other. The resulting infection cost him his leg. Then there was the time he fell face-first off his van lift in his power chair. These are all small potatoes compared to losing his parents. "We were a close family and watching them die was very hard, maybe worse than getting shot."

So what has he learned?

"This happened for a reason. I got to be a dad and raise my kids 24/7. Now I get to help people. I used to really hate my chair. Then, when it broke down and went to the shop, it became my best friend. It's power to get me where I want to go. It gets me front row seating a lot and makes me stand out. People remember me, and that helps my business. Without it I'd be stuck in bed. "

Setting goals, he says, has helped him live fully since his injury.

"Life is short. It helps to keep your eye on what you want down the road. Because of that I've been able to do so much. I was a drummer in a band and did studio work. I was on TV. I got to be a dad. Now I'm becoming a businessman. Having these goals gives me a reason to get out of bed and have something to do, something to look forward to. They keep me busy and when I reach a goal I feel like I've accomplished something. That's rewarding.

"I've been able to do so much," he repeats. "I've been blessed." ■

Dan Wilkins

Dan Wilkins has worked hard to get where he is, especially when no one wanted to lend him money to start a business selling T-shirts and posters based on humor and disability. What could possibly be funny about disability, they asked? But his business, The Nth Degree, is funny. Funny enough, in fact, that he's got a T-shirt in the Smithsonian and a demand for personal appearances that just keeps growing.

While many of his wares are very humorous, at heart Dan's a political animal fighting systemic and attitudinal discrimination. His underlying purpose is serious, his potential constituency vast.

"The shirts and posters speak to the fact that we're all trying to get from stigma to pride," he says. "People with disabilities come from all generations, religions, genders and races; we're an amalgam of America."

Luckey, Ohio seems an unlikely source for T-shirts with slogans like "Piss on Pity" or "Camp Can't Feel My Legs." Yet in the midst of the soy and cornfields of western Ohio is where I find Dan and The Nth Degree.

I wheel through the garage of Dan's 100-year-old house, past boxes of T-shirts, up a ramp and into a large office with new wood flooring, new age music playing and a big new Apple computer sitting on the long work counter. I'm struck with how sunny the house feels, even though it's overcast outside. Maybe it's all the stained-glass suns hanging from the walls and windows. Maybe it's the Halloween decorations. Maybe it's the little kid who lives here.

Off the kitchen in what could easily be a large bedroom is an enormous bathroom, so big that Dan jokes about occasionally hosting bathroom parties. This is a comfortable house, one that instantly puts visitors at ease. And Dan, his wife Beth and son Taylor are all so friendly that you can't help but feel relaxed.

It's early afternoon. Dan has been up since 7 this morning and at the computer since 9 or so, tending his business, taking orders, designing shirts, talking with people around the country. Some days he's in Toledo at the local center for independent living or attending grad school at the University of Toledo's Disability Studies program. About two weeks out of the month he's on the road at conferences, board meetings, trade shows and consumer expositions selling his shirts, or speaking to groups of educators, businesspeople, military planners or medical professionals who pay to hear his thoughts. He tells them about quality of life, the importance of high expectations, the fact that we're all connected.

Dan was introduced to disability when he fell asleep at the wheel late one night and rolled his Camaro. It was 1980, he was 20, and now he had a C5-6 injury. After nearly two months of acute care and surgery, he headed off to Ann Arbor to begin rehabilitation at the University of Michigan. It wasn't exactly what he or his parents expected—young nurses and aides dressed in civvies and a Birkenstock-wearing doc with whom Dan has since traveled the world. The philosophy there was to work with whatever function he had, to get on with life and to only look forward. That wasn't necessarily what he wanted to do at first.

"All I was focused on was what I thought I'd never do again," he says. "Like skiing or running with my dogs or hiking or falling in love or owning a business, all the things I've done since then. I felt that life was over, that maybe I'd rather be dead. Some fears left the first time I laughed, more went away when my PT taped a pen in my hand and I began drawing again. I realized I could do lots of what I had done before; I realized that many of my fears were unfounded and that I was in control. I was able to let go of that 'fate worse than death' mindset fairly quickly."

A Year of Enlightenment

But Dan's progress wasn't exactly a straight line. His halo was installed without benefit of Demerol and because the bolts weren't tightened properly, they constantly scraped his head and caused intense pain. Later, when the intern went to remove the halo, he began to tighten rather than loosen the screws, giving Dan his own personal crown of thorns. After six months in Michigan he returned home and lived with his parents for three years where, he says, dependency was a great seductress. It was just too convenient to be with his folks and collect SSI and SSDI.

"It gets real easy sometimes when there's someone there to do everything for you. You forget about how independent you were."

Dan's story line kept bottoming out on his road back to that independence. His attempt at reconciliation with his ex-wife ended in Alabama when she abandoned him there, leaving him to spend a day alone, lying in bed with no catheter, waiting for his family to come get him. There were several other horror stories as well, often due to

miscalculations or things out of his control. Jobs were scarce in the early 1980s and no one would hire him. Before the days of cell phones he nearly froze while stuck on an icy ramp outside his house during a whiteout, dressed only in a suit. He finally melted a path for himself with urine over the course of an hour. He once spent a day stranded on the south 40 of his parents' place before getting his brother's attention by using the chrome armrest of his old E&J chair as a signal mirror.

"I sometimes forgot I was a quad before figuring out I could get in some *really* bad situations," he recalls. "But most of my horror stories are about the way we're treated and how we have to overcome not disability but other people's attitudes about us."

The limitations of living with his parents finally began to become apparent about three years post-injury, when he began what he calls his year of enlightenment. He started driving. He reconnected with old friends and old hobbies. He helped found a support group. He started on his spiritual journey and began letting life in.

And when he did, Dan's fears and misconceptions evaporated, one by one. He got outside his comfort zone by traveling, by flying, by dealing with inaccessibility, by getting creative in a pinch. These were major learning experiences. He began to see with bigger eyes as he learned what was real in the world and in people.

"Going out and doing all the things we do—drinking with old friends, maybe getting laid, winning a game of pool from my chair—all these things shattered what I thought disability was. I was figuring out who the 'new' Dan Wilkins was.

"I found that if I put energy out there, things would happen," he says. "Nothing changed in me under that Camaro. What changed was how others saw me, what they expected of me. The world hadn't expanded to include me. It was powerful to realize that my disability wasn't going to hold me back. Instead, it gave me purpose and propelled me. Your perceptions change when you begin to realize that you still belong."

A good friend told him he had sat around too long and encouraged him to return to college. With help from Voc Rehab and the VA, he got his degree in psychology. He accepted a job with a Toledo center for independent living running a grant designed to push people with disabilities beyond their own perceived boundaries. Three years later he founded *The Nth Degree*. He is active in the National Spinal Cord Injury Association, writes, gives lectures and figures he has traveled the equivalent of 20 times around the world. He recently began course work in the University of Toledo's new Disability Studies program, and plans to eventually teach.

Life and Learning

It's been 24 years now. What's he learned about disability?

"I've dismissed every belief I've ever had about disability; they simply aren't true. Disability, I've come to learn, is such a natural part of life, something that gives back, something of which to be proud."

About walking?

"Walking is over-rated."

About things he can't do?

"What I can do is way more important than what I can't do."

About navigating the healthcare and benefits system?

"It's *not* designed to help you. You need to be strong and resourceful in order to make the system work for you."

About independence?

"It's not the holy grail. It's more a state of mind and who's in control than about actually doing things without help. Interdependence and connection are more important."

About employment?

"There's a great deal of dignity in working and making a contribution."

About the right way to do things?

"There are at least six right ways to do everything."

And the future?

"I'd like to write a book. I'd like to slow down, travel less and spend more time with my family, maybe have another kid. I want to teach. I want to keep doing what I'm doing. I want to continue making a difference."

Advice to people who are newly injured and in rehab?

"Remember to laugh. Lean on others when necessary, but don't get hooked on dependency. Remember that this isn't just about you. Unlearn what you think about disability because it's not a fate worse than death. Be creative and find ways to express yourself. The three things that helped me the most were a sense of humor, a belief in myself and strong family support." ■

Phillip Mann

Phillip Mann sees himself as an ordinary guy on wheels who's been fortunate enough to have some good opportunities come his way.

"I think I'm something of wheelchair ambassador," he says. "I want to be the most positive disabled person I can be because I might be the only disabled person other people ever see."

Phillip, at 50, gets around more than most nondisabled people. He worked in the Bibb County, Ga. Sheriff's Department for 27 years before retiring recently. On the side, he earned a master's degree at night school. He's been married for more than 30 years and is now helping his two daughters get through high school and college. He's been to England, South America and throughout the U.S. for sports competitions. He teaches Sunday School. Busy, busy, busy.

Don't be fooled by the photograph; this is one happy, upbeat, energetic and positive man. He still uses leg braces to stand, he hasn't stopped mowing the lawn, he continues to travel alone and he's not planning on giving up hunting or fishing any time soon. Tooling around in a lightweight chair with off-road tires, he may talk a lot about slowing down, but he shows few signs of actually doing so. His polite ways and Southern accent let you know he's from the South; Macon, Ga. to be exact.

Though no longer working, he's still up at 7 each day to have breakfast with his daughters Jana, 20, and Katherine, 17, before he sees them off to school. For a good part of the day he's busy doing maintenance around the house. A couple of times a month he stops in at the Sheriff's Department to visit and have lunch with his pals there. "It reminds me that retirement is good," he says.

One Bad Day

In 1977, when Phillip was a Deputy Sheriff, he and his partner were dispatched to a disturbance at the local food stamp office. In the process of being cuffed, the perp grabbed Phillip's partner's gun and shot Phillip twice point blank before wounding a bystander. Though on the floor and wounded in both his arm and abdomen, Phillip got off two shots and dropped the shooter.

Phillip was receiving medical care within 15 minutes. The reality of his T11-12 injury took a bit longer to sink in. Feeling caught in a bad dream during his month of acute care, he faced all the usual questions of survival, employment and the possibility of having and supporting a family. His wife Elaine, however, shared few of these uncertainties. Hearing from the doctor that he'd never walk again but that his mind was intact, her first words were "That's good enough." Once he got to rehab at Shepherd Center in Atlanta, and around so many others in chairs, Phillip agreed with her and started getting on with it.

"Seemed to me I had two choices," he says. "I could either accept the disability and go on with my life or I could constantly complain and be a pain to be around. That's not much of a choice, really."

Buoyed by constant visitors, fellow officers as well as "zillions" from the community, he jumped back into life. Friends made his apartment accessible while he figured out his work options, which ranged from retirement to part-time or full-time work.

With worker's comp, Social Security and Sheriff's pension, why not just kick back and watch the grass grow?

"Actually I *had* to work, either with the department or somewhere else. I was too scared not to and would have been a miserable person if I didn't. Going back to work was the best thing I ever did. I was very nervous at first, petrified actually, but it was great. I had a 9 to 5 schedule. I felt productive. I had fun. Dispatching was even better because it let me be very involved. I heard everything that was going on and felt like I was still one of the guys—without having to be out in the wet and the cold. I had a great career and a wonderful time. I had one bad day."

Back to full time work in less than a year, he first did record keeping and administrative work. Four years later he moved over to dispatch, where he stayed for 20 years and became director of communications. When he was offered early retirement three years ago he jumped at the chance to spend more time with his girls.

"I'm 50 years old and retired. That's amazing to me."

Like most of us, Phillip has his stories of the joys of dealing with the government. Worker's comp balked at his post-retirement plans to work part time as a bailiff for the county. Social Security initially told him he wasn't disabled enough to qualify for SSDI when he applied last year. But he still wants to return to some kind of part-time work. He's just too antsy not to.

Finding Sports

Not long after Phillip was shot, about the same time he was getting back to work, his friends had him covered with camouflage, on an ATV and hunting with them. Bolting a used chair onto a boat seat got him fishing again. Over time, he came to believe he could find a way to do almost anything.

Like figuring out how to mow the lawn by fashioning hand controls for his riding mower so he could cut his acre of grass. Like playing with his power tools and his 12-inch gas chain saw, which he uses to cut up firewood to burn in his heater.

"I s'pose that's kind of stupid and dangerous," he acknowledges, "but I really enjoy doing it."

A big change in Phillip's life came when he found Shepherd's sports program and quickly got into basketball, racing and tennis. Being surrounded with active, sportsminded people was the hook that kept him involved for 20 years. He qualified and wheeled the Boston Marathon in '87, one of six marathons he raced during a two-year span. In '89 he went to England to compete and in '90 to Venezuela for the Pan Am Games. Hanging with other people with SCI reassured him and served as an alternative owner's manual for the sitting life.

In 1983 Elaine and Phillip became proud parents of their first daughter, Jana. When Katherine followed three years later, he began to realize how much sports were interfering with his time for the three women in his life. He cut back to handcycling, and recently biked across Georgia in stages, one week at a time.

He'd camped a lot while growing up, and continued to go camping with his newer family—first in tents, then in inaccessible pop-up trailers and finally in an accessible Coleman with a ramp and 30-inch door he hauled with his minivan. He was settling down.

Finding Peace

While work, sports and family all helped Phillip keep moving forward, he says the most significant piece of the puzzle fell into place when he accepted the Lord into his life. Asked to read a scripture during an Easter service while in rehab, he tried to cut a deal: walking in exchange for reading from the Bible. No dice.

"The people I knew who had the Lord had something different than me," Phillip says, "but I didn't know or care about Him much. After that Easter service I tried out a Baptist church, but that didn't work either."

A year later, feeling very uneasy, he stopped in again. After speaking to the pastor at length and accepting God into his life, he says, everything changed .

"I get a great deal of peace and serenity from God, as well as unconditional forgiveness and fellowship with others. I believe God allowed this injury to happen so I'd become a Christian. We may not have a choice about being in a chair, but we can choose how to act once we're there. I'd rather have my relationship with God than be up and walking and being who I was."

Philip takes his faith into Sunday School, teaching scripture and being a role model to adolescent boys.

"Many of these kids don't have any positive role models," he says. "It's good for them to see adults like me screw up, admit to making mistakes and then talking about how to correct them and make them right. I think that my being in a chair is a plus for them."

Faith and love have gone together for Philip, and he appreciates that. "Having a catastrophic injury is mind boggling. We can rationalize why we have or haven't made the best of our situations, but I'm convinced that my success is because of the unconditional love my family gives me. Elaine and I have been sweethearts since the 10th grade and she's the kindest and most compassionate person I've ever known. She certainly fits the Biblical description of a Christian wife in Proverbs 31 and I've never regretted marrying her."

His faith may not have him walking but long-leg braces have him on his feet, and

Phillip's been putting them to work for him for the past 25 years.

"They let me hug my wife and I love doing that," he says. "I stand to do the dishes, to cook, to do weight shifts and for exercise. On the road, I'll sometimes stand to do a bowel program. I'd feel like a new injury without them. It's amazing to me that people who can use them don't."

After all these years of SCI, how tough has it been?

"This really isn't that bad," Phillip tells me, "and I can think of lots worse things. At first I couldn't imagine living with some of this stuff, like having to cath for the rest of my life. But being surrounded by positive, motivated people and by my wife and family all helped. Over time life just kept getting better. More places became accessible. I experimented and found ways and shortcuts to do things. I just got used to it. I've been very fortunate."

What's so fortunate about being in a chair?

"I've got a great family—an amazing wife and two wonderful daughters. I have good friends. I had a good job and so many people there who were flexible and accommodating and wanted me to come back to work.

"People who've just been injured need to know that things get better and life goes on. The chair will open up doors to college or travel or job opportunities. When those opportunities come, you have to take them and then prove yourself. I think that because I've been willing to experiment I've been able to do everything I've ever wanted to do." ∎

Dennis Bossman

In 1984, when Dennis Bossman was just a few months out of rehab, he got his first SSDI check, a whopping $408. His roommate looked at him and said, "Dude, you gotta get a job." He's been working ever since.

I met Dennis 10 years ago, when he was a salesman working the floor at a medical supply store. After listening to a few playfully disparaging remarks about how pathetic he found quads like me, I knew I liked him. Now he's a few months into a new job, selling and marketing modified vans and equipment at a suburban Denver conversion shop. His days are long: up by 5:30 or 6 for a shower, on the road by 7 for the one-hour commute, home about six in the evening.

His modest home sits in a quiet, working-class neighborhood about a half hour south of downtown Denver. Short ramps lead up to the breezeway and into the house, where I'm greeted by two curious dogs. The interior design is open, with hardwood floors that invite wheeling. A huge deck off the dining room looks west to the mountains. Because he uses the garage as a woodworking shop, his pickup and vintage El Camino are parked outside.

In 1983 Dennis was 28 and living in Steamboat Springs, Colo., pounding nails and working the tourist trade as a river guide in the summer and sleigh driver in the winter. One night on his way home from the bar, he hit some loose gravel and swerved off the road, rolling his jeep and flying through its soft top. Because the jeep came to rest down an embankment some distance from him, it was several hours before anyone found him. T9 injury; acute care in Denver for surgery and rods, then on to rehab.

Where did you do acute care?

"Holy Tony's by the Sea," he says. That would be Saint Anthony's, which is next to a lake.

Rehab? "St. Wheelchair Hospital." That would be Craig. "Back then rehab was still

wild and fun. Instead of making ceramic bunnies or remote controlled cars we played poker most of the night. On weekends my friends would visit with cases of beer. That stuff kept me grounded and let me know I could still do what I wanted and I wasn't different. Now it feels all tense and serious and, well, like a hospital. I'm glad I rehabbed when I did."

Biggest questions and thoughts in rehab? "The first was, 'I gotta stick my finger where?' followed by 'I did this to myself.' I was never pissed off. I didn't have time to sit around and whine or worry about the future."

Hard First Years

Upon discharge, he visited his family back in Missouri so "everyone could see me in a wheelchair." Herman, Mo., a town of 2,000, is the home of a sheltered workshop that makes Chinese Checkers and most of his friends and relatives assumed that that's

181

where he would work. Within six weeks he had a plane ticket back to Denver and was asking a friend for a place to stay.

"I couldn't go back to Steamboat because there were too many bad things to ingest, especially for someone with too much time on his hands," Dennis says. "Getting hurt slowed me down and made me grow up. With a weak body I had to rely on a strong mind, and I knew it was time to get a little more serious and hold myself accountable. My friend Butch put me up in a tiny studio apartment with an inaccessible bathroom for about six months."

His living conditions were anything but ideal. To use the bathroom he would poke his chair into the doorway, have his friend transfer him onto the toilet and then onto a five-gallon bucket with a cushion so he could shower. To stay busy, he helped his roommate do repair work at a nearby apartment building.

"Butch really stepped up for me," he says. "Needless to say, when he calls now he gets whatever he wants."

Eventually Dennis found Section 8 housing near Denver's city center. Far from white-bread Steamboat Springs, he was a stranger in a strange land, one of only a few Caucasians in a minority neighborhood. What was that like? "Champions adjust. You have to be flexible and figure things out."

That answer tells you all you need to know about him. This is a man who takes things in stride, rarely gets hung up on adversity and spends most of his time looking for positives. He's always smiling.

He spent his days that first summer wheeling downtown, having a couple of beers, playing cribbage, hanging out for hours and generally just putting in time. To keep fit he would wheel around the lake of a local park, first on his everyday wheels, then in a secondhand racing chair. When he ran into a Denver Parks and Recreation Department staff worker, he began water skiing with that program.

"Things snowballed and kept me from becoming a potted plant," he says. "I got out and started meeting people. I got a job, I stayed busy. I took care of myself and never got sick."

Because health insurance companies denied coverage to people with pre-existing conditions back then, he needed Medicare. In order to support himself, he had to bend the rules for 11 years, working cash jobs answering phones or doing desk work at auto repair shops.

"I had no choice," he says. "The system made me an outlaw. I needed the system until I outgrew it. It's so screwed up. When I told Social Security I was working, they kept sending me checks; then years later, they wanted it all back."

When Medicare's work disincentives were relaxed in the early '90s he began working full time at the medical supply and equipment store; within a few years he was the general manager.

Dennis feels strongly about crips in the workplace.

"Barring thresholds of pain and medication, most of us can work," he says. "I know a guy in a sip-and-puff chair who uses a mouthstick and works full time as a computer analyst. All my friends in chairs work. Everyone needs to be productive. If I won the Lotto I'd probably do a mobility clinic or buy a liquor store. I can't sit still."

For several years he went to Mexico, first with a church group and then with The Mobility Project. With both he taught sports camps as well as repaired and gave away wheelchairs. He still goes out of town for tennis tournaments or to spend a day rafting a river, but since hooking up with his partner three years ago and buying a house, he's become more of a homebody. Accordingly, kicking back now means playing tennis, riding his handcycle, woodworking or cooking either on the outside grill or in the kitchen.

He met his partner Terry when she worked as an account executive for a wheelchair manufacturing firm and Dennis was buying for the store. They quickly began a long distance courtship—she in Pennsylvania, he in Denver—by phone and e-mail until he "sweet-talked her into flying out here." Within six months she moved to Denver with her son Bill.

"I'd never been married, never lived with a woman, so having a partner and living with someone is a big change. My Tru-Luv takes real good care of me and I'm getting spoiled."

Rules for Living

How do you define coping with SCI? "Sucking it up, moving on, keeping a sense of humor and not being a pain in the ass," he says. But ... "My Tru-Luv says I'm a pain in the ass."

That no-nonsense philosophy has served him well over the past 20 years. He went from a shady job to a real one, from subsidized housing to home ownership, from chasing women to settling down with one. When asked how he got here, his answer is simple: be productive, get a job, stay busy, take care of yourself and be responsible. Don't look for sympathy about being in a chair from Dennis; he'll tell you to figure it out.

"Not long after I got hurt I'd go to watch the Nuggets play basketball," he recalls. "I would see guys there with legbags around their necks. When I sold equipment I'd see guys who were filthy and smelled. They don't work and they sit around all day smoking weed and watching the tube. They've got no self-worth. I don't know how anyone can live like that. You have to have some pride."

Lots of people worry about losing friends after they get hurt, but Dennis never gave it much thought. Because he doesn't think much about his chair, his friends don't either—probably because he's so good at putting people at ease.

"People have always been there for me, especially my friends," he says. "Some of them pulled away a bit at first. I think they were a little nervous about how I'd react to being in a chair. Once we went rafting, things were fine."

In Dennis' version of "Don't let the bastards get you down," the bastards are *everything*—disconnected catheters, bowel accidents, flat tires, inaccessible places. Without a sense of humor, dealing with those things can be pretty miserable, he says. "You've got to be able to laugh at yourself."

And he remembers how it might have been. "I could still be in Section 8 housing and rolling up the street to get food stamps and surplus food," he says. "I can't ask for much more than what I've got, except maybe a better forehand."

Were there any surprises after injury? "I couldn't believe how many guys in chairs were with hotties or that women I didn't know could be attracted to me," he says. "You just gotta go for that."

Hot tips for newbies? "You don't need college to get a good job," he says. "If you stay busy and get out every day and do things, you build confidence that you can deal with anything. You've got to keep your mind going so you don't feel sorry for yourself. And you've got to have recreation to feed your mind, body and soul. Besides, chicks dig it. It's true that anything is possible. Job, house, love, you can have all those."

What are you most proud of? "Staying out of jail and keeping my sense of humor."

Any good stories? "Well, there was this girl, a bathtub and some handcuffs ...."

Never mind. Anything you miss? "Standing up to pee."

Got an answer for everything, don't you? "Yup." ∎

Brian Johnston

Since breaking his neck 30 years ago, Brian Johnston has worked in risk management for a major rehab hospital, at a center for independent living and owned and operated a successful mail order business. For a time, he did all three. He's sold durable medical equipment. He's worked as an accessibility consultant and wheelchair sports coordinator. He purchased and renovated, and now manages and maintains the eight-unit apartment building he calls home. In his spare time he restores and rebuilds 50-year-old Harley-Davidsons.

"I'm getting pretty tired," he says, "but I can't seem to slow down."

And at 46, he's showing few signs of slowing down. Using his real estate savvy, he found, bought, remodeled and accessibilized a condo in Cocoa Beach, Fla., so his parents have a place to spend winters and he has a place to visit. He's got five acres on a river near his home and he's now clearing a driveway and turnaround on it, using an all-terrain chair he built that's towed by an old self-propelled power mower. Did I mention that he was a serious, sponsored road racer for a number of years, began a wheelchair hockey league, played quad rugby, and was an enthusiastic camper and kayaker before wearing out numerous body parts? He's done all this as a complete C5-6 quad with little more than a high school education. He's completely independent and lives alone.

He's no couch potato.

Hawglets and Gimplements

Brian's home 25 miles west of Milwaukee sports few modifications. The kitchen cabinets are intact, the counters are normal heights, no roll-under stovetop or sinks. The commode seat and bath bench, along with the rope with velcro cuffs which control his leg spasms at night are the only indications that a wheeler lives here. A long roll-under work table holds his computer and gives him a place to write. When I was there, two small Harleys and a Honda were sitting in a corner of his living room. Make no mistake; a bachelor lives here.

Shortly after he purchased this building, Brian set out to renovate and modernize each unit. He did a lot of the work himself, tearing up carpet and transferring to the floor to sand and paint. If the work went less than five feet up the wall, he did it. He still does much of the maintenance, sometimes with the help of tenants. If the chair gets in the way, he hires outside help.

A few years ago he began fulfilling a lifelong fascination with cycles when he came across a 1949 125 cc single-piston Harley-Davidson Hummer.

"The Hummer is small enough to be manageable and I can work on it from my chair," he says. "I looked at it and thought, 'I can do this.' "

He liked them so much that he's restored many Hummers since. Then he started taking on small, 50 cc Hondas and old Schwinn bicycles. Something about turning wrenches and working with his hands does it for him, he says. He's a purist, always insisting on original parts. He approaches cycles the way he approaches everything: he learns as he does.

Brian's spare bedroom serves as his motorcycle and equipment repair shop. Shelves full of parts and tools line the walls, a racing chair and parts hang from the ceiling. Two old bicycles stand in one corner, a drill press and bandsaw in another. A small motorcycle leans against another wall.

He recently rebuilt two Hummers into such good shape that they were featured in a book commemorating Harley's 100 year anniversary.

"I found a couple bikes in November of 2002 and started working on them," he says. "Fixing, making and replacing parts. Then I ran into the book people in spring of '03, and they wanted to feature them, so I had to really start working hard. I went full time from May until August to get them done for the photo shoot, everything but the wiring, so they're in the book. It's not like I made the cover of *Rolling Stone*, but it's close."

The two anniversary Hummers rotate between a friend's local Harley dealership and various bike shows. He's got four other bikes on display at another friend's cycle shop and two more in his living room. Any for sale? "I'm not hunting down any buyers but money talks. Big money is really loud!"

The mail order business mentioned earlier, which he named Innovator of Disability Equipment and Adaptations Inc. (IDEA), was a natural outgrowth of his active, problem solving mind. He already had a knack for making gimplements and crip helpers—button hooks, shoe pullers and bedtime leg holders to manage spasms. Over time, sixteen items grew into more than 300, most of which he invented himself.

Like a Glacier

When he was 16, Brian broke his neck in a diving accident. After six weeks in acute care, he went to Denver to rehab at Craig Hospital for nearly four months. He came home very weak in March of 1974, and could barely sit up for an entire day. He wore ankle weights on his arms for two years to build up enough muscle to drive.

Those first four years were a dark blur of drugs, alcohol and hell-raising. When his parents had had enough, they kicked him out of their house and he moved to nearby Pewaukee to live with his sister.

"Because she worked, I was alone all day," he recalls. "When she came home, she'd always ask me what I did. I needed to tell her something, and that gave me the motivation I needed, so I began doing things—making a sandwich, cleaning up the apartment, doing transfers or learning how to do my self-care. As I slowly figured all of that out I gained more confidence and tried doing more. When I went out, I saw people doing things I wanted to do and thought, 'why not me?' Trial and error teaches you your talents."

When his sister got married, Brian was on his own but still not totally independent. He tried a roommate for a while, then had a live-in girlfriend who helped him with some care. When that relationship ended he went on to master his transfers, dressing, external catheters and night bags. None of it happened overnight. In fact, it seemed to take forever. It wasn't unusual for him to sleep in his chair or go to work without socks. When he got his first van it took him nearly 90 minutes to transfer out of the driver's seat and into his chair. Seventeen years later he bought a pickup truck; he's in in 60 seconds and out in 30.

"I figure if I can do something once, I can probably do it quicker the next time," he says. "It's all a matter of strength, coordination and technique."

Listening to him describe all this, I think of a glacier—the movement is almost imperceptible, but the long-term effects are huge and lasting.

Progress was slow, just like that glacier, but eventually he learned it all. He is a patient and persistent man with a strong work ethic and a lifelong belief that he could improve and do things better and quicker.

Carpe Diem

I picked Brian's brain about what 30 years in a chair have taught him. Initially, he says, his "it's all over so who'd want to be with me?" attitude held him back with women. He began to get over it when a friend introduced him to the woman he eventually lived with for four years. Now he thinks that meeting and dating from a chair is easier for him than most AB's, maybe because wheels make him less intimidating. He's had his share of relationships and one night stands and says his heart's been broken more than once.

Back in '73 his doctor had told him he'd probably be dead by 25 and certainly wouldn't see 30. Thirty years later he's still kicking, due in no small part, he believes, to a good diet and a rigid hygiene routine. He's become something of a crusader for healthy living.

"I see so many guys who eat lousy, only do a bowel program when they feel like it, take all kinds of over-the-counter drugs and then wonder why they feel so lousy," he says. "When I stopped taking so many prescription drugs I began feeling a lot better.

"Most of the health stuff is common sense. I learned from doctors, experimented to see what worked for me, then stuck with it. I let my mind be my sensation from the nipples down. What you eat, your routine, who you associate with, that's who you are. Staying active kept me healthy, still keeps me healthy. Now my only concern is having a doc younger than my injury."

That quest to stay healthy and keep active now has him rebuilding a couple of British Corgis, the civilian model of WWII folding motorcycles that were airdropped to troops on the ground. This glacier grinds on.

"These things fall in my lap and I can't say no, but it is getting harder," he admits. "I can psyche myself up for things like doing the bikes for the book; I still got it when I need it. But I don't have the gumption to bundle up and go out a lot in the winter unless it's with someone."

Any advice from an old pro?

"People need to get out and do things because you never know who or what you'll meet—a friend, a lover, a job opportunity. In those early days, it seemed like every time I went out I'd meet a key person in some field. In '79 I met a guy who began an independent living center in Milwaukee. He asked me to serve on their board of directors, and that's where I met the CEO of the hospital where I later worked. I met people through racing and a lot of opportunities came from them. The people from Eagle Sportchairs sponsored me. The people from Shepherd flew me to Atlanta to speak. Every time you go out it's an opportunity. I've said yes to a lot of things, and most of them have come from being out there. I'm amazed at people who don't take advantage of opportunities. I get out of bed every day because I'm afraid I might miss something."

What about independence?

"Rehab was a great growth experience for me," he says. "I probably learned at least as much hanging out in hallways with others in chairs as I did from doctors and therapists. I learned to listen to others, take orders from the pros and take care of myself with routine, rest, a good diet, lots of liquids. I think rehab was better 30 years ago. They pushed you harder. You couldn't say no to therapy."

What about the future?

"I can honestly say I've done or tried to do most everything I've wanted to do. I didn't want to check out without being able to say that. Now I want to design and build a house on my land before my parents die."

Anything else?

"Don't dive into shallow water." ∎

Bobbie Humphreys

Life is a series of grand adventures for Bobbie Humphreys. She got over her fear that men would reject her by having her first date in ICU. She built her confidence in the larger world by taking a 10,000 mile cross-country road trip. Once, out of curiosity, she competed in the Miss Wheelchair New Jersey pageant.

She remains as excited about life and learning and contributing at 47 as she was when she sat down 30 years ago. Her philosophy?

"Jump into the deep end, then learn to swim."

In 1973, Bobbie was 17 and a junior in high school when she crashed a dirt bike trying a jump. No blood, no bruises, only two small marks on her neck from the helmet. And a broken vertebrae at C5-6.

"I knew what happened immediately and told the guy I was with that I had broken my neck," she says. "When help arrived, I had to calm down the cop and tell him what to do."

She spent a few days in the ICU of a nearby New Jersey hospital, six weeks wearing the ever-popular Crutchfield tongs, and three months in an acute care hospital waiting for a bed at Kessler Institute for Rehabilitation in West Orange, N.J. Hurt in April, she lived in hospitals until December.

"In 1973," says Bobbie, "that's how things were."

When her parents told her she was going to Kessler, she only heard the word institute, thought institution and figured they were sending her away for good. When she got to rehab, the sight of so many people in chairs, especially teens, did little to calm her down or answer her questions about marriage, children, housing and employment. Her sex education in total: "Well, you could have an involuntary bowel movement or get pregnant."

She found PT frustrating due to her limited function, but enjoyed OT because of its can-do mentality. She couldn't imagine dressing or brushing her teeth or applying her own makeup, but the OTs had answers for everything.

Yet her best rehab, she says, went on in the evenings behind closed doors blocked by power chairs. These soirees were often filled with tears and baring of souls and plenty of fun, fueled by liquor and other abusable substances. In 1973, that's also how things were.

"We would sit around and make up stories to tell the 65-year-old shrink who wanted to know what our lives and childhoods were like," she remembers. And that guy she met in the ICU? "He was a PT student. He kept coming back and we dated for a year. He was the best drug possible."

She was happy to leave rehab, but frightened as well. Returning to high school was difficult and the real world was scary. She refused to be seen with other wheelers and kept her chair out of sight when she wasn't in it.

The Impossible Comes First

Bobbie's a pretty stubborn person and gets tunnel vision whenever someone suggests her injury might stop her from doing something. This bring-it-on mentality has served her well.

Despite very limited hand function, she taught herself crewelwork, needlepoint and how to use a loom. Despite her mom saying her that calligraphy was impractical for her, she learned. Despite her diminished lung power, she sang onstage in several theatrical productions. Despite constantly sweating until a rhizotomy 10 years after injury, she dated the entire time.

Within a few months of discharge she was working a switchboard for two doctors and a funeral home. No, she says, the three were *not* partners. She manually pulled old-fashioned phone plugs in and out of the jacks, a neat trick for a quad.

"My logic was to do a nearly impossible job first," she says. "I figured anything after that would seem easy. I find my limits by taking on more than I can handle. How else do you find out all that you can do?"

Bobbie says she struggled with her disability for years, in part because she had no disabled women for role models, but she seldom let that or anything else stop her from partying "any and every way" possible those first few years. She remembers one time when her chair broke down: "My sister tossed me into a wheelbarrow and pushed me to the local tavern."

She decided that senior prom night was an appropriate time to lose her virginity, so she and her date retired to his apartment. As he undressed her, he inadvertently pulled out her catheter. Bobbie thought it was funny. He didn't.

"He got all upset and started running around, asking 'What do we do? What do we do?' He carried me out to the car, and when he remembered his car keys he dropped me on the lawn, got the keys, jumped in the car and took off. I was still on the ground. He came back in a tizzy, put me in the car and drove to the ER. Everyone there was convinced we were newlyweds because of the white prom dress and tux, so we went back to his place and acted like it."

A Balanced Whole

Four years post-injury, when a friend suggested that Bobbie try college, she enrolled within a month. With financial aid from Ramapo College, she lived on campus, away from her family, and learned how to supervise the aides who did her care. She loved school, did well studying theater and music, and broke new ground as the first wheeler to perform onstage there. Her debut appearance in "Guys and Dolls" required her to play three parts and do 14 wardrobe changes for each performance. A few years later she had the lead role in "Julie's Song." Theater remains part of her life today.

"College was amazing," she recalls, "and theater was very exciting. I was just one of the actors, no special treatment. I met so many great people."

When she finally got a van that she could drive in 1980, seven years after injury, she broke it in with Bobbie's Excellent Adventure—a 10,000 mile, eight-week cross-country road trip with her sister. They stayed at KOA campgrounds, slept in a tent, and with her sister's help did all her self-care in the van—bowel program, cath changes, everything.

"The trip had a huge impact on me and I came away much more confident," she says. "We never thought or worried about what might happen and just dealt with things as they came up. In the Grand Tetons my sister and three friends pushed me up to the top of a 9,500 foot mountain. That was awesome. I learned that asking for help was OK and that people get something out of it when they help others. I saw how my attitude affected others. After that, I felt that I could do anything."

Despite the power of that trip, Bobbie's progress continued in a pattern of two steps forward, one step back. To end a bad relationship at college, she returned home a semester shy of graduation and quickly resumed dating the wrong men and keeping the wrong hours. After a year of that, her mother told her to either change her ways or find another place to live. Jumping into the deep end again, she did both.

First she found subsidized housing in nearby Parsippany and moved into a small one-bedroom apartment. Shortly after that she met Pete, her partner of the past 20 years, in a biker bar. He was smitten.

Pete doesn't really fit the biker image. He's quiet, conservative and cautious in contrast to Bobbie's rambunctious, risk-taking nature. Yet they were an item within months, and two decades later their new-love infatuation is still evident. They're total opposites who add up to a neatly balanced pair.

"She wrote a pamphlet years ago called *How to Survive a Broken Neck*," Pete tells me, rolling his eyes. "If I wrote one it would be *How to Survive a Pain in the Neck*. I can't keep up with her."

Pete's a trained home healthcare provider, paid through Medicaid, and has provided all of Bobbie's care throughout their relationship. "Nothing's ever bothered him or grossed him out," Bobbie says, "but after all these years it's getting harder. I'm doing less and he's doing more."

Bobbie's SSI and Medicaid benefits have forced her to volunteer more and work for wages less. She has worked backstage and in the ticket office for her theater group, and performed with a traveling troupe for a couple of years. She's done motivational speaking on peer pressure with high school kids, orientation programs for rehab employees and nursing students, volunteered with kids who have AIDS and helped battered women.

"Helping others makes me feel good and I'm always wondering who I'm going to help today, always wondering who I'm going to visit next."

Shower the People

Bobbie concedes that she's slowed down the past few years, but she continues her volunteer work even as recurring skin sores keep her in bed more than in her chair. She's most proud of creating Kessler's peer counseling program, which she began in 1991 after lobbying professionals there for more than a decade. Despite being nearly 20 years post-injury when the program began, she became one of its primary beneficiaries.

"My intent was to help people with new injuries," she says. "I never thought I'd have to talk about myself or my feelings. I thought I'd just tell people how I did things. Answering all their questions forced me to deal with my own issues, all the things I couldn't do, all the memories of what I used to do. I hadn't realized how much denial I was in. Facing all those questions was very tough. The program helped me come to grips with things."

She worked with wheelers and family members at Kessler two or three days a week for about eight years, but now is there less frequently due to those skin sores. She sees driving in to Kessler, being active and wearing a dress and makeup as ways to show others what's possible. She both welcomes and enjoys being a role model.

Many people talk about college or driving or a first job being the turning point that helped them to start feeling better and knowing they were going to be OK after injury. People usually name activities that took place over a period of time that helped them. Bobbie talks about an exact moment.

"I dropped a record [12-inch vinyl, this was the '70s] and it took me a long time to pick it up. All the while, James Taylor's 'Shower the People You Love with Love' was playing over and over again. What I heard in the lyrics was that you get back what you put out and I decided to try that."

As her outlook and approach changed, she says, so did the way people saw her.

"I began doing more around the house and going out and meeting more people. I decided to be more positive and to try to be a better person. I figured that if I didn't like any of this new behavior I could always go back to the old me. It took people awhile to get used to this and some took longer than others, but more and more of them began to come around. As I became more happy and positive, I started wanting to be around myself more."

A lot has changed for Bobbie since that switchboard job over 29 years ago, but she's still learning new things and going back to old ones. She says her goal remains doing the stuff of life—working, going to school, volunteering, maintaining a 20-year relationship—whatever most helps her feel productive. As she's aged and her function has changed, the way she defines being productive has changed as well. With less energy to be out helping others, her attention is now on writing an autobiography.

"This is the hardest thing I've ever done because I have to write about my feelings," she says. "It's brought up so many issues I'd successfully forgotten, like how much my injury affected the people around me. I started writing this about 20 years ago and it's helped me fight some of my demons.

It's been very good for me."

Bobbie recently observed the 30th anniversary of her injury. Any regrets?

"Not many. I wish I'd finished college and got a degree. And I hate that I can't be married because of all the SSI and Medicaid and Section 8 rules."

What's in her future? More adventures in the deep end.

"Finish my book. Do an exercise video for quads. Take some classes and learn something I don't know yet." ∎

Marina Conner

Marina Conner is a maverick. In past lives she's been a model, a dancer, a nightclub singer and a rebel. A woman who loves men but finds them too hard to live with. And now a doting grandmother. For 31 of her 59 years, she's been paraplegic.

"Some of my women friends call me a Bitch on Wheels," she says, not without pride. "I'm not your average person. If I were in a movie, I'd be the mysterious, curious, complicated person filled with contradictions. Cher would play me."

Marina is a busy woman, working full time as a customer service specialist for a money order company. When things go wrong, orders disappear or money gets lost, she fields the irate phone calls. Her job as the liaison between customers and the company is to fix the problems that no one else can—scams, fraud, drug money laundering, all of it. She speaks several languages, including Spanish and Portuguese, and much of her work entails phone calls to bank officials in Central and South America.

Because her work day begins at noon, she sleeps in until 8 a.m. and lounges through her morning, watching the international and financial news and a soap or two before sitting down to brunch and phone calls to friends. Home from work at about 9:30, she takes in the news and Letterman before sleeping. Weekends are for the grandkids and baby-sitting them with museums, movies or bookstores.

"I don't bake cookies and I don't spoil them," she says. "I do educational things like teach them music. I run a tight ship."

Discharge to Hell

In 1972, Marina, a native of Panama, was a 28-year-old mother of four living in Colorado Springs. After catching her husband in an affair, she turned to a friend looking for a shoulder to cry on. What she got was a Fatal Attraction. Her friend decided that if he couldn't have her nobody could, and he shot her.

Vitals: T5-6 injury, six weeks of acute care, several surgeries and four months of rehab at Craig. During that period her husband departed the state, took their kids with him and left no forwarding address.

"Everything was so hard at first and I didn't believe the rehab people when they told me how much I would be able to do," Marina remembers. "I didn't believe anything would ever get better. Now I laugh about it because so much of this feels more like an inconvenience now."

Having nowhere to go after rehab, she says she was discharged to hell.

"I was in a nursing home for months and went back and forth to outpatient rehab therapy. I was devastated about losing my kids; not knowing where they were was horrible. It was almost a year before I got an apartment. I had modeled and sung professionally since my teens and was very proud of my body, especially my legs. When I was injured I was very angry about losing my legs and very angry about the wheelchair."

With a new SCI and without her kids for so long, it's no surprise that Marina got into Johnny Walker, valium and partying. But she also got into making friends, socializing and taking courses at the community college.

"I started dating some and it felt good finding out I was still a woman and could still have fun," she says. "I was even engaged for a time but broke it off. I was so focused on getting my kids back that I really didn't have time for a relationship. I'd built this wall of protection around myself so I wouldn't get hurt again. I thought alcohol made me sane but I partied so hard that sometimes I felt I was losing control."

Beyond Negativity

When the anger, the chair, the partying and the loss of her kids all ganged up on her, she attempted suicide. Seeing her survival as a second chance, she took a job as a nursing station secretary at Craig and began more college courses.

"I tried peer support, but what helped me the most was talking to a counselor at the hospital when I was working there. He

kept telling me I had to be strong because when I got my kids back they would need me. It was difficult because I was never the type of person to speak freely about myself or my feelings."

Marina's many trials had turned her into a cynical and angry crip who felt superior to other wheelers. Working around so many others using chairs was good medicine for that. A woman with a fashion-maven history—she insisted on wearing jewelry and makeup even to surgery—she continued to dress and accessorize stylishly. No baggy sweats for her. Competing in the Miss Wheelchair USA competition and singing with a trio at local clubs put her in the limelight again and helped her build confidence.

"Being around so many people in chairs at the hospital, it was like a brotherhood," she says. "I did a fashion show for the female patients so they could see that how they looked mattered. I wanted them to

know that they could still dress up to bring out the lady in them and that they could still look good and be the center of attention. The dating, the classes, the job and the singing all got me out and helped make me feel normal again. Those things were all part of my therapy. I began to realize I was the same person."

Even though her in-laws denied it, Marina figured her husband had the kids with him at his parents' place. Since her children were out of state, Legal Aid in Colorado could do little, and because she wasn't a citizen, the federal government could do less. She went four years before learning that her kids were, in fact, in Oregon and another year before seeing them. They had been told, alternately, that their mother had either died or abandoned them. When she filed for divorce, her ex filed for alimony. Finally, after seven years, she got the children back and started over as a single mom of four, who now ranged in age from 8 to 17.

With her kids back, she had a reason to get her act together and set an example, and now her life changed even more dramatically. She began working two jobs and acting like a drill sergeant with the kids. Like so many others featured here, Marina's attitude changed for the better every time her circumstances changed—getting her own place, going to school, working, getting assertive. Feeling more in control, she exerted more control.

While the jobs have changed over the years, they've all been full time and have utilized her strengths as a good listener skilled in dealing with people. She has worked in hospitals, done customer service and for years ran a travel agency, all the while learning to adapt, be flexible and always have backup plans. When her travel agency school booked her an inaccessible room and had meetings in inaccessible places during a weeklong training in Atlanta, she improvised, found the help she needed and made it into a good time. Visiting Panama without a sliding board, she found a furniture maker to build her one. When flexibility, initiative and contingency plans weren't enough, she returned to an old solution.

"When everything else failed and I needed something to carry me over, I eventually came back to God," she says. "I'd let go of Him and the church for years while I partied, but now I feel He protects me and guides me toward a less stressful life." She also uses the yoga she learned in rehab to manage and reduce stress, focusing on deep breathing to stay calm and connected with the positives of life.

"I deal with angry people all day long and need to get away from that. Yoga helps me recuperate from all the negativity. I practice in my chair at lunch or in bed in the morning. It gives me peace."

Earning Peace

Because family is the most important part of her life, Marina says losing her children was her deepest sorrow, getting them back and raising them her greatest motivation, and now grandchildren her biggest joy. These feelings extend to her larger family as well.

"For years I didn't tell my family in Panama what happened," she says. "I was afraid of getting the crippled treatment, but most of the pity I was afraid of was in my head. I wish I'd let them be more a part of this."

She'll tell you that advice from other wheelers was very helpful. She'll tell you that being around positive people was important. She'll tell you that knowledge and vigilance is a better way to deal with SCI than being afraid of what might happen. She'll tell you that she's had several things worse than SCI happen to her. And she'll tell you with a large smile that muscle spasms can improve your sex life. She'll never tell you it's been easy.

"I wouldn't have believed anyone who told me that being in a chair could be OK," she says, "but it is. Don't get me wrong, I don't like the chair but I've learned to laugh at everything that comes with it because it's all an adventure. I've also had a lot of help and have learned to listen to the medical people about taking care of myself.

"In the beginning I was a pushover and would cry when things didn't go well for me. I was asking too nicely when I was trying to get my kids back and I didn't get any respect at work until I got very assertive. Sometimes I had to talk like a truck driver. I wish it didn't have to be that way, but sometimes it was them or me. I earned that name, Bitch on Wheels, because I had to become pretty tough. If you don't fight, things will drag you down. Now, when I get fired up, watch out!

"My advice? Go to school and enjoy the experience. Have a goal, something to focus on and to live for. Find things to do so that you can start liking yourself again. Believe it when people tell you this is just the beginning and things will get better, because they do. It took me 20 years to get hold of this and sometimes I've been my own worst enemy. It's been a hard road, but I've learned a great deal.

"I also have peace of mind. I've got my family, my health, a job and a place to live. Sometimes when I'm outside getting in my car for work, I look around and it's beautiful and I say 'Yes!'" ■

Anne and Paul Herman

Risk-taking behavior is a popular route to spinal cord injury. That's how Anne and Paul Herman both got hurt. It's also how they both got better.

"Life follows fun," says Paul, a T5-6 para. "If you're not having fun, you're no fun to be with."

"If you don't take risks, you don't grow," says Anne, a C6-7 quad. "I've always liked excitement and I think recreation is much more important than any PT or OT or counseling."

It pays to listen to these two. Between them, they have 67 years on wheels, every one filled with adventure. Both have had accomplished careers, traveled extensively and are successful parents and athletic competitors. While they're anything but wet-behind-the-ears kids, they might be just getting started.

We're in Long Beach, Calif., where Anne and Paul have driven from their home in San Diego so Paul, 55 and now retired, can race in the PVA Wheelchair Games. Anne, who's 54, is a part-time social worker at Sharp Rehabilitation Center in San Diego, where she has worked for the past 10 years. Both were injured in motor vehicle accidents, Anne at 18 in a rollover, and Paul at 20 while racing his motorcycle.

Anne

In 1968, when Anne was a freshman at Western Michigan University in Kalamazoo, the friend she was with rolled his Jaguar on the way home from a fraternity party and she was thrown from the car. Following a three week stay and a laminectomy at the local hospital, she went to the 13-bed rehab ward of the University of Michigan in Ann Arbor for three months, then home to Flint for three months, then back to Ann Arbor for another three months of therapy.

Her future looked bleak. She feared that most of what she loved and wanted—skiing, college, marriage, family and especially swimming—were all out the window. Eventually she got them all back, and much more as well.

Ignoring her doctor, who told her to forget about swimming, Anne found a coach and started getting wet. Then she got Voc Rehab to pay for a couple of courses at the community college in Flint. Eighteen months post-injury, she was in New York swimming in the National Wheelchair Games. While there, she met other disabled athletes and began to get a feel for what life could be like.

Wayne State, Michigan's only accessible university at the time, came next, and she was soon meeting people again. She also joined the school's wheelchair sports team.

"Being with people was good and I felt normal again," Anne says. As so often happens, her peers were her best instructors. "I learned intermittent catheterization, transfers and adaptive clothing from other women in chairs there." While she stresses the importance of education for anyone with a disability, she says there were other advantages to being a student: "Being away from home helped me grow up and get independent. That was probably more important than the book work or who I met."

Paul

While Anne was getting an education, Paul was serving four years in the Air Force, including a tour in Vietnam. Once home from the war, he raced motorcycles on the professional circuit. In 1971, he dumped his bike on a dirt track in Toledo, Ohio. The fall wasn't all that bad, but getting run over a couple of times afterward was. Broken back, surgery, Harrington rods and six months flat on his back at the VA in Iowa City, followed by a year at the Hines VA Medical Center in Chicago. He spent six months of that year working with braces and crutches.

"I'd walk two hours each morning and then two more each afternoon," he says. "In the end, walking just wasn't very practical but I think that attempting to walk was part of my adjustment. I had to find out for myself if I could do it."

With Social Security and VA benefit checks coming every month, Paul stayed in Chicago for four years deciding what was next.

"I loved not having to think past the next day," he remembers. "You know, just kicking back and getting those checks every month. I'd been working since I was 14 and then when I got hurt I didn't have so many money worries any more. All I had to do was learn to drive and be independent. My circle of friends was other vets. I shared an apartment with another wheeler."

He did much more than just cash checks. Though he'd grown up on a farm, Paul felt his future was in the city so he began taking architecture courses at a community college. He also took up

chairs helped me go from feeling negative to being excited about life again. I liked what I saw when I saw Paul, so I followed him from party to party. He was special from the beginning and he's probably the best thing that's ever happened to me."

Family First

They quickly began long distance dating after the '74 Games, with Paul driving to Michigan or Anne flying to Chicago. Eventually he moved to Flint. They lived together for six months, got married in '77 and moved to San Diego two weeks later.

wheelchair racing, which at that time consisted of cruising down sidewalks in 50-pound chrome E&Js. When he was three years post-injury he met Anne at the 1974 National Wheelchair Games in Detroit.

By this time Anne was six years post-injury and hitting her stride. She'd been to Germany as part of the 1972 Paralympic team, was traveling and competing several times a year, and working full time as a Voc Rehab counselor and social worker. She smiles when she talks about meeting Paul.

"I'd been getting more active and doing things to feel better about myself," she says. "Working and getting to know others in

"It was good timing for both of us," Anne recalls. "I was 10 years post when we got married, Paul was eight. We were both pretty well adjusted by then and knew what to expect."

"Marriage was life-changing for me," Paul tells me. "Sharing my life made it much more meaningful."

After a few courses, Paul decided architecture wasn't for him ("You have to know how to draw and enjoy doing it eight hours a day.") and once in California he tried computer classes. Within two years he had an associate degree and steady work as a systems analyst, writing business applications for manufacturing software. The field has given them a comfortable life.

"Work was important to me," he says. "I liked the job and it helped me feel good about myself. Another important thing was that the job was practical, given the chair. I see so many people struggling in careers where they're destined to fail. How practical is it to be a truck driver in a chair, or a speech therapist with CP? It's very cool that they're trying to work, but you have to be realistic. And my job gave me the resources to have some fun. We wanted a family and you have to have money to raise kids."

Their son Donald came a year after Paul started working. I wondered if getting pregnant required any special machinations. "Is that like gyrations?" Paul asked. Well, not exactly. "We didn't have to do anything special for Anne to get pregnant. Donald was a miracle, right Anne?"

"I always hoped for kids," says Anne, "but we weren't sure Paul was fertile. My doctor recommended against even trying and told us that raising a child would be too hard. We were very lucky."

And very conscientious. Both of them did their pre-birth homework, gathering information, taking positive parenting classes and finding out from other disabled parents what to expect. Paul built a wooden changing table and made other modifications in anticipation of the event. Once Donald arrived, they worked hard to make raising a child from wheels work.

Much of the burden fell on Anne, and after returning to work for three months, she found the combination of employment and parenting too much. She quit her job and spent years volunteering as a counselor at Donald's elementary school. When he went to high school, she went back to work part time as a social worker.

"She was trying to do it all," Paul says. "When Don was a baby most everything fell on her because I was working full time to support us. Parenthood changed my life. I never worked late and family always came first. This hotel room is my idea of camping, but I took him camping with the scouts every year, solely for him. Having a child made me much more responsible."

Anne remembers the frustration and all the planning being a parent required.

"It was hard to be in a chair and one of the moms," she says. "Not all the homes in Donald's play group were accessible."

They both lined up play groups with other parents. They hired teens to take Donald swimming or for walks. Anne took him to the mall so he could walk safely, away from traffic. They took him everywhere—water skiing, snow skiing, Scouts and back to the Midwest a couple of times a year to visit family. They both embraced parenting with gusto and suspect they probably did more as parents than many of their ablebodied friends.

"He was our priority," says Paul. "We may have raised him more sanely because some things, like clean hands, just weren't that important. I think it might not have been until he was in high school that he truly realized we were in chairs."

Now, nearly 25 years later, they speak with pride of Don's graduation from UC Irvine and his work for a biomedical firm.

But isn't being a two-chair family cumbersome? Paul says there are upsides.

"If the house is set up for one wheeler, it's set up for two," he says. "I think it's probably kept us more independent. I see friends in chairs who depend on their AB spouses for everything, so much that they wear them out. We can't do that. And we never expected Don to help us."

These two just might be the Joneses everyone, including all their ablebodied friends, are trying to keep up with.

"Seems like every time we did something, our friends would do the same thing shortly after," Paul says, laughing. "We had our son then they had kids. We'd remodel our house, then they'd remodel theirs. We would travel and then they'd start traveling."

The Long Haul

Aside from Paul's recent retirement, following a 25-year career, neither of them has slowed down much or lost that sense of adventure. They continue to travel several times a year for professional conferences, where Anne does presentations and posters, or to see family, ski or attend the Veteran Wheelchair Games. Both are firm believers in doing what's fun and feels good.

After 16 National Veterans Wheelchair Games, Paul continues to compete. He's won gold five times in each event he entered and has wheeled more than his share of marathons.

"I'm not so serious about racing anymore," he admits. "Now I show up, compete and have a good time."

Anne's still working part time at Sharp, often putting in more hours than her paycheck reflects. Her job consists of outpatient social work and working with groups for women with disabilities, including a cross-disability support group.

"SCI women have unique needs in areas like stigma, self-esteem and self-determination," Anne says. "They need to find other women for support and to do things to empower themselves. I've found a good deal of satisfaction in work and helping other people."

Swimming is still important enough to her that she's willing to spend more time in the locker room changing than the 45 minutes she actually swims. The '72 Paralympics was no fluke; she competed in the '76 Games in Canada, the '96 Games in Atlanta, and the Mexico City Pan American Games as well. Her success has earned her spots in the Flint Sports Hall of Fame and the San Diego Hall of Champions.

They both still hit the slopes at ski areas in California and, more recently, Purgatory, Colo. Neither is about to stop any time soon and Anne's still as enthusiastic as ever, even though she recently broke her scapula skiing.

Post-injury life hasn't been totally clear sailing. Just prior to college graduation, the stress of a romantic breakup combined with heavy duty anxiety about finding work and the prospect of facing the cruel, non-campus world sent Anne into a major depression. She didn't want to eat, was unable to get out of bed and incapable of making decisions. Slow to seek treatment, she took a while before righting herself and getting back on track.

"I think I might have suppressed a lot of sadness and not taken the time to grieve my injury," she says. "It's okay to grieve. Living with spinal cord injury is hard."

Twenty years later she began to notice a hearing loss that eventually resulted in total deafness in one ear. Over the past 10 years she's gone through five hearing aids for the other ear, each progressively stronger. Counseling and support groups, she says, have helped her cope with this latest loss.

The broken scapula forced her to rely on home health assistance for three months, and now neck pain and scoliosis are forcing her to make other lifestyle and personal care changes.

"I'm slowing down some and things are a bit more difficult," she says. But she's also better equipped to adjust to change.

Paul's recent retirement was forced, in part, by increasing pain and stiffness from thirty some years of wheeling and 25 years at a desk. The past few years at work, he had to prop up his feet for several hours a day to lessen lower-leg swelling. When the job stopped being fun, he knew it was time to cash it in.

But they're not about to start retreating from life. They're planning more travel, more skiing, more racing and more swimming. What few lifestyle concessions they've made have been primarily to keep the adventure going.

The Most Important Thing

Did such full lives seem possible shortly after injury?

"I thought I was done, that I would never have fun again," Paul says. "I wanted to be a race car driver and I knew that was over. I'd grown up on a farm and after rehab, whenever I went to visit my parents there, I couldn't get around without hurting myself, so I knew that was out.

"That first year was so scary. I was anxious all the time. But when I began taking risks, connecting with others and being assertive, my attitude totally changed."

A lot of people say there's a reason they've been paralyzed. Not Paul.

"I just don't think of life that way and don't take it that seriously. I never planned it, it just sort of happened. I've never looked too far down the road and honestly couldn't tell you what's going to happen next year."

Anne, on the other hand, is fairly certain her injury was meant to be. Otherwise, she'd have too many connections to explain.

"I've sensed an apparent plan since the beginning," she says. "I went to Western Michigan because a friend recommended the school, and he ended up in a chair too. Before I was injured, I double dated with the daughter of the man who would be my surgeon. I began a support group after seeing an old friend who needed one. I think SCI, work and various activities I've pursued all seem like they've been for a reason."

Life with SCI has changed enormously since Paul and Anne were injured. The equipment's better, accessibility has improved and medical advances have increased quality of life. But even with all that, Paul tells me he feels SCI research is not much closer to the cure than it was 30 years ago. Which brings him back to the importance of taking risks and having fun.

"Once you start having fun, other things fall into place," he preaches. "When I began trying things, finding out what was fun and then doing them, I started moving on. It's a process that takes time. The answers don't all come in two weeks. I spent six months trying to walk before I figured out that I wouldn't be able to. There are so many things like that you have to figure out for yourself."

After three and a half decades of risk-taking and adventure, Anne's advice to newbies is similar and not surprising.

"I tested myself and took risks, even when I was afraid," she says. "I learned from my mistakes. Sports influenced every aspect of my life and helped me build the self-esteem I needed to have the life I wanted. Sports helped me feel young. All those things helped me feel more in control and better about myself. People need to celebrate *any* success, and they need risks and adventure in their lives.

"Whenever I wanted to do something—swimming, going to school, having a child—I found another quad who had done it and learned from her. I figured if they could, so could I."

Paul says it differently. "Having fun is the most important thing," he says. "That's what sports did for me. Don't worry about the job, don't wait for the cure. Just start having fun."

Paul and Anne continue to walk the talk and remain much younger and more adventuresome than most people 20 years their junior. Their risk and adventure formula works for them and they're sticking to it. ∎

Don Dawkins

Don Dawkins denied he was a gimp, denied his paralysis, denied its permanence and denied himself. He did it for years until one day, in a support group filled with old-timers, a long-term survivor asked him a key question. Was his injury going to be a chapter in his life, or the whole book?

"That's when I decided I wasn't going to let this be my life," he says, "but it took me close to a decade to get hold of this."

Saturday morning in Sarasota, Fla. is kick-back time for Don. He needs those weekends to recover from his demanding work weeks. He commutes over an hour each way to his nine-to-five job in Tampa as director of outreach services for the Florida SCI Resource Center, an information clearing house for people with new and old injuries. The 81,000 miles logged on his two-year-old van speak to how much he travels as an advocate, peer mentor and lobbyist.

He's passionate about his work with new injuries, and passionate about the sorry state of rehab today. Frustrated by his clients' ever-shorter rehab stays, he often takes on the job himself, telling and showing people with new injuries how to dress or do transfers. He sits with patients and parents in intensive care units explaining the possibilities and offering hope, encouragement and options. He tells me he's angry with cure-crazy politicians who fund cure research at the expense of rehab and quality of life, and that he may have had more advantages and opportunities during the 1960s and '70s than people who are injured now.

"I didn't spend half my life in this field to watch today's kids being denied half a chance," he says. "A lot of new injuries think this is the way it is. They need to understand that they can fight back. Where's the democracy here?"

Don, 56, has worked for 20 years as a therapeutic recreation specialist, a counselor and a program manager at four different facilities. Prior to his rehab career, he owned and ran a bookstore and sold durable medical equipment. He's an old-timer himself now.

He was out with friends in 1965 when the car he was riding in rolled, leaving him with a T4 injury. A broken bone cut an artery and he nearly bled out before reaching the hospital. He eventually did his rehab at Mary Freebed Rehabilitation Center in Grand Rapids, Michigan, where the care was excellent despite what he calls an aged facility reminiscent of a Dickens novel.

Every day, his mom made the 100-mile round-trip bus ride to visit, and never flinched as he took his anger out on her. He was depressed, lost nearly 50 pounds and couldn't sleep.

"It was total denial," he says. "I thought breaking your back was like breaking a leg and that eventually it healed. I thought if I didn't accept the paralysis, it wasn't real." He refused to participate or cooperate with therapists, and left rehab knowing very little about how to take care of himself. Upon discharge, he holed up in his parents' home and stayed close. He felt no connection to other wheelers.

"I stayed that way for years," he says. "I'd cross the street to avoid other gimps."

He had lost his identity as an athlete. He'd lost the future he'd imagined in the Marine Corps or as a cop, and he feared he'd lost the ability to make his own way. He couldn't look at himself in the mirror.

Discoveries Small and Large

Don's slow metamorphosis began a year after discharge when he moved to Milwaukee, lived on his own, cared for himself and worked a 50 hours a week factory job. He began to date, but continued to struggle.

Another step in his evolution came after his return from Milwaukee when he enrolled in a community college. Voc Rehab and other benefits sources were flush and generous in those days, giving him a stipend, offering to buy him a van and paying for school. But he had no study skills, no experience applying himself to course work, and was fairly certain college was about partying, women and good times. Don had never been a scholar and his roommate Dan had to explain to him that book learning might also be involved.

"I didn't have a clue until he said, 'Look, you fool, it's like a job. You go to class, you read, you study, you take tests.' I understood that and began to catch on. I got about a year's credit in two years."

Yet Don was still going through the motions with no joy or flavor to his life. He didn't much care about anything, so skin breakdowns and surgery quickly followed. His doctor diagnosed him with FIS, or 'f--k it syndrome.' He began to find the cure for that when he transferred to Michigan State and discovered wheelchair basketball.

"I'd heard of wheelchair sports but figured they were beneath me," he remembers. "When I went to that first game all the sounds and smells in the gym brought back memories. The athletes had skills and used strategy. They had jobs, cars, careers and wives. They were happy and I wanted that; I wanted it like dope. It was a real epiphany, and for the first time I thought I could have a life. Seeing these guys made it all real for me. I started playing right away and it changed my life."

He also went to a disability support group, and that forced him to deal with his denial. When he did, things changed more and faster.

"Those old-timers bitch-slapped me around," he says. "They called me a whiner and told me I wasn't the only guy with problems. One guy with a Bronx accent told me, 'Don, youse is very narcissistic.' I had to go home and look it up. When the guy asked me whether the chair was a chapter or the whole book, it really opened my eyes."

Peer involvement, he was learning, was essential. "Old-timers don't coddle you. They tell it like it is. Most of what I needed to learn came from the give and take, the stories, the camaraderie of other paras or quads. I realized I didn't survive that accident so that my life could be miserable."

Even so, Don's recurring pressure sores forced another surgery in the mid-'70s. He spent months on a wild SCI unit, in a room with drug dealers, ex-cons, booze, sex behind the curtains. He fit right in.

When his doctor saw how well Don connected with others, he encouraged him to mentor them. His nondisabled friend Dan Adams says that was the start of Don's counseling career. More importantly, that's when he met his future wife Marj, an SCI nurse who has become his emotional cornerstone and helped him regain his sense of confidence.

"She got me past a lot," Don says. "I couldn't blame anyone for the chair any more. I started taking responsibility, realizing that my attitude and happiness were choices. I began feeling some pride about who I was and what I'd done. I learned having a disability was OK."

Don and Marj married 27 years ago, a few years after they met. Ten years later, not long before they moved to Florida to care for his aging parents, they became parents to Jill, who he calls the joy of his life. He says his daughter, marriage and extended family are what he's most proud of in his life, the best things he's ever done.

"I was working when Marj called and told me she was in labor," he remembers. "We met at the hospital, where a sleepy resident asked me, 'Do you want in on this?' The next thing I knew I was in the delivery room with Jill in my arms. That was maybe the greatest moment in my life. Marj and I have worked hard and we've made a great life for ourselves."

A Positive Passion

Don has his horror stories, including 28 surgical procedures, approximately four years in bed and all those conflicted years of denial. At least 15 of the surgeries were for repeated skin breakdowns, which he says were secondary to his own stupidity. A botched surgery to correct scoliosis cost him a kidney and four months in the hospital. "I'm still paying for mistakes I made in the first few years," he says.

What has 37 years on wheels taught him?

He ticks off his answers: "I've developed an almost perverse sense of confidence about being able to deal with what life throws me. I know I can ride the whitewater. SCI is not a fate worse than death, and walking doesn't define who we are. We all do what we have to do and we all choose if we're going to be victims or survivors. Nobody's a hero here."

How can a newly injured person find a way to understand all that?

"We're not widgets; everybody does it their own way," he explains. "For me it was a combination of things—wonderful parents, friends who wouldn't cut me any slack, maturity, education, life experiences, seeing others in chairs moving forward."

Don still gets choked up recalling how his family and friends simply refused to abandon him after his accident. He expresses deep gratitude and credits them for helping him through his changes. He knows how rare that kind of loyalty is. His friend Dan points to Don's gift of sharing, calling it a fair trade-off.

"He didn't want any special treatment," Dan told me, "and in return we only saw him and not the chair."

Is there a process for learning this?

"I think you've got to have contact with other wheelers," Don says. "They teach you what life can be like, what's possible. PVA knows this; that's why they hook people up in rehab. Knowing other survivors might have sped up the process for me because I didn't put any effort into it until those guys confronted me and I had to accept what I was. It may sound trite, but quality of life is proportional to the effort you put into it."

Is employment essential to that sense of engagement?

"No, not everyone can work. Success is being productive and active. There's incredible value in volunteering. Success could be travel or a hobby. Success is having a positive passion for life.

"If someone in rehab had shown me a video of how my life would eventually turn out, I never would have believed it. I couldn't imagine that I could have a graduate degree or a wife who gives me unqualified love or a great kid or even be happy. I hate to say it, but I'm probably a better man for this. I'm very grateful." ∎

Fred Fay

In 1981, after nearly two decades of quadriplegia, Fred Fay had it all. Still only in his 30s, he'd already done long and successful advocacy moving the country toward accessibility for people with disabilities. He had a great job at Tufts University. He'd been showered with national recognition, fathered a child and joyfully embraced being a dad.

Then the bottom fell out. First he and his first partner separated permanently. Then a cervical cyst that had been drained years earlier grew back and compressed his spinal cord. In less than a year he went from a manual chair to a recliner to a power recliner to a stretcher as he progressively lost function and sensation. Whenever he sat up, he experienced increased pain and severe autonomic dysreflexia.

At first he continued to commute daily to Tufts, but as his condition worsened he rented an apartment next to the hospital, wheeled to work on a gurney each day and only went home on weekends. Despite four surgeries, his cyst continued to progress. Twenty-three years later he remains flat on his back.

In putting this project together I made a conscious effort to steer clear of superstars, mostly because they make the rest of us look so bad. Though Fred is clearly a superstar, his is a story that needs to be shared.

Still, all I could think about was the bed. It scared me, just as I suspect our chairs frighten so many nondisabled people. Within two minutes of wheeling into his home, Fred had me so comfortable that my apprehensions vanished.

He lives in Concord, about a half-hour from Boston, in a comfortable old house he and his second partner Trish remodeled and expanded when they got together in the early 1980s.

His bedroom is a techno-geek's dream. Within arm's reach are a VCR, stereo, phone, keyboard and controls for a computer. A television and computer monitor are mounted overhead and facing

the floor. The ceiling is mirrored, letting him see the keyboard on his chest. An environmental control unit allows him to open and close windows and doors, raise and lower shades and blinds, light the fireplace and operate all his other equipment. He's able to run most of the house from his bed.

That bed, complete with a hinged mirror mounted above his head so he can maintain eye contact during conversations, sits atop a power wheelchair base. Using a long, heavy-duty extension cord, he cruises throughout the house and onto the deck on sunny days.

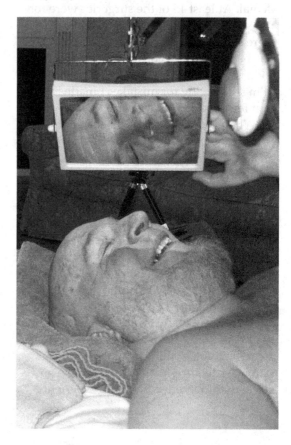

Some might define hell as looking at the ceiling for more than two decades. Not Fred, the ultimate optimist and spinmeister.

"Most people dream about breakfast in bed once a year," he says. "I get all my meals there. And I never get stuck in traffic."

When I ask him if his injury was the worst thing that ever happened to him, he just laughs. "No. That would have to be the stock market. Quite honestly, I don't see my disability as all that restrictive. Though it's certainly affected who I've become, it's a very small part of who I am."

A Rapid Ascendancy

Fred was 16 when he lost his grip on a backyard trapeze in Bethesda, Md., fell 10 feet to the ground and landed squarely on his head; broken neck at C5-7, complete quadriplegia. That was in 1961, before the days of SSI, Medicaid or extensive vocational rehabilitation. Following surgery as a research patient at the National Institutes of Health in Bethesda, Fred rehabbed at Warm Springs, the center in Georgia founded by President Franklin Roosevelt. He wasn't sure what the future held, but like so many of us, he ran into a key person who gave him a good idea.

"I met Larry Kegan who had been in a chair for a few years and he told me about his life and the many things he'd done with it," Fred remembers. "At some point he asked, 'You know you'll never walk again, don't you?' I said something like 'Yeah, I suppose.' He kept asking until I couldn't deny it anymore. That night I sobbed and sobbed, but woke up the next morning with a vision of what my life could be—school, work, marriage, family—and began working to get strong and learn what I needed so I could have those things."

Forty years ago anyone out in public using a wheelchair was an oddity, a spectacle to be openly stared at. Fred's reaction to that kind of attention? "I learned that I could either get angry with those people who stared or ignore them and go about my business," he says. "I chose the latter."

His immediate business was to have 3,000 business cards printed up and co-found a peer support group with a friend in the D.C. area. He formed networks with 65 community groups to make sure the proposed Washington subway system would be accessible. But he was just getting started.

After earning a degree at the University of Illinois, he worked at IBM for three years evaluating hardware and software, then returned to the U of I for a Ph.D. in psychology. His graduate work examined architects' attitudes toward disability and their willingness to design buildings with built-in access. His findings? Attitudes don't matter much. The best way to get what you want or need is by asking, and he's spent much of his life doing just that. He lobbied tirelessly for access to public transportation (Urban Mass Transportation Act of 1964), public buildings (Architectural Barriers Act of 1968) and inclusion (Rehabilitation Act of 1973). He also worked for Jimmy Carter's election in 1976.

"Back then," he says, "every curb was like the Berlin wall and air travel was next to impossible. Whenever I ran into a problem I'd keep going up the chain of command from the flight attendant to the captain to the airline vice-president to get what I needed."

Doctorate in hand, Fred became a consultant for the Massachusetts State Rehabilitation Commission, founded the Boston Center for Independent Living and, as a senior research associate for the Urban Institute think tank in D.C., did a giant needs assessment survey on independent living. In 1975 he was appointed to his position at Tufts University. In 1977, he was named one of Boston's Ten Outstanding Leaders.

One year later, based on his work with the American Coalition of Citizens with Disabilities, he received a coveted U.S. Jaycees Leadership Award, which goes each year to 10 outstanding young Americans under 36 who have excelled and made significant contributions. Previous winners include John Kennedy, Ralph Nader and Elvis Presley. Many other awards followed.

"The awards were all real ego trips," he says. "The U.S. Jaycees Award event was three days of celebration and meeting important people."

It's All Between the Ears ... or on the 'Net

Fred was riding high, then the cyst hit him. He says coping with it was much harder than adjusting to his original injury. After 20 years of schooling—and barely 10 of working—he was on his back, separated from his partner and unemployed.

"I went through a severe depression when I retired from Tufts," he says. "I was in tears constantly from medication. I was taking methadone for pain and then went through withdrawal when I quit. I was pretty numb and don't have much recall of a couple of those years. Getting free of all the prescription drugs and learning self-hypnosis and meditation helped me get back on track."

I know people who never got back on track after losing a job. How do you get back on track when you're flat on your back?

"I usually hope for the best and prepare for the worst," he says. "I would imagine having less and less function, until I was only a disembodied brain. Once I convinced myself I could get by on intellect alone, then the loss of function became easier to deal with. I've always been grateful for having a spinal cord injury rather than something that was more progressive. Things could always be worse."

He uses self-hypnosis and meditation, along with positive affirmations and biofeedback to stay relaxed enough to ward off the blues and depression.

"Imagining something is almost as powerful as the real thing," he says. "When I go out on my deck I can get myself into such a relaxed state that if I focus, I can be in the Bahamas in about 30 seconds." Warp speed and cheap.

Fred's been too busy to physically go to the Bahamas. Instead, he partnered with Trish and threw himself into activism and advocacy. He helped elect a governor in Massachusetts, worked extensively with Justin Dart by phone and on the Internet for passage of the ADA, served as chairman of the Americans with Disabilities for the Clinton/Gore campaigns in 1992 and '96, affected disability provisions of the Democratic Party platform and influenced several White House appointments. Along the way, he received the prestigious Henry B. Betts Award, a $50,000 recognition given to the person who "embodies innovative dedication to improving daily life for people with disabilities worldwide."

He credits technology for much of what he does. He's either online or on the phone constantly, and sends out frequent e-mails and alerts about disability-related legislation to thousands. His friends suggest that he's more productive now than when he was sitting up.

"The computer and Internet give me access to the world," he says. "They can really liberate people with disabilities."

Considering *What* Circumstances?

As Fred reviews his life, he reiterates that taking responsibility for his own happiness and health has made a lot of things possible.

"Attitude is so important," he says. "I believe I always have a choice in how I see things, and that things usually work out for the best. I've chosen to be optimistic and see severe disability as an opportunity to learn about dependence and pain management. Reading *Man's Search for Meaning* [Viktor Frankl's account of his years as a prisoner in a Nazi concentration camp] reinforced this for me and made clear to me that we can choose how to react to things.

"When a doctor told me I had a 1-in-200,000 chance of fathering a child, I experimented until I was able to ejaculate. Taking responsibility for that gave me my son Derrick, and nothing I've done comes close to being as important as him."

Fred always finds the positives, quickly rattling off several about staying in his bed and his home: never late for meetings because they're always at his house, no rush-hour traffic, being his own boss and deciding when to work or play. He points out that if you don't mention the bed, most people will jump at those perks.

He and his partner Trish met in the hospital when he was dealing with complications from the cyst and her husband was dying of cancer. They got to know each other, fell in love over time and have been together for 20 years. They still act like a couple of smitten teenagers. Could that be part of the reason he smiles so much?

Together, they manage a household, watch movies and occasionally rock out with their home karaoke machine. They listen to music on his 400-CD changer from his vast and eclectic collection of tunes.

Fred counts his parents' high expectations as a huge blessing. Foregoing college, even in the tune-in-and-drop-out '60s, was never an option for him. Those expectations rubbed off and he only seems to have raised them over the years.

He sees that peer encounter at Warm Springs as a very significant point in his life, and feels it's essential for wheelers to know other wheelers. He suggests political involvement as a great way to gain peer support and get in touch with something larger than oneself.

"I learned that if I was going to make progress I needed to stick my neck out," he says. "You've got to be willing to take risks if you want to get ahead."

Fred is about as happy, positive and easygoing as anyone I've ever met, and there's certainly no need to qualify that description with "considering the circumstances." And his good humor is contagious. He was out on his deck in the sun as I drove off, and it was easy to imagine him smiling, with a drink in hand, soaking up the Bahama sunshine. ∎

Charmaine Brown   *A Royal Flush*

Wally Dutcher

About a year after he was injured, Wally Dutcher's Voc Rehab counselor gave him a vocational aptitude test. The results indicated he had a future as a pilot, real estate agent or mortician. Instead he went on to design homes, organize and manage a mutual fund and run a successful cabinet-manufacturing company.

He also founded two local chapters of what is now the National Spinal Cord Injury Association, started a competitive swim club for kids, helped found a successful center for independent living and now works on disability issues with his local government in St. Petersburg, Fla., where he's lived since 1961.

"Life is about fun, challenge, resourcefulness and opportunity," Wally says. "I've never been afraid to try new things or check out new areas. I go with what's available and transfer skills from one setting to another."

The way he sees it, success is about being ready when opportunity knocks. He does the research, becomes knowledgeable and then goes for it when the time is right.

"You never know when the spaghetti will stick to the wall," he says.

Curious, bright, assertive and very willing to take risks, a straightshooting guy who doesn't sugarcoat anything, he's fun to talk to on the phone and more fun to spend time with. How does he describe himself?

"I can be your best friend or your worst enemy. Just don't try to hose me."

When Wally sat down in 1956, forty-seven years ago, the world was a different place. Most of the people in this book weren't born, the Dodgers played in Brooklyn, the Lakers played in Minnesota, computers were bigger than houses, music came on vinyl and phones were all wired to the wall. Survival for quads was iffy.

He was 19 and on active duty in the navy when he broke his neck diving into a pool. Complete C5-7. Rehab, such as it was, came after four months of acute care and a couple more waiting at the SCI Center at the Hines VA Hospital just outside of Chicago. He moved to the Woods VA rehab hospital in Wisconsin, spent four months in bed before he ever sat in a chair, and wryly offers that at that time occupational therapy consisted primarily of keeping people occupied.

Watching others in rehab showed him what he should and shouldn't do. Some adjusted and pushed the envelope. Others withered. He paid attention to it all. After 22 months in hospitals, he returned to his parents' home northeast of Milwaukee.

Even though he has a complete injury, needs physical assistance with many activities, and didn't drive for the first 25 years of disability, it's hard to imagine a more independent person.

"Everyone can be independent in how they think," he says. "Independence is utilizing what's available to achieve your goals and get the job done. I've never been afraid to ask for help. It's an opportunity to meet people. Everyone's dependent in some way."

For Wally, family and VA benefits are what made school and work possible. "I might have ended up in a nursing home without them," he says. "I wouldn't have done much without my parents and Chris. My parents and sisters were very supportive and when Chris and I married, she assumed my care. Now that she uses a chair herself because of bad knees and emphysema, I'll hire someone to help. It's always about getting the job done."

Opportunity Knocks, Knocks, Knocks ...

I visit Wally and his wife Chris in the big, open St. Petersburg home he designed and had built in 1978. The only sign of adaptation is the biggest roll-in shower I've ever seen, complete with a 6-foot sliding glass patio door. It's the third home he's designed and built for himself, and he got it right. (His first opportunity came with his parents, when he designed a barrier-free home they built with a quadriplegic contractor.)

What sticks out about Wally is his ability to see opportunity in everything. He expects success once he gets started on any project, regardless of any barriers along the way.

While many would have seen the institutional architecture of the 1950s and '60s as an obstacle to higher learning, Wally saw it as an opportunity. Getting up to third-floor classrooms at a local Milwaukee college was an occasion to meet other students and offer them a workout on the stairs. Nearly 10 years later, before the advent of vans with lifts and accessible public transportation, he got to classes at the University of South Florida in Tampa by finding three students to drive him to school. He routinely thumbed his way around the inaccessible campus, meeting new people to assist him.

Upon discharge from rehab, and again when he moved to Florida, Wally saw the lack of peer support as an opportunity to organize local chapters of the National Paraplegia Foundation—now the National SCI Association—in Milwaukee in 1959 and Pinellas County in 1961.

There was another knock at the door when he needed some in-home care and PT.

The Visiting Nurses Association sent Chris, the woman he eventually married in 1961. He immediately began a campaign to date her. Despite what he calls his obvious charms, she declined.

"I was impressed with his attitude," she says, "but I had a policy of not fraternizing with patients. He was very persistent."

Chris relented, Wally prevailed, and they dated for nearly two years before marrying. They visited Florida shortly thereafter, liked what they saw and decided to stay. After they'd spent seven years fighting the negative attitudes of the day about people with disabilities adopting, their daughter Dana entered their lives when she was six weeks old. They were in heaven and Dad passed out cigars.

You'll See It When You Believe It

Wally turns the old phrase "I'll believe it when I see it" on its head. He sees things happen because he believes he can make them happen. His formula for doing well sounds like a cross between self-help books, the Boy Scouts and, of course, your mom and dad.

"First you need to know what you want," he says. "Then you have to be prepared and do your homework. You have to know what you're talking about and how to be resourceful. You have to take advice and suggestions and then figure out how to use them to get what you want."

Rather than viewing the almost universal inaccessibility of the '60s and '70s as an employment obstacle, he saw it as a chance to work in a different way.

He turned the absence of broadcasting jobs for people with disabilities into a reason to start a mobile disc jockey business. When a neighbor asked for his help in putting together a mutual fund, he saw both employment and an opportunity to learn securities law and the investment world. When asked to run a cabinet-making operation about a dozen years later, he saw a chance to learn about managing a business, which he did successfully for several years. Since then he's continued to consult on home design modification from his home office.

He credits his employment success to his two philosophic linchpins, SWAG (sophisticated wild-ass guess) and RAM (rearrange, adapt, modify). The sophistication is in the learning and homework necessary to make those wild-ass guesses happen. RAM is about being flexible, getting along with others and creating win/win situations.

If idle hands do the devil's work, Wally's got an express ticket to the land of the saints; the guy is always busy. When he's not working he's volunteering in his community.

When his daughter expressed an interest in competitive swimming, he helped found St. Petersburg Aquatics, a cooperative effort with the city, and got them to kick in $30,000 in seed money. He drew up the incorporation papers, and served as president of the board of directors. The program ultimately produced an Olympic gold medallist. He proudly speaks of his daughter and her accomplishments in the water, which include being a member of both the Junior National and National teams, a two-time Olympic trials participant and an NCAA All-American 14 times. Hard to know how much of that would have happened without the swim program.

He kept looking outward as much as inward. Using his business acumen, he organized and co-founded the Caring and Sharing Center for Independent Living, and served multiple terms as both president and secretary. That organization has grown in the last 10 years from its original 600 square feet and one employee to a 7,000 square-foot facility with about a dozen employees. And he serves on an advisory committee advising the mayor on access to services, facilities and programs of the city.

Wedded to his sense of opportunity is a deep curiosity about almost everything. Questions from his daughter about God prompted Wally and Chris to check out the local Unitarian-Universalist Church. His curiosity ("I'd never taught religion before, so why not?") led him to teaching the kids' religious education program as he learned. Eventually he and a group of friends formed a new Unitarian-Universalist Fellowship.

His lifelong love of singing led him to a performance of the Alumni Singers, a local group that concentrates on African-American spirituals. Not wanting to disturb the dynamics of the group, he asked the director if he might practice with it, but the director insisted he join the group. Twenty years later, he's still singing with them.

Bet on the Next Hand

What does Wally think is his strongest asset?

"Knowing how to solve problems," he says. "I always have to ask the next question. It's not really about the chair so much as about life—you show up, you make a good impression, you know what you're talking about, you ask questions and learn. You've got to take things seriously, know what you're doing and enjoy it while you're doing it.

"You have to learn to advocate for yourself and know what you need in terms of healthcare or benefits or anything else. You have to challenge decisions and be willing to go up the chain of command. Peer support may not be for everyone, but you can learn a lot from others."

Most 65-year-olds are afraid of computers. Wally's on his up to eight hours a day.

"I got my first one in '89," he remembers. "I've always been curious about technology and how things work. As a kid I had to know how bowling-pin setters worked. I'd go to the circus and watch the gaffers to see how they orchestrated everything."

His best advice to newly injured people?

"You've got to accept what's happened and move on," he says. "There's always another hand to be dealt, that's how life is."

After spending a day and an evening with Wally, I know I've met someone whose life has been filled with achievement by any standard. It's easy to believe him when he calls most of his 47 years of using a chair more inconvenience than imposition. I can't imagine spending time with him without enjoying myself.

He's adventurous, opinionated, irreverent, creative, funny as hell and always looking forward. He's also generous, engaged in life, eager to contribute and give to others.

Before I say good-bye I have to ask what more is left for him to do.

"Oh gosh. I've got so much to do and I'm running out of time. Each day is a new opportunity." ■

CHAPTER SIX
SCI and Meaning

No discussion of disability would be complete without asking people what disability means to them. Because living with a spinal cord injury affects people emotionally, spiritually and culturally, making sense of that experience and finding some meaning in it might be called a philosophical, spiritual or religious pursuit. Then again, maybe it's no more than a physical condition absent any meaning.

Q: Is there any meaning, purpose or lesson to be learned from your SCI?

- Things happen for a reason or as part of God's plan
- This is all quite random, without any reason
- This has made me a deeper, stronger, wiser person

Vague questions beget vague answers. Most people saw this as two separate questions, one about why they'd been injured and another about what they'd learned. Many say their accidents happened for a reason, though they often struggle to articulate one. Nearly everyone will tell you they have learned more than a few lessons since sitting down.

As a species, we seem to want reasons for most everything; in the face of calamity, that imperative is amplified. But wanting something doesn't make it so. About half these people believe their injuries had some reason or purpose, the most specific explanations revolving around one general theme: "So I can teach other people" or "So I can be an example for others" or "God chooses strong people for this, and I was chosen to be an example." Joel Lorentz, injured shortly after shaking his fist in defiance of God, however, doesn't totally discount the possibility of divine retribution.

Many continue to search. When pressed about a reason or purpose, they often respond by saying "I haven't figured it out," "I'm still learning the reason" or "I know there's a reason, but I haven't found it yet."

Many, like Gretchen Schaper, simply want some order to both life and the universe. "I think I'd go crazy knowing that everything happens randomly," she says. "So much of what's come into my life—the motorcycle, Peter, my art, the dogs, my house—they're all the result of SCI. I believe those things were supposed to happen, like a complete chain of events."

Like Gretchen, others sensed a purpose or intent, even if they are unable to put their finger on what it is. "I've seen an apparent plan since the very beginning," Anne Herman says. "I chose my college on the recommendation of a friend who later became disabled, I double-dated with the daughter of my eventual neurosurgeon, I started a support group because a friend needed one. I don't think it's all coincidence."

In contrast, about one-quarter of this group sees their accidents as totally random, rejecting out of hand the suggestion of some reason or grand design. "I hate it when people go there," says Richard Famiglietti. "This was an unfortunate accident." Karen Hwang finds no meaning in her injury or disability either and compares her life to an absurdist drama. "Things are what they are," she says. Ditto for Paul Herman: "I just don't think like that."

Pat McGowan's been on both sides. He suspected a reason at first, then changed his mind. "Maybe I was grasping for a rationalization," he now says. "I don't look for a reason anymore. Life is random."

Wally Dutcher, as usual, has his own take, and focuses on the practical more than the philosophical. "I don't look for a meaning or reason," he says, "because if you're constantly looking for one, I don't think you'll ever go forward."

This group may be vague about why they were injured, but they have few doubts about learning from the experience of being disabled. On this topic, they are reflective, sincere and talkative. Answers ran the gamut from the sunny—they'd learned patience, gained strength, become more positive about life or valued their family and friends more—to very overcast and foreboding lessons of the high cost of living in the fast lane or getting out of gang life.

Michael Slaughter learned he has fewer limitations than he thought. Benj Anderson now looks for opportunity everywhere. Curtis Lovejoy gained a new focus and commitment to doing the right thing. Keith Davis now finds daily meaning in positively impacting others. "SCI was having a mid-life crisis at 17," he says, "with the right to make mistakes."

Fred Fay feels losing progressively more function over his now 40-plus years of disability brought out the best in him and helped him become even more productive. "There's a lot of acquired wisdom that comes with this," he says convincingly. "If you live through it, you've got something to teach."

Some people create reason or meaning. "Look," Angel Watson says, "as long as I have to deal with this, I can at least be a good example to others, to young people." SCI drove Phillip Mann to commit "to be the most positive disabled person I can be."

Mark Bussinger and Joel Irizarry see SCI as a daily test of grit, adaptability, patience and empathy. "I'm still learning every day," Mark says after 24 years.

"You make of life what you want," says Jason Regier, "and it can be an enlightening experience. You benefit and learn from it." Dan Wilkins says SCI confirms many popular observations for him, "like most of life being small stuff, that strength comes from adversity, that if I can do this I can do anything."

Some speak of lessons in vulnerability, humility and resilience. Anne Marie Hochhalter says SCI is a reminder that we're all at risk all the time. Vincent Dureau says he finds comfort in man's ability to cope, and is humbled by the reminder that "shit happens and sometimes we face challenges that are bigger than us and defeat us."

While some claim disability made them better people, that's exactly where others like Susan Douglas and Mark Bussinger draw the line. "I'm skeptical of this concept of wisdom or learning being a result of suffering," Susan says with a sigh. "I didn't need this to be a better person." Mark says he might have needed some improvement before he was injured but adds, "I don't think I need to be a saint."

Regardless of beliefs about reason, purpose, randomness and lessons learned, sooner or later people are faced with decisions about whether to go on after injury and how to go on. That's where Don Dawkins says things get simple. "You make a choice to be a victim or survivor," he says. "It's not complicated."

The people on these pages were selected because they're doing well and because they're happy with their lives so it's not surprising that they've found positive lessons and meaning in their experience of disability. The broad range of the lessons they've learned and meanings they've found, along with their resilience and trust in the future, should offer hope and promise to us all.

Having asked "Why?" and "Why me?" and having found or created answers they can live with and lessons they could learn from, they've moved forward. For them, the operative question became "What's next?"

Charmaine G. Brown *A Royal Flush*

These people all wondered about what life might have been like had their injuries not happened, about those roads not taken. That kind of speculation is inescapable for anyone who finds himself on a road *so* different as this road of wheels.

It's easy to find the downside of paralysis. Hell, the list is endless. But is it also possible that paralysis has an upside? Without getting preposterously sappy, can something good arise from this extreme kind of disruption? If people were able to find positive lessons and meanings, might they find opportunity as well?

Q: Did any positive opportunities come your way that would not have if you hadn't been injured?

- Many general positives
- Sports
- Good people
- Education
- Travel
- Job
- Being a role model

The responses people gave to this question go a long way in explaining why they've coped so successfully. They've all done well both in finding positive opportunities and outcomes to their injuries and then seizing those opportunities as they came. They took advantage of being a role model or example for others, getting closer to family members, seizing the chance to reevaluate life or get serious and responsible about living it. They spoke with gratitude of the positive and influential people who'd entered their lives. Some pointed to the doors wheelchair sports opened, others to the benefits of a college education that otherwise would not have come their way.

Before his injury, Jason Graber had no plans for his future. Now, with his college degree in hand, he sees nothing but big things: "I expect something good to happen to me every day because of my chair."

When he was shot at 17, Felipe Antonio was living on the edge of gang life. Seven years later he's working and going to college, neither of which seemed likely

before his accident. "Sometimes our disability gives us opportunities like college or being a role model," he says. He's running with both of them.

Disability gave Robert Statam the courage to put drugs and alcohol behind him, start anew and get an education.

James Lilly, Joel Irizarry, Juan Garibay and Felipe Antonio all went from gang life to classroom with the help of disability programs and Vocational Rehabilitation. Juan and Felipe both used California's fee waiver program to cover tuition.

"I never thought I'd go to college," says Juan, who earned his GED in prison. "The campus environment is so positive and so different from the gangs." With his coach's encouragement, Felipe enrolled at a junior college and likes how it's changing him. "People there are different, more accepting of different cultures and more accepting of me," he says. "That motivates me to be more open-minded and less prejudiced."

Others like Pat McGowan, Dan Wilkins, Greg Adcock and Don Dawkins might never have gone (or gone back) to college had they not been injured. Pat was a ski bum, Greg was detailing cars and Don wanted to be a cop. With Voc Rehab footing the bill, they took classes and found good jobs. Dan's now a disability advocate and businessman, Greg's an engineer, Don's an outreach worker. Pat, who's an economist in Manhattan, says "I wouldn't be in this field if I hadn't been injured."

Joel Lorentz didn't go to college, but instead went from a dead-end job painting water tanks to a good one dispatching cops. Not only does he like the work, but it keeps him clear of his drug past as well.

Dan Wilkins doubts that anything he could have done if he hadn't broken his neck could be as meaningful as the advocacy and empowerment work he does now. "Every day there's joy and the promise of doing something good and having fun doing it," he says.

Susan Douglas's car accident didn't change her plans to become a doctor, but the personal victories of medical school and professional achievement are far sweeter because she earned them using a chair.

Sports has been very, very good to many in this group. Curtis Lovejoy contemplated suicide after he broke his neck and before swimming took him around the world and brought him gold. "I had asked God for opportunities," he recalls, "but I never imagined that they'd come in this kind of package." Ryan McLean got to compete in the Paralympic swim trials, model and appear on television, all due to her accident. Quad rugby gave George Taborsky some great friends and the chance to travel. Phillip Mann competed in England and South America in pursuit of his sporting life; Jason Regier and others traveled throughout the U.S. with quad rugby teams, and Wardell Kyles and Joel Irizarry have played basketball and football all over the country. Thanks to wheelchair sports, all their lives have been enriched.

Both Anne and Paul Herman were athletes before their accidents but their opportunities, competitive and otherwise, increased enormously afterwards. Anne competed internationally for more than 20 years, while Paul's still at it nationally. A blue collar Vietnam vet, he took advantage of free schooling and turned his back on harsh Midwest winters for a good computer job and life in sunny San Diego. And oh yeah, there's that minor matter of 25 rewarding years of marriage and parenthood.

The donations and support of thousands of people she has never met made going to college much easier for Anne Marie Hochhalter. More important, she says, in the aftermath of Columbine she's found Christianity, a positive outlook and a refreshingly appreciative perspective on life.

Greg Adcock and many others say that disability brought them great people, great bonds and great friendships.

Nearly every person I interviewed spoke of some unforeseen positive change or good from their accidents. Many offered comments such as, "Now I have goals and rely on myself more," "I'm happier now than I was before I got hurt" or "I never imagined I could have had a life like this." No one claims that being disabled is like winning the sweepstakes or that using a

wheelchair is their idea of the good life, but nearly all say that disability, along with big challenges, gave them big opportunities. Many also add that, truth be told, their lives weren't exactly gum drops and lollipops before they got hurt.

Call it denial. Label it blind optimism. Say it's a case of people seeing what they want to see. It doesn't really matter. These people are convinced they've found positives and opportunities because of their accidents. Not everyone has succeeded in making the most of these chances, but no one mentioned regretting taking advantage of whatever came their way. Almost everyone claims to have gained *something*.

This group has recognized and built on what disability has brought them. They have taken risks, seized opportunities and run hard with them. They've done well because they've found opportunity in the so-called trash of misfortune and then forged it into something good and useful. That's the stuff of hope.

Q: What's your greatest accomplishment? What are you most proud of?

- Career and personal accomplishments
- Successful adjustment
- Marriage and family
- Education
- Independence
- Lifestyle changes

Amit Jha says it's his marriage and career. Wally Dutcher includes founding several community organizations, his advocacy work, and managing the first Dow Jones index mutual fund. Juan Garibay and Robert Statam speak of turning their lives around. For Bobbie Humphreys it would be the combination of her trip across the country, founding a peer support program and her partner Pete. Jason Graber puts his college degree at the top of his list. James Turner lists a trio of marriage, college degree and becoming a minister. Nothing ranks higher for Marina Conner than raising four kids. They're all talking about their finest accomplishments, the ones they're most proud of. Their answers tell us who we are and who we can become.

Less than one-third of this group ranks injury-related issues like financial or physical independence as their best accomplishments, and most measure success the same way they did before injury. In terms of pride of achievement, disability plays a minor role in their lives.

Vincent Dureau, who spends half his time traveling the world, says his pride comes from helping found a successful international company and signing paychecks for 450 people. The travel, he says, "is what most executives do, so doing it from a chair is not really exceptional."

Mark Bussinger's success as a realtor is much more important to him than having done it as a quad. Pat McGowan points to his success in graduate school and his ongoing job success as an economist. "I work hard and I'm good at it." Richard Famiglietti says helping change the law so people in Connecticut can work and buy into Medicaid is the accomplishment and the contribution he's most proud of.

Aric Fine holds world records in disabled water skiing and has competed internationally for years, but being a husband and father are what make his chest swell. Fred Fay has been an effective advocate for decades and won both the 1978 US Jaycees Award as one of the Ten Most Outstanding Young Americans and the prestigious Henry B. Betts Award, but he knows his greatest accomplishment. "My son," he says. "Without a doubt, my son."

Fred is not alone in citing family first. Don Dawkins doesn't pause before answering, "My wife, my daughter, my family. We've made a great life for ourselves." Audrey Begay says giving birth to her daughter was not only her finest accomplishment, but also the defining moment of her life. "She turned my life around in such a positive way," Audrey says. "Hannah's my motivation and makes me responsible."

Life-altering events are often cited. "I belonged to a gang and was living the life of a thug," James Lilly remembers. "I turned that around. Now I have a wife and two

great boys and make a good living telling kids about how I did it. I'm very proud of that." Joel Lorentz made similar changes, going from a life of drugs and alcohol to one of satisfying work and home ownership: "Getting back on track by finding work, supporting myself, living on my own, filling time; those are a big deal to me." After being shot in a drug deal gone bad and doing a year of hard time, Wardell Kyles smiles about his life four years later. "I'm on the right side of the law and others see me totally differently," he says. "Now I'm doing positive things like mentoring and sports."

Keith Davis was an elite wheelchair racer for years and competed in the Paralympics. But those are "just things you put on a résumé," he says. "I'm most proud of living every day to the fullest and trying to be an example of what's possible." It's the everyday things that do it for Matthew Seals, too: "I work a job like everyone else and I love my kids," he told me. "I make sure I don't take advantage of my disability or feel sorry for myself. I live a relatively normal life and that's what I'm proud of."

The longer people live with SCI, the less their injuries seemed to interfere with their lives. Some who are younger and have newer injuries are still making adjustments, changes and accommodations to both SCI and life. Anne Marie Hochhalter, five years after her injury, says "I live on my own, I drive, I have my family, my friends, I go to school. I have goals." At 22, Ryan McLean's still getting started and is proud of going to college, working, having an apartment of her own and coaching swimming. Six years after his injury, Jason Regier sees staying positive enough to finish college, go to grad school and remain active as major achievements. Others point with pride to getting back to high school or college quickly, graduating on time, remaining the same people and avoiding major depressions.

We reveal ourselves in the telling of our accomplishments, often saying as much with what we don't mention as with what we do. People in this group speak of jobs, marriages, families and such individual achievements as lives turned around, ones lived to the fullest or those steered back on to the right road. The point? This group measures their success in much the same way they did before their injury. They measure success by their educations, relationships and careers. Disability, they say, is only one of many factors in their lives.

This narrative began with first impressions and early expectations, most of which were grim and meager. In the beginning we're too quick to fear that our possibilities will be greatly diminished or that our lives are effectively over. Not so.

The lives of the people on these pages speak to the fallacy of those early assumptions. Instead of limits, loss and concessions, they found possibility, opportunity and hope. Through effort, diligence and tenacity, they were able to create lives based not on loss but filled with education, work, marriage, children, sports, travel and positive contributions. They speak with genuine pride of their lives and their accomplishments. They'll tell you they're ordinary people living ordinary lives. They say that if they can do these things, others can too. That's good news. ∎

Finding Meaning

When I was first injured, I thought scratching my nose was a major feat and feeding myself warranted a celebration. The first time I wiped my butt, I called family and friends across the country to share my good news. These were major accomplishments then and remain so now. To this day, I sometimes find myself smiling after managing to button a shirt, tie my shoes or use a pair of scissors with one hand.

People told me lots was possible while I lay in rehab unable to feed or dress myself, but I wasn't buying it, not at first. As things changed and I was able to do more, more seemed possible. It was hard to believe, startling really, because in the beginning doing anything at all was so hard to imagine, much less actually accomplish. I may not have thought life was over, but I wasn't sure much was left. I was so wrong. There was so much left, so much more than I expected. I found that life was still here for me, still as full of possibilities as ever. Of course it was; where else was it going to go?

Mine is not a singular experience, but something I share with almost everyone in this group. Their lives also continue to be full and rich and rewarding, and the treasures that now fill them are much greater than scratching noses, using utensils and wiping butts. Little of it comes easy, but we continue to strive because we must. We strive because we need more. We need meaning.

Shortly after I got to rehab, my brother pinned a cartoon to my bulletin board. It was a panel of drawings showing a guy happily walking down the street, only to be crushed by a giant hand from the sky. Confused, he asks, "Why me?" The answer is a thunderous, "Who better?"

"Why us?" we ask. We feel we've been screwed, and think we got a raw deal.

That cartoon came to mind a few years later as I was reading *Man's Search For Meaning*, Viktor Frankl's account of his imprisonment in the Nazi concentration camps during World War II. A physician and psychotherapist, Frankl witnessed and experienced unspeakable atrocities and lost everything—his wife, mother, father, brother—while living on a subhuman level and surrounded by deprivation, torture and death. He somehow maintained his will to live and his faith in the future by asking what he owed life, what he could be grateful for, what his purpose might be. He came to realize that even in the face of losing everything material and corporeal, we—all of us—can still choose our attitude, behavior, dignity and morality. His search for meaning became his purpose for life.

Meaning and purpose are the engines that drive human endeavor. They allow us to believe the future will be better. Without meaning and purpose, what's the sense in living?

Frankl's legacy to us all is his assertion that our prime directive is to seek meaning and value for our personal lives and then incorporate both into how we live them. That's a tall order, certainly a higher and more spiritual mission than merely gratifying our basic drives and instincts or adapting to society and environment.

In the beginning, most of us hold on tooth and nail, just trying to survive until tomorrow. Once we get our lives stabilized we find ourselves wanting and needing something deeper and more meaningful than simply the next day. Those wants and needs can become our search, our spiritual quest. Our task isn't so much to ask "Why me?" as it is to decide what to do now that it *is* me. Meaning, purpose, fulfillment and perhaps even the self-actualization Maslow wrote about all lie in that deciding and doing.

"It is a peculiarity of man that he can only live by looking to the future," Frankl wrote. Because our mission lies in the future, we must look forward and only forward, to what can and will be, not back to that which is no more.

I have to believe that if Frankl could find meaning and purpose while facing death at Auschwitz, surely we can do the same while living with paralysis in 21st Century America.　■

CHAPTER SEVEN
A Summary

After all the interviews and questions, after all this group's years of disability, is it possible to identify what people who do well after SCI have in common? I think it is. Here's a brief summary of the attitudes, mindsets and behaviors that this group appears to share.

They demanded full lives

They found goals, activities and work that helped them feel good about themselves. They expected good things to happen to them, and insisted on living lives that were rich by any standards.

They focused on the present and the future

They accepted SCI and moved forward, incorporating disability into their lives without denying its effects and limitations or allowing it to become the focus of their lives.

They took their time

Early after injury, most progressed slowly and incrementally, building step by step on each accomplishment before progressing to the next. Most took at least two years to work SCI into their lives and feel comfortable with it.

They put first things first

They learned the basics of self-care, benefits and staying healthy before moving on to schooling, employment, relationships and larger plans for their lives. By celebrating minor successes they gained confidence that bigger successes were possible and likely.

They took control

They took charge of situations and made things happen. They developed a strong internal sense of control and believed they could influence their future for the better. They refused to be victims and took responsibility for their lives.

They valued faith, spirituality, meditation

Faith comforted many of this group and helped them find meaning in their experience of disability. Others found meditation, yoga or visualization helpful. It should be noted that none of these are requirements. Many did well without them.

They found humor in themselves and SCI

They made abundant use of laughter and humor to defuse the intrusive demands of life with SCI and avoid taking themselves and their disabilities too seriously.

They stayed busy

This group kept busy with school, volunteer work, advocacy, sports, personal projects, parenting and employment. Their high level of activity exposed them to new opportunity and provided structure for their early days of SCI.

They took advantage of benefits and education programs

They tapped into government programs and benefits while transitioning to life with a disability, getting an education, finding employment and learning to make their own way.

They found peer support

They connected with support groups and long-term SCI survivors who served as informal mentors and helped them see possibilities, solve problems and avoid common pitfalls.

They learned good problem-solving skills

This group analyzed problems and fixed them. With or without help, they saw obstacles as problems to be solved, then solved them.

They valued pragmatism

This group's style is flexibility and a willingness to change habits, diets and entire lifestyles to make things work. They see problems as specific and temporary, and their solutions are pragmatic.

They passionately pursued their interests

They threw themselves into what they cared about. This commitment and engagement helped them succeed in school, work, and relationships, and feel productive and fully alive.

They made effective use of computers

This group used computers and the Internet as equalizers that kept them connected to the larger world, compensated for loss of mobility and provided inexpensive communication and access to information.

Recurring themes

As people described their lives, and life with a disability, recurring themes emerged. These themes were central to how they coped and reconstructed their lives after injury.

The quest for meaning

"Everything happens for a reason" was a familiar, but far from universal, refrain in this group, perhaps satisfying a need to feel that providence or a blind universe wasn't playing games with them. This often led to deeper religious faith, a strong desire to help others or significant changes in lifestyle.

The test

Many saw SCI as a test of resourcefulness, character and will. Some saw it as a test of their faith in God, some as a challenge to live a life of high moral standards, others as a mandate to live up to their full potential.

The lesson

Almost all saw lessons in SCI, although the lessons learned varied widely. Examples: They felt they'd gained patience, compassion and empathy, or learned to overcome limitations, seek out opportunity and keep a positive outlook. A few found value in the experience of adversity.

The second chance

About one-quarter of this group said SCI had given them a fresh start, a needed sense of direction, a chance to right past wrongs or get their act together. This was particularly true of people who faced major changes such as leaving drugs or gang life behind.

The acceptable risk

Having lost and gained so much, failure seemed less threatening now. As one person put it, "What are they going to do, take away my birthday?"

The life reappraisal

For some, SCI forced a reevaluation and subsequent journey of self-discovery. They became more aware of what was important to them, what and who they loved, and what they wanted to do with their lives. ∎

Appendices

Appendix I. Government Benefit Programs

Of this group:
- Over 80 percent have accessed benefits at one time—SSI, SSDI, Medicare, Medicaid, Pell Grants, PASS, 1619b, etc.
- Over 50 percent say government support was essential for them
- Over 50 percent say dealing with the system was difficult
- Forty percent continue to receive benefits
- Over 20 percent think benefits can make you dependent

Nearly everyone used at least one government program for assistance after their injury and most people used several. Almost half still rely on at least one program—most commonly SSI and/or Medicaid—and probably will forever. A few who are now retired receive SSDI and Medicare or long-term VA benefits.

Unemployment is astonishingly high among people with SCI, and money problems are common. It is not easy for people with disabilities to find jobs they qualify for, especially jobs that offer both a decent wage and adequate health coverage. Jobs that pay well enough to cover personal assistance services are especially rare. And since almost any job will cause a disabled worker to lose SSI and the health insurance provided by Medicaid, there is every disincentive to avoid working. A few in this group, 15 to 20 percent, do manage to work and retain Medicaid coverage by keeping their income under a prescribed limit.

While dealing with the system can be at best a major challenge and at worst the stuff of nightmares, government benefits are a fact of life, a necessary evil and an ongoing reality for many in this group. Most find the process of applying for and keeping benefits hostile and adversarial. Some say dealing with the programs has not been so onerous, and most eventually get what they need if they stay at it long enough.

Rules of the game

To find programs that can help, you must learn as much as possible about which programs will best meet your needs for daily subsistence, medical coverage, subsidized housing, personal assistance services, education or qualifying for and finding work.

How to find out? Any way you can, but preferably *before* getting that letter telling you you're disqualified. Because so many in this group were so young at the time of injury, their parents often did the homework and research. That was great, they said, until it came time for them to live on their own; then they had to scramble to learn everything in a hurry. If you must rely on government programs, learning the fine print and the rules is as important as learning self-care. If you need benefits to survive, the quicker you learn how to acquire and keep them the better off you'll be.

People get their information from a variety of sources. Many learn the ropes from social workers or family services experts while still in rehab, others learn during the first few months out of the hospital. Some learn everything on their own while others seek out seasoned wheelers for advice. Some rely on what they're told by Social Security workers and some get their information from independent living centers or the Internet. It's always a good idea to get a second opinion.

A good place to start is the Social Security Administration's toll-free information number (see below). Workers reached through this number can answer general questions about enrollment procedures, the location and phone number of the nearest SSA branch office, and other basic information. If you go to an SSA office, be prepared for long lines and long waits. Avoid the busiest days like Mondays and the first and last of the month. Be sure to explain your situation clearly and completely, so you get the right forms for the right program. Ask every question you can think of, then ask a few more. Once you have what you need, be sure to fill out forms accurately and completely, since any omission or error will cause delays. The SSA processes millions of applications and claims each month, so it's easy to get lost in the system. Once everything is completed and returned, the waiting begins. It's a good idea to call occasionally and check the status of your claim.

An independent living center is another good place to get the help you need. Their advocates can often walk you through the application process. Since ILCs are mostly staffed and administered by people with disabilities who know your rights and know how to work the system, they're a resource you'd be foolish to ignore. Anyone with a physical or cognitive disability is a potential client.

Going to an ILC can also be a genuine education for anyone new to disability. ILCs are not warm and fuzzy like rehab and are staffed by committed crips working for disability rights and social and political change. They're the kind of people behind the passage and enforcement of the Americans with Disabilities Act (ADA) and many of the entitlement programs that make independent living possible. Every state has a network of federally funded ILCs. See resources below.

Keep in mind that information regarding these benefits comes from people, often ones just like that person you speak with who works for your cable, credit card or insurance company. As such, the information you get is only as good and as reliable as the person giving it to you. It's a good idea to approach this information the same way you would approach major surgery—analyze the information carefully and always consider getting a second opinion.

A Short List of Government Programs

Supplemental Security Income (SSI) is a means-tested SSA entitlement program administered by individual states. Eligibility is affected by any assets you may have (e.g. stocks, cash, possessions) and benefits are affected by earned income over a specified amount that differs in every state. If you qualify for SSI you also qualify for Medicaid. Contact www.ssa.gov/notices/supplemental-security-income/

Medicaid is the federal government's medical insurance program for the poor and disabled. This is bare-bone coverage, although unlike Medicare it does cover prescription drugs. Eligibility guidelines impose strict income and asset limits. Contact www.cms.hhs.gov/medicaid/

Social Security Disability Insurance (SSDI) is an earned benefit requiring a work history of at least 40 quarters (10 years). If you worked and paid taxes for that long, you're eligible regardless of any other benefits you receive. Expect a five month waiting period before benefits begin; the amount may be offset by worker's comp benefits, depending on which state you live in. If you qualify for SSDI you also qualify for Medicare, although there's a two-year waiting period before Medicare benefits begin. Contact 800-772-1213 or www.ssa.gov/disability/

Medicare is the federal government's healthcare program for the elderly and the disabled. Most people who qualify for SSDI receive Medicare. Like Medicaid, Medicare is minimal coverage, with very limited drug coverage. Contact www.cms.hhs.gov/medicare/

Student Earned Income Exclusion allows a person who is under age 22 and regularly attending school to exclude up to $1,370/month ($5,520/year maximum) of earned income before benefits are affected. Limited to SSI recipients.

Benefits for Disabled Children can provide benefits to those who became disabled *before* the age of 22, the adult child's parent worked long enough to be insured under Social Security, is receiving retirement or disability benefits or is deceased. Good way to gain access Medicare through parents' benefits.

Plan for Achieving Self-Support (PASS) is a Social Security program making it possible to work and save money for future employment goals without losing SSI or Medicaid/Medicare benefits. The

Do-It-Yourself PASS Kit by Barb Knowlen contains everything you need to know about writing a PASS plan. Check out her web site at www.barrierbreakers.com for more information.

Vocational Rehabilitation Services are federal programs in each state, designed to assist people with disabilities obtain jobs. While services vary from state to state, programs often provide assistance with tuition, transportation, housing or other aspects of preparation for and entering the workplace. Some offices can be rigid and arbitrary with their benefits, and it's good to have in hand as much information about your rights as possible *before* going in and asking for help. Much of the needed information is available at local ILCs. Barb Knowlen's *How To Kick Butt and Win* is something of an underground classic on the subject of getting the help you want from Vocational Rehabilitation no matter where you live.

Section 8 Subsidized Housing is a federally funded program normally administered on a local level by cities, counties or regional housing authorities. Certain housing is designated as subsidized and offers low rentals for seniors and people with disabilities. Units are often very limited and waiting lists are often long. But if you can get a unit, rent is normally no more than 30 percent of your gross income.

The Ticket to Work program provides expanded access to employment services and extends Medicare coverage for SSDI an additional 4.5 years (8.5 years total).

Employer Subsidy assigns a percentage value to any extra supervision or assistance given to an employee with a disability, allowing you to earn that percentage above the allowable wage ceiling.

1619B allows SSI recipients to work and maintain their Medicaid coverage as long as their medical expenses and cost of in-home care, combined with their earnings, remains under a ceiling set by their respective state.

Employment Related Work Expenses (IRWE) are disability-related expenses deducted from gross income. Gross Income minus IRWEs = adjusted income.

• Social Security Administration information: 800-277-1213 or www.ssa.org

• Veterans Benefits Administration information: 1-800-827-1000 or www.vba.va.gov/

• Search for nearest ILCs: www.ilru.org

• Additional good ILC sources: www.wid.org.www

• Benefits information: www.disabilitybenefits101.org ∎

Appendix II. The Model Systems Spinal Cord Injury Rehabilitation Centers

The Model Spinal Cord Injury System program, sponsored by the National Institute on Disability and Rehabilitation Research (NIDRR), US Dept of Education, provides comprehensive medical, vocational, and other rehabilitation services to meet the needs of individuals with spinal cord injury. Sixteen Model System Centers across the United States work together to demonstrate improved care, maintain a national database, participate in independent and collaborative research and provide continuing education relating to spinal cord injury.

Alabama
Spain Rehabilitation Center
Amie B. Jackson, M.D.
University of Alabama at Birmingham
Dept. of Physical Medicine & Rehabilitation
Birmingham, AL 35249-7330
Contact: Pamela Mott
Voice: 205-934-3283
Fax: 205-975-4691

California
Santa Clara Valley Medical Center
Tamara Bushnik, Ph.D.
Rehabilitation Research Center for TBI & SCI
950 S. Bascom Avenue, Suite 2011
San Jose, CA 95128
Contact: Tamara Bushnik, Ph.D.
Voice: 408-295-9896
Fax: 408-295-9913

Rancho Los Amigos National Rehabilitation
Center
Robert L. Waters, M.D. and Rod Adkins, Ph.D.
 7601 East Imperial Highway, HB 206
Downey, CA 90242-4155
Contact: Robert L. Waters, M.D.
Voice: 562-401-7161
Fax: 562-803-5623

Colorado
Craig Hospital
Daniel P. Lammertse, M.D. and Gale G.
Whiteneck , Ph.D.
3425 South Clarkson Street
Englewood, CO 80110-2811
Contact: Scott Manley, Ed.D.
Voice: 303-789-8214
Fax: 303-789-8219

Florida
Jackson Memorial Hospital & Miami Project to
Cure Paralysis
Marca L. Sipski, M.D.
PO Box 016960, R-64
Miami, FL 33101-9844
Contact: Marca L. Sipski, M.D.
Voice: 305-324-4455 ext. 4433
Fax: 305-243-3395

Georgia
Shepherd Center, Inc.
David F. Apple, M.D. and Lesley M. Hudson,
M.A.
2020 Peachtree Road, NW
Atlanta, GA 30309-1402
Contact: Lesley M. Hudson, M.A.
Voice: 404-350-7580
Fax: 404-355-1826

Massachusetts
Boston Medical Center
Shanker Nesathurai, M.D., FRCP(C) and Holly
Ditchfield
One Boston Medical Center Place, Room F-511
Boston, MA 02118
Contact: Holly Ditchfield
Voice: 617-638-7895
Fax: 617-638-7313

Michigan
University of Michigan Hospital
Denise G. Tate, PH.D., A.B.P.P.
300 North Ingalls, Room NI2A09
Ann Arbor, MI 48109-0718
Contact: Martin Forchheimer, M.P.P.
Voice: 734-763-0971
Fax: 734-936-5492

Missouri
University of Missouri-Columbia
Kristofer Hagglund, Ph.D.
One Hospital Drive, DC046.10
Columbia, MO 65212
Contact: Joanne Willett
Voice: 573-884-7972
Fax: 573-884-2902

New Jersey
Kessler Medical Rehabilitation Center
Joel A. DeLisa, M.D. and Steven Kirshblum, M.D.
1199 Pleasant Valley Way
West Orange, NJ 07052-1499
Contact: David S. Tulsky, PH.D.
Voice: 973-243-6849
Fax: 973-243-6861

New York
Mount Sinai Hospital
Kristjan T. Ragnarsson, M.D. and Ralph Marino,
M.D.
1 Gustave Levy Place, Box 1240
New York, NY 10029-6574
Contact: Audrey Schmerzler
Voice: 212-659-9369
Fax: 212-348-5901

Pennsylvania
Thomas Jefferson University Hospital
John F. Ditunno, Jr., M.D.
132 S. 10th St., 375 Main Bldg.
Philadelphia, PA 19107-5244
Contact: Mary Patrick, R.N.
Voice: 215-955-6579
Fax: 215-955-5152

University of Pittsburgh Medical Center
Michael L. Bonniger, M.D.
Human Engineering Research Laboratories
7180 Highland Dr., Bldg. 4, 2nd Floor
Pittsburgh, PA 15206
Contact: Rosemarie Cooper
Voice: 412-365-4850
Fax: 412-365-4858

Texas
The Institute for Rehabilitation and Research
(TIRR)
William H. Donovan, M.D. and Kenneth C.
Parsons , M.D.
1333 Moursund Street
Houston, TX 77030-3408
Contact: Karen A. Hart, Ph.D.
Voice: 713-797-5946
Fax: 713-797-5982

Virginia
Medical College of Virginia Hospital
Virginia Commonwealth University
William O. McKinley, M.D. and David X. Cifu ,
M.D.
Dept. of Physical Medicine and Rehabilitation
Richmond, VA 23298-0677
Contact: Michael A. Tewksbury, M.B.A.
Voice: 804-828-0861
Fax: 804-828-5074

Washington
University of Washington Medical Center
Diana D. Cardenas, M.D. and Charles
Bombardier, Ph.D.
Department of Rehabilitation Medicine
Seattle, WA 98195-6490
Contact: Cynthia Salzman
Voice: 206-685-3999
Fax: 206-685-3244

Appendix III. Department of Veterans Affairs Spinal Cord Injury Centers

California
DVA Medical Center
5901 East 7th Street
Long Beach, CA 90822
562-494-5701

VA Palo Alto Health Care System
3801 Miranda Avenue
Palo Alto, CA 93404
650-493-5000

VA San Diego Health Care System
3350 La Jolla Village Drive
San Diego, CA 92161
619-551-8585

Florida
James A. Haley VA Medical Center
13000 Bruce B. Downs Boulevard
Tampa, FL. 33612-4798
813-972-7517

VA Medical Center
1201 NW 16th Street
Miami, FL 33125
305-324-3174

Georgia
Augusta VA Medical Center
One Freedom Way
Augusta, GA 30907
706-823-2216

Illinois
Edward Hines VA Hospital
5th and Roosevelt Road
PO Box 5000-5128
Hines, IL 60141
708-216-2241

Massachusetts
Brockton/West Roxbury VA Medical Center
1400 V.F.W. Parkway
West Roxbury, MA 02132
617-323-7700 ext. 5128

Missouri
VA Medical Center
1 Jefferson Barracks Drive
St. Louis, MO 63125
314-894-6677

New Jersey
Department of VA
New Jersey Health Care System
385 Tremont Avenue
East Orange, NJ 07018
973-676-1000

New Mexico
VA Medical Center
2100 Ridgecrest SE
Albuquerque, NM 87108
505-256-2849

New York
Bronx Veterans Affairs Medical Center
130 West Kingsbridge Road
Bronx, NY 10468
718-584-9000

VA Hudson Valley Health Care System
Castle Point, NY 12511
Castle Point , NY 12511
Phone: 845- 831-2000

Ohio
Louis Stokes VA Medical Center
10701 East Boulevard
Cleveland, Ohio 44106
216-791-3800

Puerto Rico
San Juan VA Medical Center
10 Casia Street
San Juan, PR 00921-3201
787-758-7575

Tennessee
VA Medical Center
1030 Jefferson Avenue
Memphis, TN 38104
901-577-7373

Texas
South Texas Veterans Health Care System
Audie L. Murphy Division
7400 Merton Minter Boulevard
San Antonio, TX 78284
210-617-5257

VA Medical Center
4500 South Lancaster Road
Dallas, TX 75216
214-302-6702

VA Medical Center Houston
2002 Holcombe Boulevard
Houston, TX 77030
713-794-7128

Virginia
Hunter Holmes McGuire VA Medical Center
1201 Broad Rock Road
Richmond, VA 23249
804-675-5128

VA Medical Center
100 Emancipation Drive
Hampton, VA 23667
757-722-9961

Washington
National Spinal Cord Injury Headquarters
VA Puget Sound Health Care System
1600 South Columbian Way
Seattle, WA 98108-1597
206-768-5401

Wisconsin
Clement J. Zablocki VA Medical Center
5000 W. National Avenue
Milwaukee, WI 53295
414-384-2000

Appendix IV. Resources
Organizations

American Association of People with Disabilities
The largest national nonprofit cross-disability
member organization in the United States. 800-
840-8844
http://www.aapd.com

Center for Research on Women with Disabilities
A women's research center focused on health,
aging, civil rights, abuse, independent living and
promoting full participation in community life
for women with disabilities.
800-44-CROWD
http://www.bcm.tmc.edu/crowd/

*Christopher and Dana Reeve Paralysis Resource
Center*
A comprehensive, national source for
information about health, community
involvement and quality of life.
800-593-7309
www.paralysis.org

The Disability Rights Education and Defense Fund
A national law, research and policy center for
disability rights.
510-644-2555
www.dredf.org

*The Independent Living Research Utilization program
(ILRU)*
A national center for information, training,
research and technical assistance in independent
living. Look for a nation-wide list of ILCs
searchable by location. 713-520-0232
www.ilru.org

Independent Living Centers USA
A listing of independent living centers
throughout the country.
http://www.ilusa.com/links/ilcenters.htm

Mobility International USA Promotes international
exchange, community service, youth programs
and travel for people with disabilities. Publisher
of *A World of Options*, a guide to international
opportunities. MIUSA, PO Box 10767
Eugene, OR 97440
541-343-1284
www.miusa@igc.apc.org

National Center for Independent Living
Provides essential information to assist people
with disabilities to live independent lives.
ncil@tsbbs02.tnet.com

The National Coalition for Disability Rights
Sponsors grassroots responses to threats to the
civil rights of people with disabilities.
202-661-4722
www.adawatch.com

National Organization on Disability
Comprehensive information source on
community involvement, jobs, technology,
housing, access to health care, transportation,
education and the law.
202-293-5960
www.nod.org ability@nod.org

National Spinal Cord Injury Association
A mother lode of information, support and
resources. NSCIA sponsors support groups
through its many local chapters. Impressive
resource center and links.
800-962-9629
www.spinalcord.org

*Parent Advocacy Coalition for Educational Rights
(PACER)*
An agency providing information, resources and
referrals to parent training centers in all states.
Also a source for information on ILCs, vocational
rehabilitation and educational aid.
4826 Chicago Ave. S. Minneapolis, MN 55417
952-838-9000
www.pacer.org

Paralyzed Veterans of America
National service and support organization for
veterans with local chapters throughout the
country. Good information and support services.
Call 800-424-8200 for chapter nearest you
www.pva.org

World Institute on Disability
A research and public policy center promoting
the civil rights and the full societal inclusion of
people with disabilities. Good links and
resources. 510-763-4100
www.wid.org

Useful websites

There are many websites with information on SCI and disability issues. Most sites provide you with links to many more. Here are a few of the more popular ones.

www.access-able.com
Access-Able Travel Source has good information and resources for traveling with a disability. 303 232-2979 303 239-8486 (fax)

www.assistivetech.net
The Center for Assistive Technology and Environmental Access is a resource for assistive technology (AT) and a link to disability-related information for survivors and their family members. 800-726-9119 404-894-9320 (fax)

www.bentvoices.org
BENT: A Journal of CripGay Voices is an online magazine of and for gay men with disabilities.

http://carecure.atinfopop.com/4/OpenTopic
CareCure Community forums provide the latest information on SCI and related conditions and feature the research of Dr. Wise Young. Good bulletin boards and chatlines.

www.craighospital.com
Craig Hospital, a leading Model Systems Center, offers good basic information and is perhaps the best source on health, wellness and aging. Check out Research Department info. 303-789-8000

www.DisABILITIESBOOKS.com
An online bookstore for new and out-of-print disability-related books. 617-879-0397

www.disabilityinfo.gov
The federal government's portal is a directory of disability-related links, information and resources relevant to people with disabilities, their families, service providers and other community members.

www.dsusa.org
Disabled Sports USA offers nationwide sports rehabilitation programs to anyone with a permanent physical disability. 301-217-0960

www.jan.wvu.edu.
Job Accommodation Network a free employability consulting service for people with disabilities. Worksite accommodations solutions, technical assistance regarding ADA and other legislation, and self-employment options 800-526-7234

http://www.jfanow.org/
Justice For All's email network site for activists and disability-rights information.

www.lookingglass.org
Serves families with disabilities with links, publications, bulletin boards and more. Good info on adoption. 1-800-644-2666

http://www.makoa.org/
Disability information and resources with links to discounted prescription medications.

www.mentalhealth.org/suicideprevention
The National Strategy for Suicide Prevention provides suicide prevention information and links to state prevention programs. 800-SUICIDE

www.miamiproject.miami.edu
The Miami Project to Cure Paralysis publishes the latest in research news, along with basic information and good links. 305-243-7108

www.mscisdisseminationcenter.org.
Model Spinal Cord Injury Systems Dissemination Center site provides information from the entire Model Systems network including a database of resources, newsletters, journal publications and more.

www.nlm.nih.gov/medlineplus/spinalcordinjuries.html
The National Institute of Health's Medline site is a mother lode of searchable medical information and links to other sites. A great starting place.

www.nod.org/religion
Religion and Disability Program advocates for the removal of barriers to religious participation by people with disabilities. 202-293-5960

www.paincare.org
National Foundation for the Treatment of Pain is a good source on pain management, complete with helpline and referral list. 831-655-8812

www.pva.org
The Paralyzed Veterans of America service and support organization for veterans is a good source for information on disability rights and law, accessibility, sports, recreation and more. 800-424-8200

www.sath.org
The Society for Accessible Travel and Hospitality provides information and links to travelers with disabilities. 212-447-7284

www.sexualhealth.com
Informative site on the physical and psychological nitty-gritty of sex and disability.

www.sci-info-pages.com
Comprehensive information on most aspects of SCI, run by a quad. Resources, links and more.

www.scipilot.org
The SCI Peer Information Library on Technology is a database of tips from consumers on purchasing and using assistive devices; descriptions of practical, homemade inventions to solve real problems. 416-597-3422 ext. #6264

www.spinalcord.uab.edu
The Spinal Cord Injury Information Network is a comprehensive site run by Spain Rehabilitation Center. Good resource, good links.

www.spinalinjury.net
The Spinal Cord Injury Resource Center offers a vast amount of information explaining basic anatomy, physiology and the complications resulting from spinal cord injury.

www.spinal.co.uk
The Spinal Injuries Association is a British organization devoted to quality of life for SCI survivors.

www.spinlife.com
SpinLife.com is an online medical equipment store. 800-850-0335

www.survivingparalysis.com
A great place to connect with other quads, ask questions and solve problems. Run by a quad.

www.360mag.com
A good online magazine for young people, with great links and resources.

www.va.gov
Department of Veterans Affairs. Good for pertinent veterans' information on compensation, education, health, vocational rehabilitation, benefits, medical center locations and more.

www.wid.org
The World Institute on Disability is devoted to research on social issues facing people with disabilities.

www.wheelchairjunkie.com
Fun site for power-chair users. Tales and photos designed to amaze and amuse.

Magazines

Disability Studies Quarterly
A scholarly journal on disability issues and rights; Society for Disability Studies, c/o Professor Carol Gill, Department of Disability and Human Development, University of Illinois at Chicago (MC 626), 1640 Roosevelt Road #236, Chicago, IL 60608-6904; www.afb.org/dsq/index.html

Mouth Magazine
All disability rights all the time; a good source for activists. Contact Mouth, PO Box 558, Topeka, KS 66601; 785-272-2578; www.mouthmag.com.

New Mobility
A well written and informative monthly devoted to disability culture and lifestyle—people, recreation, sports, travel, equipment, health, the arts and disability rights. Check out their website for selected magazine articles, message board, chatrooms and more. Contact No Limits Communications Inc., PO Box 220, Horsham, PA 19044; 800-675-9134 or 215-675-9133; www.newmobility.com

PN
A monthly magazine with a focus on SCI for veterans—recreation, travel, research, rights and benefits. Contact Paralyzed Veterans of America, 2111 East Highland Ave., Phoenix, AZ 85016; 888-888-2201 www.pvamagazines.com/

Ragged Edge
Excellent magazine focusing on disability rights. Contact Ragged Edge, PO Box 145, Louisville, KY 40201 www.ragged-edge-mag.com

SCI Life
An online magazine published by the National Spinal Cord Injury Association. Lifestyle, research, info on chapters. NSCIA has a good SCI hotline. 800-962-9629; www.spinalcord.org.

Sports 'N' Spokes
Concentrates on adaptive recreation on sports. 2111 East Highland Ave., Phoenix, AZ 85016; 888-888-2201; www.sportsnspokes.com

Books

Authentic Happiness by Martin Seligman. A guide for identifying personal strengths and using them to increase well-being, satisfaction and happiness. A follow-up to *Learned Optimism*. Free Press, New York; 2002.

Beyond Ramps: Disability at the End of the Social Contract by Marta Russell, a hard look at the politics behind disability, funding for social programs, and civil rights. Common Courage Press, Monroe, Maine; 1998.

The Body Silent by Robert F. Murphy. Murphy, a sociologist, examines how progressive quadriplegia from a spinal tumor changes his role in society. W.W. Norton, New York; 1990.

The Caregiver's Guide by Greenberg, Boyd and Hale. Directed to caregivers for the elderly, but don't discount it for that reason. Useful advice on management of time and stress. Nelson-Hall, Chicago; 1992.

Caregivers and Personal Assistants: How to Find, Hire and Manage the People Who Help You (Or Your Loved One!) by Alfred H. DeGraff. Definitive book on hiring, firing and keeping the help you need, written by a quadriplegic who has hired PCAs for 30 years. Saratoga Access Publications, Inc., Colorado; 800-266-5564; 2002.

The Creative Visualization Workbook by Shatki Gawain. A resource for stress management through visualization. Whatever Books, San Rafael, CA; 1982.

CripZen: a Manual for Survival by Lorenzo W. Milam. Written from the trenches with wry gallows humor. A good survey of the emotional minefield of disability. Mho & Mho Works, Box 1671, San Diego CA 92176; poo@cts.com; 1993.

The Directory of National Information Sources on Disabilities 8455 Colesville Rd, Suite 935, Silver Spring, M.D. 20910; 800-346-2742; www.naric.com.naric

The Do-It-Yourself PASS Kit by Barb Knowlen. Available through Barrier Breakers, 4239 Camp Rd., Oriskany Falls, NY; oneoftwo@borg.com; 1993.

Easy Things To Make ... To Make Things Easy by Doreen Greenstein. Simple do-it-yourself home modifications to make life easier and maximize independence. Brookline Books, Cambridge; 1997.

Enabling Romance by Erica Klein and Ken Kroll. How-to tales of sex and disability told by people with disabilities and those who love them. Excellent. No Limits Communications Inc., PO Box 220, Horsham, PA 19044; 1992.

The Feeling Good Handbook by David Burns. Stress management techniques from yoga, visualization and meditation to power naps. Plume Books, New York; 1990.

Financial Aid for the Disabled and Their Families. Details more than 900 scholarships, loans, grants, awards, and internships for people with disabilities and their families. $39.50 plus $4.50 shipping from Reference Service Press, 5000 Windplay Drive, Suite 4, El Dorado Hills, CA 95762; 916-939-9620; www.rspfunding.com; 2004

Financial Aid for People with Disabilities offers information on post-secondary education programs for people with disabilities. HEATH Resource Center, One Dupont Circle NW, Suite 800, Washington, DC 20036-1193; 800-544-3284; 2001

From There to Here by Gary Karp and Stanley Klein. Survivors tell their own stories of how they made sense of their accidents and put their lives back together. No Limits Communications, Inc., PO Box 220, Horsham, PA 19044; 2004.

Full Catastrophe Living by Jon Kabat-Zinn. Excellent advice on managing stress and pain using meditation and yoga. Techniques have been used clinically with an impressive record of success. Dell Publishing, New York; 1990

Hiring Someone to Work in Your Home. Basic guide on hiring home health help. The Women's Bureau, U.S. Department of Labor, 202-219-6652.

How To Kick Butt and Win by Barb Knowlen. Manual for getting what you want from Voc Rehab. Barrier Breakers, 4239 Camp Rd., Oriskany Falls, NY 13425; oneoftwo@borg.com; 1994

Learned Optimism by Martin Seligman. A well written guide to increasing optimism, decreasing depression and responding positively to the negatives of life. Free Press, New York, NY; 1990.

Life On Wheels by Gary Karp. A cross-disability reference book covering aspects of life with disability, e.g. selecting a chair, staying healthy, home access, legislation and more. O'Reilly & Associates, Sebastopol, CA; 1999.

The Luck Factor by Richard Wiseman. This systematic investigation of what lucky people have in common suggests that attitudes, beliefs and behaviors all affect luck. Hyperion, New York; 2003.

Man's Search for Meaning by Viktor Frankl. Frankl's riveting account of his survival in Germany's death camps is a primer for his therapeutic methods. More than inspiration, Frankl provides concrete coping tools for us all. Simon and Schuster, New York; 1959.

Minding the Body, Mending the Mind by Joan Borysenko. A good resource book for stress management and stress reduction. Addison-Wesley, Reading, MA; 1987.

Moving Violations by John Hockenberry. Hockenberry has been around the world and back covering stories for radio and television. Injured at 19, he tells the story of his journey through rehabilitation, employment, romance, career and life. Instructive, insightful. Hyperion Books, New York; 1995.

No Pity: People with Disabilities Forging a New Civil Rights Movement by Joseph P. Shapiro. A seminal look at disability discrimination and the history of the fight to find its remedies. Times Books, New York; 1993.

Pathways to Health: a Book About Making Healthy Choices is an easy-to-read primer on many aspects of SCI from the researchers at Craig Hospital; 303-789-8202; HealthResources@craighospital.org www.craighospital.org; 2000.

Personal Assistance Services Guide, information on hiring, managing and supervising personal assistants. 435-979-3811; 1998.

The Ragged Edge: The Disability Experience edited by Barrett Shaw. A collection of articles from 15 years of *The Disability Rag*, later renamed *The Ragged Edge*. The Advocado Press, PO Box 145, Louisville, KY 40201; 1994.

The Relaxation and Stress Reduction Handbook by Davis, Eshelman and McKay. Step-by-step guide to stress-reduction techniques. New Harbinger Books, Oakland, CA; 1995.

The Sensuous Wheeler by Barry Rabin. A good basic guide to sexual adjustment and intimacy following SCI. Self-published. Long Beach, CA; 1980. Available through Amazon.com

Spinal Network, Third Edition by Barry Corbet, Jean Dobbs *et al*. If you can only buy one book, make it this one. Overflowing with information, resources, stories, been there/done thats. The bible for mobility impairment. Nine Lives Press, PO Box 220, Horsham, PA 19044; 1998.

Staring Back: The Disability Experience from the Inside Out by Kenny Fries, ed. Good collection of writings from writers with disabilities. Plume, New York; 1997.

Taking Care of Yourself while Providing Care by Richard Holicky. A comprehensive guide for family caregivers of newly injured SCI survivors. Craig Hospital; 303-789-8202; HealthResources@craighospital.org, or www.craighospital.org; 2000.

Taking Charge: Teenagers Talk About Life and Physical Disabilities. Open discussion of self-esteem, communication, independence, relationships, dating, body image, sexuality and family life. New Mobility bookstore, 800-543-4116, newmobility.com or your local bookstore. $14.95.

Waist-High in the World: Life Among the Nondisabled by Nancy Mairs. Memoir of marriage, faith, art and life with MS, from an informed female perspective. Beacon Press, Boston; 1996.

Women and Disability: The Experience of Physical Disability Among Women by Susan Lonsdale. Extensive discussion of the issues facing women with a disability. St. Martin Press, New York; 1990.

Yes, You Can! A Guide to Self-Care for Persons with Spinal Cord Injury by Margaret Hammond *et al*. Excellent primer with the focus on the individual with SCI. A good resource for the entire family. Available in Spanish. Published by the Paralyzed Veterans of America, Washington, DC; 888-860-7244; *www.pva.org/pvastore/*; 1989.

A Personal Note

This project began over 30 years ago. In 1972 I was living in a commune in Portland, Maine and occasionally fantasized about traveling cross-country and interviewing people who, like myself, were living alternative lifestyles. I envisioned writing about it, making videotape and sharing the information along the way. A few years later I did travel across the country, but it was to start a new, post-hippie life in Colorado. When PVA so generously agreed to fund this project in the spring of 2002, I realized once again that fantasies, though often deferred, need not be abandoned. Occasionally they can be realized, though not always in the form we envision.

This has been a personal adventure and priceless learning experience for me. How could I not learn from such a qualified group of teachers? I'm humbled by the trust the people here have shown in telling their stories. I sit in awe of how far they've come, all they've done, the resilience they've demonstrated. Their willingness to share their lives benefits and instructs us all. They continue to move forward, to explore and risk and achieve. Their stories are all our stories.

I initially dismissed this project as impractical for a mid-50's quad, envisioning only what might go wrong in traveling the country. All the misadventures I feared, as well as a few I failed to anticipate, did in fact happen—cancelled room and car reservations, missed flights, automobile accidents, endless traffic jams and countless episodes of being hopelessly lost in seedy sections of strange towns. In all, I traveled a combined 17,000 air and highway miles and stayed in motels in various stages of disrepair. In the end, none of that mattered. I lived to tell about it and am immeasurably better for having done so. I learned once again how much more I'm limited by lack of imagination than by wheels and along the way often wondered why I had waited so long to do this. In hearing others tell their stories I relived mine numerous times. I come away with more gratitude and a different understanding of disability.

> We shall not cease from exploration
> And the end of our exploring
> Will be to where we started
> And know the place for the first time
>   T.S. Eliot

We are, all of us, wounded healers. Many of us begin this journey thinking life is already over, only to discover that what awaits us far exceeds the hopes we fear must be abandoned. We incorporate loss into life and learn that the pain of that loss need not be the first thing to enter our mind each morning. Though the loss may never truly leave us, its pain and impact lessen over time. If we're open to it, we come to understand that disability does not preclude quality of life and that the two can reside together quite comfortably.

We owe ourselves opportunity, adventure and success. We owe ourselves laughter and challenge and goals that exceed our grasp. And we can have them, probably not today, maybe not tomorrow, and almost certainly not as we once pictured them. But we can have them. We have only to begin.

∎

Printed in the United States
By Bookmasters